SPECIAL EDUCATION
IN
CANADIAN SCHOOLS

Ken Weber

 IRWIN
PUBLISHING

Highland Press
151 Highland Park Blvd., Thornhill, Ontario L3T 1B8
Telephone (905) 889-6608

Distributed exclusively in Canada by
Irwin Publishing
1800 Steeles Avenue West, Concord, Ontario L4K 2P3
Telephone (905) 660-0611

ISBN 0-9693061-5-6 (Highland Press)
ISBN 0-7725-2106-9 (Irwin Publishing)

Canadian Cataloguing in Publication Data

Weber, K. J. (Kenneth Jerome), 1940 –
  Special education in Canadian schools

Includes bibliographical references and index.
ISBN 0–9693061–5–6

  1. Special education – – Canada.   I. Title.

LC3984.W43 1994   371.9' 0971   C94–900188–0

Printed and bound in Canada.

1 2 3 4 5 T-G 97 96 95 94

Table of Contents

Foreword

Special education is not a subject in the sense that history or science are subjects. Nor is it a strategy like behaviour modification, or a skill like carpentry or spelling. Rather, special education is a concept, a principle, a particular conviction that *every* individual student has unique needs, abilities, and interests, which schools have a moral and practical obligation to meet.

Administrative procedures and classroom practices in Canada are built around this conviction. Legislation in the provinces and territories guarantees access to public education for all students regardless of their needs. Individual districts, boards and schools in Canada — at least ideally — are set up to deliver special education through an extensive variety of support that ranges from modifications of student programs, to allocation of special resources, to changes in building design. Classroom teachers and teaching assistants — again ideally — are able to draw on special training and on their own resources and talents to bring all this together for students with special needs.

Like all systems put together by human beings, Canada's special education has functional impediments and design faults. But the system is dynamic. It changes; it develops; it adapts. And most of the time, it improves. In any case special education, not just in Canada but everywhere, is only as good as the people who make it work. Ultimately, special education can only succeed as a concept, as a principle, and most importantly as a practice, through the actions of professionals who are committed to the belief that *every* student has a right to the best that schooling can offer. The ideal of special education is, in effect, to put itself out of business. The goal for which it strives is a system in which adaptation and accommodation for the needs of every student is automatic, and in which the very notion of "special" education is unnecessary.

Ken Weber,
30 March, 1994

1

Special Education Today

Room for Everyone

Larin was born with ataxic cerebral palsy. By the time he was two years old his parents had concluded he would never walk or stand or even sit without help. Larin did not speak, and although they had no medical confirmation, his parents also thought he was blind and deaf.

Therefore, until he was four years and ten months old, this little boy lay in a cardboard box in a corner of the kitchen where he was born.

Larin's parents were not abusive or malicious. But they were extremely unsophisticated, having had very little experience with education and none at all with community services. From the very beginning there was little reason, in their opinion, to expect that Larin's world would ever develop beyond the confines of a cardboard box. So as best they could they fed him, and cleaned him, and from time to time, when the weather was pleasant, they slid the box from the corner to an open doorway so that Larin could feel the warm sun on his tiny, wasting body.

The box might have remained the limits of his world forever had it not been for a singular event in mid-September, 1989. Larin's only sister had begun kindergarten the week before. She showed up on the first day and never returned so the kindergarten teacher stopped by to see what could be done. It was a visit that changed Larin's life forever. Not only did it signal the end of the box, it also marked the

beginning of his formal education, for within a short time, the same big yellow bus that once more picked up Larin's sister each morning, also took Larin — box and all for the first while — to school.

Three years later, the power of this development in Larin's life was reflected clearly in what his teacher told the school's Support Team in an end-of-term report:

"Larin can now use his walker without help and except for stairs, is independently mobile. Also, the latest set of corrective lenses have made an enormous difference to his field of vision.

Speech patterns continue to be difficult to understand but this could be my fault in part, since the other children seem to comprehend better than I do. However, I have no difficulty when the context is clear (e.g., counting: Larin can count 1—? with ease). Academic progress is steady, albeit slow. His favourites are still math, story time, and music. What is most encouraging is Larin's sunny disposition. He delights in absolutely everything that goes on, especially in the companionship of other children. (The delight is mutual.)

I am convinced that Larin has at least normal intelligence, and may be brighter than we know. Certainly he can learn to read.

It has been a challenge, but a pleasant one, to teach Larin this year and to watch him grow toward independence."

Larin's story reflects what are likely the two most important developments in the relatively brief history of special education in Canada. One is a very fundamental development: quite simply, the vast majority by far, of special students like Larin now go to regular community schools. The other is far more abstract, but in the long run, probably more significant: this is the undisputed conviction that Larin and other students with special needs can be educated in those schools.

Both developments are very much twentieth century phenomena, in fact, *late* twentieth century. For until the final few decades, not just in Canada but everywhere, it was entirely acceptable to look upon an exceptionality as an educationally limiting, even terminal, condition. In many jurisdictions in Canada, students like Larin, and many others whose special needs are far less intense, did not even have the legal right to attend regular schools. The schools themselves were in any case, generally unprepared, both functionally and philosophically, to educate them. The change in a very short period has been remarkable. Special education in Canada, in a span of approximately twenty-five years, has evolved from a haphazardly delivered, and frequently misunderstood 'extra' into a vital, effective, integral, and in most of the country, legally mandated part of every system.

How We Got Here From There

Before 1900

Primitive and ancient societies wanted little to do with disabled persons. Aristotle, for example, described deaf people as "incapable of reason", "no better than the animals of the forest" and "unteachable". Under Solon's law, the weak and disabled children of Athens were placed in clay vessels and abandoned. In Rome, disabled children were thrown into the Tiber. It was not unusual for wealthy families of the time to keep a mentally handicapped person for entertainment. No less a personage than the moralist philosopher, Seneca, reported that his wife kept a "feeble-minded dwarf", ostensibly for just that purpose.

There were some exceptions to this general attitude. The Talmud offered enlightened instructions regarding the blind and deaf, and Hippocrates' investigations into epilepsy and mental handicap suggested that scientific curiosity about special needs was not entirely absent. However the impact of these exceptions was limited to small, specific groups.

In the Middle Ages too, there were few bright spots. Saint Nicholas Thaumaturgos, fourth century bishop of Wyre, became known as a "protector of the feeble-minded", but there is little evidence of what he accomplished. (He was also the patron saint of sailors and pawnbrokers — and the prototype for Santa Claus!) Some monasteries and other clergy established hospices, but the superstitions of the day, along with a powerful belief in Satanic possession and the sheer demands of mere survival meant that persons with disabilities were very much on their own.

Some strides were made in Europe in the post-Renaissance Era, but they were chiefly isolated, short-lived bursts of change, the accomplishments of individuals with will and drive, rather than the product of a general amelioration in attitude. Most educators today recognize names like Ponce de Leon (1520-82) the Spanish monk who taught deaf children to speak and read, and Louis Braille (1809-1852) who adapted for the blind, a night-writing cipher system invented by one of Napoleon's officers. Jean Marc Itard (1775-1858) who "discovered" and tried to teach Victor, the wild boy of Aveyron, and Frederick Treves (1867-1923) who "rescued" John Merrick, the Elephant Man, are also among the better known. However, indifference to their efforts, or perhaps just overwhelming inertia is evident in the fact that carnival shows continued to exhibit persons like John Merrick, well into the mid-twentieth century; Itard's contemporaries actively discouraged him; Braille's adaptation was resisted, especially in North America, for almost fifty years after his death; De Leon's methods were lost and have never been found.

Still, the news was not all bad. A significant impact was made by the British philosopher John Locke (1632-1708) whose philosophy of sensationalism taught that children are not born with innate characteristics imprinted by God, nature, or the devil, but are instead a *tabula rasa*. Ever so slowly, this idea, given further impetus by other European scholars like Voltaire, Rousseau, and Goethe, began to chip away at the idea that disabled people are simply the product of some Great Plan and should be left alone, even though this kind of humanism was simply too advanced and radical for the times to take on practical, universal expression.

With the nineteenth century came some major developments — especially in Canada. Ronald McDonald, a reporter with the *Montreal Gazette*, opened a school for the deaf in Champlain, Quebec, in 1831. It was Canada's first formal special education project. Similar schools opened in Halifax in 1856, in Toronto (1858) and Winnipeg (1884). Schools for the blind opened in Toronto (1872) and Halifax (1873), and the first Canadian institution for the mentally retarded opened in Orillia, Ontario, in 1876. The 1870s also saw the opening of the Ontario Institution for the Education and Instruction of Deaf and Dumb Persons (1870) and the Ontario Institution for the Education and Instruction of the Blind (1872). In 1893, Children's Aid societies were formed in Ontario and became the model for North America.

The establishment of such institutions indicates the presence of a greater degree of social responsibility, and a developing interest in people with disabilities. Although some of the methods used then, and certainly the language and terminology, make contemporary educators wince, these were especially striking developments for the time in light of the fact that education of the so-called "normal" population was still far from universal.

Twentieth Century Developments

First, Custodial Responsibility

By the end of the first World War, humanitarian principles had become a central force in the public attitude toward people with special needs. Although the thrust was more one of "looking after the less fortunate", than one of social responsibility *plus* liberal education, at least people with exceptionalities were seen as human beings whose special needs required some kind of special accommodation. A significant portion of the curriculum at the Canadian institutions for exceptional persons, for example, was devoted to industrial training so that graduates could seek gainful employment.

Education to address other areas of exceptionality was a hit or miss affair at best. Students with a less visible need such as a learning disability (the term did not exist until 1963) or those with what is often seen now as a behavioural difficulty, were usually early dropouts. Right through to the final quarter of the century, these dropouts were regarded — and also saw themselves — as poor educational material in any case, not likely to benefit a great deal from extended schooling. Pre-computer, assembly line industry absorbed them quite readily into employment, and reinforced this perception.

For students with physical disabilities, the Ontario School for Crippled Children (now part of the Hugh MacMillan Centre) in Toronto quickly established a well-deserved international reputation for its programs. Yet the efforts did not go uncriticized, for many students with serious physical needs were considered poor candidates for education on the premise that it served little purpose, and offered only minimal return to society.

For students with major intellectual needs, the hope for liberal education was even bleaker. By the late 1890s, the Orillia, Ontario institution for the mentally handicapped, which had developed quite advanced school programs for its clientele, was involved in a vigorous struggle to keep them going in the face of wide criticism. Public education for gifted students was almost unheard of until the 1970s.

Then, a Shift to Education

All this changed dramatically by the late twentieth century. In Canada, the pivotal era of special education will likely be held by future historians to have begun in the late nineteen-sixties. It was around this time that the philosophy of dealing with exceptionalities began to change from one of socially responsible custodial care — with haphazard education — to one of social integration and universal education. The change evolved around this time for a number of reasons.

The strength of two unofficial but dominating movements diminished significantly in the nineteen sixties. One was the *testing* movement, especially the I.Q. test, which reinforced the practice of shunting less successful test-takers onto educational sidings. Although doubts about the real value — and the abuse — of testing instruments were raised as early as the 1930s, public faith in them took a long time to fade.

Simultaneous with the decline of tests as an absolute, was the decline of the *eugenics* movement which argued, in essence, that 'feeble-minded' persons should be protected in institutions, so that, even more important, society at large would be protected from genetic contamination. In 1918, a coalition of doctors, social workers and influential citizens had

For Discussion: The Case of Myndee

Shortly after Myndee's twelfth birthday, the family physician told her parents that he thought Myndee's condition just might be Prader-Willi syndrome, although he acknowledged that he'd heard about this syndrome only for the first time, at a recent conference. A symptom of Prader-Willi syndrome is insatiable appetite that can lead to obesity. Other common features are very serious tantrums, what appears to be exceptional stubbornness, speech and language problems, and pronounced learning difficulties. There is as yet no specific treatment.

Myndee is sixteen now and was recently judged to be — by another physician — schizophrenic. Since her early childhood, Myndee has also been described at one time or another, as having suspected Tourette syndrome, suspected tuberous sclerosis, and suspected autism. Whatever the (un)certainty of the medical diagnoses, Myndee's learning and behaviour seem to exhibit characteristics found in all of these conditions. If unmonitored, she will eat constantly; she is very much overweight. The tantrums have diminished a great deal over the past few years, although her stubbornness continues. Myndee has a will of granite; once embarked on a course of behaviour, she cannot be diverted. Unfortunately a lot of the behaviour is obsessive, perseverative, and usually not very productive. She will engage in a lot of rocking and humming, and if she is upset she will slap herself until she is stopped. The behaviour also manifests itself in repeated recitals of

things like multiplication tables, the Periodic Table of the Elements (which she knows much more thoroughly than any one else in her classes) and on occasion, poems discussed in class and even latitude/longitude measures from map activities.

During her elementary schooling, Myndee was moved from regular integrated classes to 'resource' classes to 'behavioural' classes, and spent one (quite successful) term in a class designed especially for severely learning disabled students. Last year, Myndee was promoted to secondary school, although the decision was taken more for social than academic reasons. The secondary school in which she is enrolled, has an 'inclusive' policy. All students, exceptional and otherwise, are in regular classes.

Whether or not Myndee is truly integrated, is open to question. Her fellow students, never knowing what to expect from her, avoid her politely. The teachers, after six weeks with Myndee, do not object to her presence, but are confused about their role. Myndee seems to be able to do some academic work — when it pleases her. She appears to be able to read, but there is no certainty about this. She thoroughly enjoys math, but generally does what she wants to do — multiplication — when the class is studying anything. The teachers have presented a petition to the principal which, essentially, asks her : "What are we supposed to be accomplishing?" The principal has acknowledged that this is a legitimate question.

formed the Canadian National Committee on Mental Hygiene to pressure the government to expand custodial facilities for the 'feeble-minded' whose spread resulted, in the Committee's opinion, from procreation by 'unsound stock', the numbers of which were being accelerated by the government's 'admittance to the Dominion of degenerate immigrants' (sic!).

Although both testing and eugenics still had their champions — particularly testing — their combined and somewhat mutual power had been minimized by the latter part of the twentieth century, when provincial governments

began to establish policies and legislation to bring about special education. In their place, the *normalization principle* championed in Canada by Wolf Wolfensberger through the National Institute on Mental Retardation (now the G. Allen Roeher Institute) became a credible and widely accepted philosophy. In essence, normalization argues against institutionalization. It contends that persons with special needs, especially those who are mentally handicapped, should be viewed more from the points on which they are similar to other persons, than from those on which they are different, and argues further, that if integrated into mainstream society, persons with mental handicaps will take on the behaviours of the norm because they will have normal models to follow.

Empowerment of Classroom Teachers

Educators in the sixties, and even more so in the seventies, began to abandon a medical model for viewing students with special needs in favour of an ecological focus. Hitherto, teachers had been led to concentrate on what was wrong with a student. Under the new focus there developed much greater interest in what is right, what a student can do rather than in what he or she cannot do. Teachers also began to recognize their own strengths and the potential power of their own contributions to an exceptional student's case. Whereas in the medical model approach, a teacher is expected to defer to some greater, outside expertise, the ecological focus grants teachers, and teaching assistants, the right to exercise intuition, knowledge, and experience.

An important consequence of this latter approach is that the student with special needs is seen as an educable entity, not as a custodial, medical responsibility for whom intellectual development and learning are secondary to coping with a handicap. Perhaps more important, ultimately, is the effect on how special education service is delivered. In a medical model, expertise is visited upon both student and teacher from above and afar. In a model that requires empiricism and hypothesis and flexibility and constant program modification,

For Discussion: The Case of Barney

Barney's principal agrees with the grade two teacher and the School Team that a special education committee should consider Barney's case. In the first place, Barney seems to have a preoccupation with sex, far beyond what most adults would consider normal in a seven year old boy. His speech is filled with sexual innuendo, which no one is sure Barney even understands, but his slang vocabulary is extensive (and he is successfully teaching it to the rest of grade two!).

A second matter is his bullying behaviour. Barney is big for his age, husky and strong. He is very aggressive in the schoolyard, fights a lot, and is particularly cruel to the kindergarten children who are terrified of him. This aggression frequently manifests itself in two other ways. One is in class where in 'group', Barney dominates. He has to be in charge. The other is grabbing — he calls it "feeling up" — the girls in class. He has even tried it with some of the older girls in the schoolyard. This grabbing is done openly sometimes, surreptitiously at other times, and is clearly not play.

The third problem seems almost pale in terms of corrective urgency. Barney doesn't seem to be able to remember things in class. He may learn a letter or a word one day and seem to have comprehended it (i.e., incorporated the learning into his long term memory) but on the next day he doesn't seem

to know it. He may print a simple story and read it to the teacher, but two days later can no longer read it. In the teacher's opinion, this deficiency is genuine. It's not some kind of avoidance on Barney's part.

There is some complication in Barney's family life. The family is from Europe. Barney has mastered English, but speaks the European language at home. Mother goes to English classes. Father has not learned English and adamantly refuses to. He has had a full time job since their arrival in Canada. Father is in his mid-forties, twenty years older than Mother. Barney is an only child.

At school, Barney describes what appears to be very rough play with his father: being swung around by the feet, tossed in the air, etc. Barney is encouraged to punch his father as hard as possible. (All the above has been verified by Mother, who comes to teacher-parent conferences willingly. Father refuses to attend, or even come to the school.)

Mother has agreed to accept the recommendations of a special education committee, but the principal candidly admits his doubts that any recommendations will succeed without some help at home. The grade two teacher, meanwhile, wants to know if it would be helpful to transfer Barney to a behavioural class.

the decision-making and the delivery of service are likely to be much more current, not to mention appropriate, if they take place on site. By the early nineties therefore, the trend in Canada had moved clearly toward management of special needs in the local community school and specifically in the regular classroom.

The Vitality of Parent Support

Political activism by parent and other advocacy groups on behalf of students with special needs, had — and continues to have — a powerful effect on the provincial governments. The strength and sophistication of lobbying efforts by groups like the Association for Children with Learning Disabilities (now the Learning Disabilities Association) and The Association for Bright Children, among others, were instrumental in motivating educational jurisdictions to improve the lot of exceptional students. Advocacy groups were a strong force in encouraging governments to enshrine educational rights for exceptional students in legislation.

At the same time, it became accepted, indeed encouraged, practice among professional educators, especially by the nineteen nineties, to involve parents far more extensively in day by day educational decision-making.

Legislation To Guarantee Education

The availability of special education for students with special needs has always been profoundly affected by legislation and public policy. In the final quarter of the century, each of the provinces and territories moved toward a position that guarantees this availability. As is typical for educational policy and practice generally in Canada, the twelve jurisdictions in the country vary on specifics. Some have very direct and detailed legislation; others rely on policy. All of them however, by the 1980s, had made special education available in a manner and to an extent that was not even contemplated before the 1960s. (For a summary, see Figure 1-A. See also Appendix A for more information on legislation and policy in each of the jurisdictions.)

The trend toward guaranteeing special education for exceptional students in Canada was given great impetus, psychologically, by legislation in the U.S.A., and both psychologically and directly by the *Canadian Charter of Rights and Freedoms*.

Special Education by Province and Territory*

Prov./Terr.	Legislation	Policy
Yukon	✔	
N.W.T.	✔	
B.C.		✔
Alberta		✔
Saskatchewan	✔	
Manitoba	✔	
Ontario	✔	
Quebec	✔	
New Brunswick	✔	
Nova Scotia	✔	
P.E.I.		✔
Newfoundland	✔	

*The Education Acts in each of the provinces and territories are continually under passive and active review, particularly in matters of special education. At the time of publication, British Columbia, Alberta, Saskatchewan, Manitoba, Ontario and Newfoundland were conducting active reviews.

Figure 1-A

Legislation in the U.S.A.

A landmark piece of legislation in the U.S.A. in 1975, 'The Education for All Handicapped Children Act', Public Law 94-142, now changed to 'Individuals with Disabilities Education Act' (IDEA) mandates appropriate education for every handicapped student, appropriate screening procedures, consultation with parents (and due process rights if they disagree with the school), a written individual education plan (IEP) for each student, placement in the least restrictive environment appropriate to the student's needs, and other features. (In 1990, the U.S. Congress amended 94-142 with Public Law 99-457, extending the protection of the original Act to infants and toddlers.)

Although Saskatchewan had established ground-breaking policy in 1971, and Nova Scotia in 1973, the fanfare of Public Law 94-142 in 1975 changed the face of special

For further information on U.S. Public Law 94-142, see Appendix A.

education forever. It guaranteed education for students with special needs; it gave huge impetus to the idea of integration, and it put special education and exceptionalities in the limelight as never before. Regrettably, it also generated a huge bureaucracy and almost overwhelming bureaucratic procedures. Nevertheless, it provided a pioneering model for other legislators to follow. Within five years, the Ontario government passed the Education Amendment Act (1980), at the time the most stringently mandatory legislation in Canada.

By the end of the 80's, all provinces and territories were providing full special education programs in the regular school systems, with all but a few having passed mandatory legislation to guarantee them.

The Impact of the Canadian Charter of Rights and Freedoms

When the *Canadian Charter of Rights and Freedoms* came into effect in 1982, advocates of students with special needs anticipated a major shift in educational practice that would clearly favour those students, and predicted that a flood of court cases would bring it about. For the first time in Canadian history, there would be legal, constitutional grounds to fight what they perceived to be discriminatory practices against exceptional students. The provisions under Section 7 and Section 15 of The Charter offered that support.

However, while there were a small number of significant challenges to educational practice across the country, especially in matters of the right of special needs students to education in a regular school (See Black-Branch 1993, Dickinson & MacKay, 1989, and others) a decade later, the predicted flood of cases had not yet appeared. One likely reason is that the wording of the Charter is ambiguous and open-ended, making the argument of cases difficult. Does the "equality" stated in Section 15, for example, mean equal access? Or does it mean equal opportunity? And what, at the core, does 'equal opportunity' mean for say, a student with special needs like those Larin has? Does it mean that his *needs* are actually *rights* which a school system must guarantee by special, appropriate placement and resources and practice — which in turn begs the question: what is *appropriate*?

Given the complexity of the issues above, it is not difficult to appreciate another reason why the Charter has not yet stirred up the amount of challenge that was first anticipated: Canadian judges have a history of reluctance to become involved in educational matters.

Perhaps the most important reason however, is that by the time the Charter became law, the provinces and territories of Canada were already moving toward legislation and policy that included students with special needs in their systems. Throughout Canada today, students with special needs have the right to an education, and generally, this education takes place in the regular school system. In the majority of those systems, integration of special students into regular classes is by far the most frequent practice. It may be possible to argue that it was the Charter which motivated educational administrators to make accommodations, provide resources, and establish practices which have gone a long way toward the equality that advocates call for. However that trend was already well-established by the time the Charter was passed. There is no question the Charter gave an impetus, but for the most part, educators were already on track.

—from the Canadian Charter Of Rights And Freedoms:

1. The *Canadian Charter of Rights and Freedoms* guarantees the rights and freedoms set out in it subject only to such reasonable limits prescribed by law as can be demonstrably justified in a free and democratic society.

7. Everyone has the right to life, liberty and security of the person and the right not to be deprived thereof except in accordance with the principles of fundamental justice.

15. (1) Every individual is equal before and under the law and has the right to the equal protection and equal benefit of the law without discrimination and, in particular, without discrimination based on race, national or ethnic origin, colour, religion, sex, age or mental or physical disability.

(2) Subsection (1) does not preclude any law, program or activity that has as its object the amelioration of conditions of disadvantaged individuals or groups including those that are disadvantaged because of race, national or ethnic origin, colour, religion, sex, age or mental or physical disability.

At the same time, the Charter also gave impetus to a practice that had developed a momentum of its own: namely, recognition not only of the rights of parents, but of the potential value of their contribution to an exceptional student's education. Many educational administrators, and parents as well, learned that very positive results can accrue when a flexible, modifiable, appropriate placement and program is established for a special student through collegial and cooperative efforts. An undeniable benefit of the Charter for students with special needs is that it tips the balance in their favour. The very fact of The Charter, with all that it implies, is in most cases, all that is necessary to ensure that all parties will try to bring about the best possible outcome without the potentially awkward side effects of litigation.

Still, a decade in constitutional and rights law is but a mote in time. The legal system in Canada is perhaps the only entity in the country that moves even slower than education, and given that experts continue to predict that there are going to be more and more Charter challenges regarding special education (Black-Branch, 1993) it may be that we have seen only the tip of the iceberg. Most educators hope fervently, that should this be the case, the challenges yet to come will be limited to matters of access and not educational practice. Ironically, a significant legal decision from, say, the Supreme Court of Canada, could actually work against special students by establishing a single country-wide standard, or common requirement in educational placement or practice. One thing that has been learned in the very brief history of special education and in the even briefer experience with integration as the norm, is that meeting the educational needs of special students requires educational responses on a by-case basis. System-wide — country-wide — policies on matters like identification, placement and program could have a deleterious effect.

The Impact of Human Rights Codes

An element in the special education mix that has yet to sort itself out in Canada is the role to be played by the various provincial and territorial commissions on human rights. The relatively brief experience in the country with these various commissions is that they seem far more willing to become involved in educational

issues than the courts are, particularly in matters of appropriate placement. Given that there are advocates who perceive the rights of special students in a very particular and focused way, it may well be that the impact of human rights codes has yet to be fully absorbed in Canada's education systems.

Today, Integration As The Norm

During the period when the education of exceptional students in the regular school system was gradually becoming normal and accepted practice, the typical administrative design was one which tended to group the students in self-contained classes, often according to what was perceived to be a common need. It was not uncommon, therefore, to see physically disabled students, for example, grouped together, not necessarily on the basis of their academic potential but on the basis of their disability. This was frequently the case even though the natures of their individual physical disabilities were often widely disparate! Classes like these were usually referred to as the "resource class" or "special class" or "developmental class". Other euphemisms abounded, although the generic term used by almost everyone was at first *segregated class*, eventually replaced by *self-contained class* or *congregated class* in educational parlance.

Needless to say, it did not take long for both the descriptions and the type of placement to take on somewhat pejorative connotations. Very often this developed because these classes were usually made up of students whose exceptional needs were very visibly different (such as physically disabled students and those with multiple disabilities), or made up of students with a variety of mental handicaps.

The principal argument for establishing such class structures is not hard to figure out: it is easier to deliver "service" (i.e., personnel, resources, and special accommodations), easier to provide a better adult care ratio and, arguably, less expensive and easier to deliver the service when there is a universal need.

Whether this kind of class structure is good/bad, best/worst, or right/wrong is moot. And given that all educators accept that exceptional pupils have a right to education, *placement* continues to be the single most contested issue in all of special education. (See especially Chapters 3, 4, and 14 for more on this.)

Over time, certainly by the final decade of the twentieth century, educators — not without some prodding by advocates of exceptional students — came to accept that this form of segregation, at least on a widespread basis, may have negative effects that can quite possibly outweigh the benefits. Not that this position was then, or is now, a unanimous one. Many advocates, particularly those who argue for learning disabled students, for gifted students and for deaf students, contend that a specialized setting is not only preferable but in fact necessary if these students are to reach their potential and live their lives in the fullest and most effective way. Nevertheless, by the nineteen-nineties, the prevailing placement for the majority of exceptional students in Canada had become the regular class. Integration had become the norm.

This does not mean that *all* Canadian students with special needs today are automatically being placed in regular classes. Common sense, and an accumulation of empirical evidence from experience with integration, teaches that for a small minority of students, a specialized environment for a period of time is often more beneficial. Rather, integration as the norm means that placement decisions have come to be made on the premise that the regular class is the preferred setting for students with special needs, and that all program planning, along with all marshalling of resources, is carried out with that objective in mind. Only after due deliberation, and in most cases, extensive consultation with parents, is a part

or full time self-contained placement chosen as a preferred alternative.

That we have generally arrived at this point in special education in Canada is significant, not because it represents a major scientific breakthrough, but rather because it represents a victory for common sense, a factor that prevails when professional educators and caring parents pool their knowledge, their intelligence and their good will on behalf of students with special needs. It is an indication of the maturing of special education.

Special Education As a Mature Force

Universal access to education is guaranteed now for exceptional students; integration is generally accepted as the most normal and desireable situation; and students with special needs are generally perceived as just that: *students*. In short, special education has become a normal, integral and functional part of education in general. For that reason it makes sense to conclude that, quite likely, the major steps for special education have now been taken. Not that continuing change and development and improvement are no longer necessary. They will always be necessary and will continue to happen. But special education is positioned now so that changes will occur in the larger context of all education. As education itself changes, special education will change with it. In that context, the future of special education will most likely be expressed in positive refinements of what has already been achieved in the past quarter century.

2

Exceptional Students in Canada

What Is an Exceptional Student?

An exceptional student is one who has special needs. To meet those needs appropriately, a school system makes certain modifications for the student.

Over the brief history of special education in Canada, special needs have tended to be grouped, for discussion and, to some extent, for systemic purposes, into the following very broad, general categories.

☐ *Intellectual differences:* including students who are intellectually gifted and those who are mentally handicapped.

☐ *Sensory handicaps:* including students with auditory or visual problems.

☐ *Communication disorders:* including students with speech and language problems. Learning disabled students are included in this category.

☐ *Physical disabilities:* including students with physical problems arising from birth defects, orthopedic conditions, and conditions resulting from disease. Generally, students with neurologically based difficulties are included in this category.

☐ *Behaviour disorders:* including students with psychoses, and those who are socially maladjusted or emotionally disturbed.

☐ *Developmental disabilities:* including students with pervasive disorders like autism and those with multiple disabilities.

It is important to note that the idea of categorization like this is a continuing controversy in special education (See later chapters, e.g., Chapter 3) especially because of what critics say are the negative connotations implicit in any such form of identification. A further difficulty lies in the fact that educational jurisdictions tend to interpret some of the above categories quite arbitrarily, so that 'developmental' for example is used in a variety of different ways in Canada. Nevertheless, categories — classifications — continue to be used in special education, principally to clarify discussion, research, teacher development and training, and scientific investigation. For obvious reasons, they are used for administrative and statistical purposes as well, usually broken down by an individual jurisdiction into the specific sub-classifications it finds most useful.

How Many Students in Canada Are Considered Exceptional?

Most professionals are wary of this question. Data are difficult to collect and even more difficult to present as accurate for a variety of reasons. Some boards of education, for example, are quite rigorous in their interpretation of what consititutes — say — *learning disability*, whereas some may be very unspecific. And there are others that use no classifications at all.

Exceptional Students In Canada (1983): Numbers and Percentages*

	Number of Pupils	% of Excep. Pop.	% of School Pop.
Mentally Handicapped	63 359	11.3	1.75
Learning Disabled	159 159	28.4 *11-15*	4.41
Behaviour/Emotional Disordered	27 298	4.9	0.78
Speech Impaired *+Language*	43 914	7.9 *2*	1.22
Visually Impaired	2 029	0.4	0.06
Hearing Impaired	5 231	0.9 *0.6*	0.14
Physically Disabled	2 971	0.5	0.08
Multiply Handicapped	11 369	2.0	0.31
Other†	244 390	43.7	6.77

* from Canadian Council of Ministers of Education, 1983.

† includes pupils in modified and remedial programs, and students who in the early 1980's were considered mildly mentally handicapped but who today are far less frequently identified as exceptional.

Figure 2-A

Differences in definitions also affect the data. What may be defined *behavioural* in one district may not be in another. (Note the differences, for example, in the classifications between Figure 2-A and Figure 2-B.) Professionals in the speech field — at least to others in related fields — seem to have extraordinarily high standards for what consititutes normal speech and language, so that to some, the numbers in the speech classification are unrealistically high. The whole field of mental retardation (even using the term) has been undergoing such change that statements of number in this classification could be regarded as at least partly subjective.

Other problems abound. For one, privacy regulations make data difficult to collect. Another is that students with more than one disability are sometimes classified (and counted) in each of the disabilities, and sometimes only in the primary one — *if* it can be determined which disability is primary! (What is primary can vary according to the context.) Geography in Canada is sometimes a barrier to collection. Hearing loss in the eastern Arctic, for example, seems to be unusually wide-spread; yet hard data on the extent of the situation are very difficult to put together. The very matter of identification is itself an issue. The validity and reliability of assessment instruments and methods are continually under attack.

A continuing irritant to professional educators is the extent of the discrepancies in reported numbers of exceptional students. The Canadian Council of Ministers of Education for instance, issued data in 1983 indicating that 15.5 per cent of the school-age population is considered exceptional. (See Figure 2-A.) On the other hand, a figure of 10 to 12 per cent has been offered in the literature for so long now that it has become an almost unquestioned truth.

The extent to which the numbers vary from one jurisdiction to another can be seen in Figure 2-B (next page). These data show four randomly selected categories of exceptionality as reported by five different Canadian provinces in 1989. The significant differences in prevalence from one province to another can only be reasonably explained by the fact that there must be significant differences in identification procedures from province to province, as well as differences in data gathering, and in other matters such as how an exceptionality is defined.

One of the as yet unsung legacies of Ontario's mandatory special education legislation, popularly known as Bill 82, may well be a readjustment in the popular notion of just how many students in a typical school-age population are thought to be exceptional. In the first complete school year after the legislation was implemented (1985-86) Ontario identified 6.5 per cent of the school-age population as exceptional. Four years later (1989-90) after this specific, stringent, mandatory legislation was solidly established so that very, very few students with special needs "fell through the cracks", the percentage of the school-age population officially identified exceptional in the province was 7.9. The percentage figure for the following school year (1990-91) and for the next

(1991-92) was almost exactly the same despite the fact that the total school-age population had increased each year. These data suggest quite strongly, that approximately 8 per cent may well be an accurate number to describe how many students in a typical jurisdiction are exceptional.

Exceptional Students in Canada (1989) Numbers and Percentages*

Province	Number of Pupils	% of School Pop.	% of Excep. Pop.
I. Learning Disabled			
Nova Scotia	12 106	7.14	64.32
Quebec	96 585	10.23	76.40
Ontario	55 768	3.10	40.90
Saskatchewan	3 665	2.95	60.92
British Columbia	6 637	1.29	10.95
II: Behaviour Disordered			
Nova Scotia	747	0.44	3.96
Quebec	13 722	1.45	10.85
Ontario	8 104	0.45	5.94
Saskatchewan	548	0.26	9.10
British Columbia	2 578	0.50	0.42
III: Physically Disabled †			
Nova Scotia	174	0.10	0.92
Quebec	1 458	0.15	1.15
Ontario	1 030	0.06	0.75
Saskatchewan	173	0.08	2.87
British Columbia	425	0.08	0.70
IV: TMR ‡			
Nova Scotia	452	0.27	2.40
Quebec	2 404	0.25	1.90
Ontario	7 600	0.42	5.57
Saskatchewan	728	0.35	12.10
British Columbia	1 254	0.24	2.06

* from Council For Exceptional Children, 1989

† 'Orthopaedic' is used in Saskatchewan and Ontario

‡ (Trainable Mentally Retarded) The term is less frequently used now across Canada and in some jurisdictions (e.g., Ontario in 1993) has been set aside by actual legislative change.

Figure 2-B

Where Do Exceptional Students in Canada Receive Special Education?

The majority of Canadian students with special needs attend regular classes in community schools. In other words, the majority are integrated, or 'included'. To use a more scientific term than "majority" is extremely difficult because jurisdictions across the country vary in what they mean by 'integration', by 'inclusion', and by 'attending regular classes'.

New Brunswick in 1986, for example, passed legislation which eliminated its Auxiliary Classes Act and mandated integration of exceptional students into regular classes. Yet New Brunswick continues to participate in the Atlantic Provinces Special Education Authority (APSEA; see Appendix A) and sends some of its deaf students, for example, to separate, specialized schools run by APSEA. Does this mean then, that New Brunswick's exceptional student population is fully integrated, or *almost* fully integrated? The distinction, for those who debate integration, is significant.

For the school year 1990-91, the province of Ontario's statistics on school enrolments reported that 157,227 students, or 7.9% of the total school population were identified as exceptional.*

However, in matters of integration or "attending regular classes", Ontario's data for that year distinguish between those students who attended regular classes full time, and those who attended part time. In those data, it was shown that 17.2% of the exceptional students attended regular classes *full time*, and that 65.2% attended regular classes *part time*. Does this then mean that in Ontario in 1990-91, 17.2% of exceptional students were integrated, or 65.2%? Or if the two types of placement are combined, does it mean that 82.4% of exceptional students in the province were integrated?

*Statistical Services Section, Ontario Ministry of Education, 1991.

For Discussion: The Case of Kerry and Krista

Until his sixteenth birthday at the end of his grade ten year, Kerry's school career had been relatively without incident, given the fact that he had been born profoundly deaf. The same smoothness can be ascribed to the school career of his twin sister, Krista. An important difference however, is that Krista's hearing is normal. Also, she was identified as 'gifted' in grade six, an identification that has been confirmed in each school year since.

From kindergarten to the present (i.e., grade ten) Kerry and Krista have been in the same class. The only exception was a period of two years, for grades four and five, when Kerry attended a residential school for the deaf. Here, he learned to sign proficiently and this is now his principal means of communication.

Both young people have always exhibited the kind of exceptional closeness frequently observed in twins, with the result that Krista has, in effect, become her brother's advocate and principal communicator with the hearing world. Otherwise, Kerry manages his own situation effectively. He is very assertive, unquestionably bright, and academically capable —although there is some suspicion that his achievements would not be quite so extensive were it not for the role played by Krista, and that without her, he would have real difficulty.

The decision that the school, the twins, and their parents are now confronting, is whether Kerry and Krista should stay together for grade eleven. Since grade six, Kerry has had a signing interpreter in class, part time. (Krista signs and interprets for him as well.) The objective at the time this assistance was set up, was that it be gradually phased out as Kerry supposedly improved his speech and developed his ability to understand without sign. The opposite has happened. Kerry's speech has deteriorated and the amount of signing has increased.

What makes this an issue is that next year, a special class will be formed in grade eleven, for students like Krista who have demonstrated clearly superior ability. This class will operate almost entirely on a cooperative learning and project basis. Kerry's history confirms his difficulty with this style. Krista, on the other hand, thrives on it.

Over the past few years there have been several discussions between the school and the family over the appropriateness of enrolling the twins in separate programs. This year, for the first time, the twins were fully involved in the discussions. Kerry is adamantly opposed to the separation. Krista is ambivalent. The parents are uneasy. The school wants to do what is best for everyone.

Generally, the trend, internationally, is to report integration rates in this latter way. Italy, for example, long regarded by special educators as the leading western model of aggressive integration, today places about 90% of its exceptional students in regular classrooms. Italy had established a practice of full integration by 1971, yet by 1977 its legislation was modified, in part to accommodate the fact that certain students were not able to benefit from it. Nevertheless, Italy continues to be regarded as a model of full integration (Ferro, 1990). In Sweden, another system regarded as fully integrated, 90% of all exceptional children attend their local community schools (Gartner et al.,

1991) but 85% of the students with moderate and severe mental handicaps are assigned to self-contained classes, as well as 64% of students with multiple exceptionalities (Grunewald, 1986). England and France follow legislation that includes an 'integration to the greatest extent possible' principle (Hegarty, 1987; Zucman, 1985) which is similar to U.S. legislation. Yet all three countries have different statistical interpretations of integration.

The difficulty of presenting scientifically unassailable data is compounded in Canada's case for unlike all of the countries mentioned above, our education systems — and the collection, interpretation, and presentation of data — are governed by the provinces and territories and not by the central government. And as can be seen in Figure 2-B, there is a remarkable lack of similarity in the numbers for a country that, with the possible exception of Quebec, has a remarkably similar culture from coast to coast.

In the end, the lack of firm, country-wide data may well be to the benefit of exceptional students and their parents and teachers. The experience with special education in general, during the past quarter century and with integration in particular, has taught the value of dealing with exceptional students on a by-case basis, of making placement decisions, developing programs and delivering service according to individual need, not according to blanket policy.

Thus while it is very unsatisfactory, statistically, to be able to say only that the *majority* of exceptional students in Canada are integrated, the description not only suggests Canada is consistent with the rest of the western world's education systems, it also suggests that for the students themselves, flexible and dynamic policies prevail.

For Discussion: The Case of Redmond

When Redmond was six, his parents separated and a family court judge decided the boy should live alternate weeks with his mother and father. Hence, Redmond has two legal addresses. Last week his father moved to a new home so that the two addresses are now in different school districts.

Redmond is ten years old in grade three. He has a fairly severe brain injury owing to a motor vehicle accident two years ago. His speech is clear but often echolalic, and his behaviour is very unpredictable. Within the same hour he can be pleasant, reasonable and accommodating, then turn fiercely angry, even on one occasion — but only one so far — violent and uncontrollable.

Academic ability is a mystery in Redmond's case. He appears to learn things but the gains seem to be short term. It is rare for him to be able to demonstrate on a succeeding day that he can repeat what he apparently grasped on the day before. What also distinguishes Redmond is an almost unbelievable artistic talent. His drawings are creative, bold, exciting, and when he wishes them to be, accurate at a level way beyond that of a ten year old or even most adults.

His parents agree that Redmond should attend only one school. The school near his mother's home has a very successful and quite elaborate resource room system; it uses behaviour modification extensively and its language development programs are a model for the board. Student programs here are very individualized and academic achievement is prized. Near the home of Redmond's father, the school is fully integrated; there are no resource rooms or self-contained settings at all. Although there is individualization of program, the school is very much a 'community' in the fullest sense. Academics are valued but social development seems to take precedence.

Both schools, by sheer coincidence, have principals who are deeply committed to fine art programs. What Redmond's parents must resolve is where to enrol him.

3

Some Contemporary Issues in Special Education

Advocacy, Litigation, and Rights

Because the notion of educating exceptional students in the regular school system was a relatively new one only twenty-five years ago, it is not surprising that there was some resistance initially, to guaranteeing them the right to such education. Before experience made clear that exceptional students are indeed educable and in effect, more similar than different, the assumption was fairly widespread that including them in the population eligible for free, public education would impinge detrimentally on the rights of so-called normal students, and would weaken the capacity of the system generally.

The movement to clear the decks of this resistance was given momentum by two factors: one was the intense lobbying and public awareness effort by advocacy groups; the other was litigation in the Canadian courts. The legacy of these two factors continues to have a significant impact on the relationship of educators and exceptional students.

The success of the huge efforts put forth by advocacy groups in the 1970's and 1980's, in the face of what many educators acknowledge was then a fairly high level of inertia in the profession, has meant that the groups continue to flex their muscles, and are seldom content with what they perceive to be only minor gains. The result is that educational — and legislative —

decisions today in regard to exceptional students, indeed in regard to all of education, are profoundly influenced by the policies of advocacy groups. For educators, this influence can be a potential concern because advocacy groups, quite naturally, have very focused objectives.

As well, the success of litigants seeking redress principally through the Canadian Charter of Rights, and under the jurisdiction of the various provincial human rights bodies, has introduced a significant trend toward the use of the legal system to bring about desired objectives. Educators must be aware that parents will turn to the civil courts, especially if there are no mechanisms of appeal in a province's education legislation, with the result that the judiciary, and not professional educators, will be asked to resolve individual educational rights issues. One difficulty with this avenue of redress is that a situation almost automatically becomes fiercely adversarial, and diminishes the cooperation so vital to the education of an exceptional person; the plaintiff may win but the victory is often a hollow one. Another is that the decision of a civil court is likely to be based on what is legally correct, and this in turn may not be what is educationally sensible. Perhaps most serious is the establishment of precedent whereby the decision in a single, unique case can alter the base of operating policy for everyone else.

To Category Or Not To Category

After a quarter century of movement toward normalization and integration, it seems quite paradoxical that the use of categories — labels, some would say — continues as a very widespread and accepted practice. It is paradoxical because the use of categories (or labels or classifications or definitions) seems to contradict the direction in which special education has been moving.

Critics of their use argue that a category by its very nature is inadequate, that the complexity of a human being cannot be summed up in a single concept such as *gifted*. Categories may exaggerate; someone who is described as *deaf* may only be hard of hearing. They are often used incorrectly; a prime and long standing example is the use of *dyslexia* as a synonym for learning disability. And they tend to propagate confusion, most especially as the result of continuing attempts to find mitigating phraseology. A classic case in point is the frenetic search for descriptions to replace *mentally retarded*.

Most insidious of all, critics say, is the potential for preclusive identity: that is, once exceptional needs in persons are classified by means of a category, they will inevitably be perceived primarily in terms of the label rather than simply as human beings who happen to have an exceptionality. The argument is that individuals who have learning disabilities for example, and are labelled L.D., will innocently and unwittingly provoke certain negative, or at least lowered, expectations in those who teach them. Therefore when they commit the kind of errors that all people do in the daily course of life, or depart from the accepted norm in even the slightest way, their behaviour will not be accepted as normal, or forgiven as a temporary aberration, but will be seen as "learning disabled behaviour". The next stage is that these individuals will then rise — or sink — to the expectations others have of them.

In that sense, labels disable.

Yet the continuing use of categories is not so paradoxical if one examines their positive side. Their users contend that the gains made on behalf of students with special needs could well disappear without a category or general,

agreed-upon way to describe unique characteristics. Certainly it is simpler and more logical to engage in academic discussion, in professional development, in in-service teacher training, in all varieties of research, when there is a clear, accepted, and understood frame of reference.

Professional dialogue about an unique remediation strategy for example, or instruction in, say, a computer-enhanced procedure, is far more likely to bear fruit if the professionals engaged in the dialogue are in basic agreement on the target audience.

Research, with its need to isolate variables as much as possible, benefits immeasurably from a shared awareness between reporter and consumer of just what subjects the research concerns.

Administrators face the inevitable factor of accountability, and despite what some feel is an uncomfortably crass reality, administrators need a mutually acceptable taxonomy of description if they are to account for their management of the public purse.

Finally, but by no means least, there is the simple matter of recognition. Advocates in the field of learning disability, for example, are aware of the gains that were made on behalf of students with this particular special need, once learning disability was recognized as a category of special education, once these students were recognized not just as obtuse or unwilling, but as people with a special set of needs to be addressed in a manner that takes cognizance of their uniqueness.

It could well be that over the next quarter century, the use of categories may become a nonissue for the simple reason that over the past quarter century, the thrust toward normalization and integration — the *regularization* of special education — has continued unabated despite the widespread use of categories. It may be reasonable to conclude that the achievements in special education to date, despite the use of categories, means that critics of the practice have not given sufficient credit to the professional quality of those who work with exceptional students, and who see categories only as a convenience for procedure and discussion and administrative decision, not as labels.

Integration/Mainstreaming*

Almost all educators agree that integration of exceptional students into regular classrooms is a desireable end. Where disagreement arises is just how, and to what extent, the desired end can be translated into reality. The most vigorous advocates of integration — including both educators and parents — regard the principle as pure and absolute: *all* students, whether their needs are special or not, should be educated in a common environment, that is, in the same classrooms. They contend that the greatest benefits accrue for exceptional students by simply being in a regular class, modelling normal behaviour, and participating in normal, age-appropriate activities.

Others — again including both educators and parents — although they may well be firm supporters of integration, do not view the matter quite so unconditionally. This group contends that circumstances may make it desirable, indeed necessary, that some exceptional students, for a portion of their program at least, be placed in a relatively more restrictive environment such as a self-contained (i.e., "segregated" or "congregated") class or school.

Proponents of absolute integration contend that the mere availability of a spectrum of settings is offensive. The very existence of alternative settings, they say, can make integration fail for the very simple reason that it does not have to work. Supporters of a range of settings, meanwhile, point to the fact that even those jurisdictions committed to integration have had to make special accommodations in some cases that amount to a form of segregated placement. They argue further that it is unrealistic to assume that total integration is possible.

Whether it is intended or not, there is a contention in the total integration position that this view is morally superior. On the other hand, implicit in the variety-of-settings view is the notion of greater practicality and educational effectiveness, short and long term, for everyone concerned.

It is ironic that a polemic should arise out of these two positions since in the end, both groups want what is best for all students. There is even further irony in that a neutral observer, with no prior information, would have some difficulty at first, distinguishing between a jurisdiction with a total integration policy

*This issue is given further treatment in Chapter 14

and one with a range of settings policy, for both, out of sheer, practical necessity and the benefit of all, will arrange special settings for some exceptional students some of the time.

Unfortunately, a resolution of the argument is not easy to achieve. Research, although it clearly points out the negative effects of segregation, also points to its positive outcomes. Experience with integration is usually very case-specific; it can be misleading to generalize from the success or failure of one, or even several situations. And empirical evidence suggests that it is almost impossible to separate the success or failure of integration from the level of commitment in individual teachers. Ultimately, since the issue of integration seems to be yet another of those educational matters wherein philosophy and practice operate in different conceptual planes, it is reasonable to conclude that whether exceptional students are in a totally integrated setting or in a modified setting, success — in whatever terms – will rise or fall on the will and on the ability of both the teachers and the students themselves.

Cultural and Socio-Economic Differences

Professional educators wince at the accusation that special education is often a depository for the children of poverty and for the culturally different. They wince because over-representation of these groups in special classes is often the case, and that flies directly in the face of everything education stands for. Yet for very real reasons it is easy to see why the special class is often regarded as an ideal placement.

Children of poverty and of some cultural minorities often have a high frequency of severe health and physical problems that affect their education. Conductive hearing loss (usually *otitis media*) among native children in Canada, for example, and eye infections affecting sight, occur at an average rate much higher than that of the general population. Children of minority groups sometimes experience linguistic difficulties that impinge on their school function in a major way. Assessment procedures that do not allow for cultural anomalies can have the effect of placing a child very restrictively in an education system. It is not unusual for children from lower income families or from recently arrived immigrant families to have difficulties simply because they are confused by the demands of the school culture. Sometimes a family's lack of precedent for educational experience as well as lack of support for it, can have a serious effect on a student's performance.

Underlying all of the above is the very frequent situation wherein heads of the families do not manage a child's case by dealing with the school, the education system, and support agencies (or confronting them if necessary) either because they choose not to, or because they lack the sophistication.

For educators the issue is one of delicate choice. From an educational perspective, these are indeed students with very special needs. And very frequently, the needs can be effectively met in a special education mode. However, the educational perspective must inevitably be illuminated by consideration of what is morally and socially appropriate. Identification and placement of a student in special education is a major step, one that can be taken with certainty if the basis of the decision is strictly educational. But when the basis is coloured by social, cultural and economic factors, there is, inevitably, a commensurate erosion of that certainty. It is a hard nut to crack, and no jurisdiction in Canada has yet done so to everyone's satisfaction.

The Gap Between Assessment and Program

In theory, where perfection is always more attainable, the assessment of a student is conducted not just for the purpose of identification, but also for the purpose of program planning. In fact, inasmuch as most exceptionalities are broadly identifiable without formal assessment at all, it may be more accurate to say that the principal purpose of an assessment, after it refines the broad identification, is to provide the information from which program planning can be developed.

For Discussion: The Case of Leeanne

Occasionally, when Leeanne is frustrated or upset, she will stab herself in the leg or arm with a pencil. These incidents have decreased in frequency over the past year but she now shows a tendency to daydream.

Leeanne is eight and a half, with Down syndrome, from a single parent family. Her mother is a medical doctor, a dermatologist, and there is one sibling, a seven year old brother also in the family.

From birth, Leeanne has been the recipient of much care and effort. She was placed on an infant stimulation program almost immediately. She goes to camp, Brownies, skating, and every day spends many hours with her nanny or her mother who, because of her sophistication and her professional position, has been able to gather a range of support services.

Presumably as a consequence of this intense interaction, Leeanne's social skills seem well developed. She speaks easily and without impediment. She is always attractively dressed, and her self-care behaviours seem typical of most eight and a half year olds. With the exception of a few aberrations — the pencil stabbing for instance (she also went through a fairly extended period of spontaneously biting her playmates) — Leeannne seems to be socially well adjusted most of the time.

Academics are another problem. Leeanne can count to 14 or 15, and has been able to for over two years. There has been no progress at all in arithmetic. She enjoys being read to but cannot, or at least does not, read. She can print her name correctly about 50% of the time, but is really only comfortable with printing the L.

The issue at present is as follows: until now, Leeanne has been integrated with her peers (for JK, SK, 1, 2). Next year, the grade 3 class in her neighbourhood school, will be in a "pod" (56 children, 2 teachers, part-time assistant). The school board has recommended that Leeanne go to a self-contained class in a school slightly farther away. (There will be a fourteen minute bus ride.) This is a regular school, with three self-contained classes. In Leeanne's proposed class, there will be six pupils, one teacher and a full time assistant. The program is high-intensity language development. The class will be mainstreamed for music, art, lunches, recess, field trips, special events, (about 50% of the day).

Leeanne's mother insists her daughter will be much better off in the neighbourhood school, in the grade 3 pod, and plans to fight for this.

Like so much of education, the practice often stumbles clumsily after the theory. It does so for several reasons. Chief among them is the strange combination of expertise and naivety that seems to prevail on both sides of the assessment/program planning issue. Psychologists or psychometrists or other assessors, without actual experience in teaching, often have either idealistic or simplistic notions of what actually occurs minute by minute in a classroom. Many classroom teachers, on the other hand, are not well-versed in assessment procedures, and frequently have difficulty coming to grips with the results of an assessment, most especially in translating the results into program.

To be fair to both sides, the number of professional, concerned, caring assessors and teachers who attempt to rise above this problem is by far the majority. Yet they are frequently obstructed by matters not of their own making. The gap begins with their own training, for traditionally, neither gets opportunity to gain more than sketchy knowledge about the other. (Many universities and colleges are taking steps to remedy this.) As well, both sides argue that the gap could easily be narrowed, even closed, by direct communication: that if the teacher(s) and teaching assistant(s) of the student being assessed can communicate directly with the assessor, the questions that need answers will at least be put on the table. Yet in many jurisdictions, this very simple expedient is impeded by bureaucracy and systems management. It is very common policy for assessors to obtain and report data only to a third party (coordinator, committee, principal, etc.). Then for a variety of reasons such as privacy regulations, work loads, or in some cases, inefficiency, these data come to the classroom, if at all, in a form that is altered or diluted or summarized to the point of irrelevance.

It is the student who falls into the gap this system creates. The assessment may well be competent; the teachers may well be effective. But unless there is opportunity for some form of direct communication, the whole point of the procedure is diminished.

Teacher Responsibility Versus Bureaucracy and Tradition

All teachers regard the academic success of their students as a high and appropriate priority. Yet very few ever stop there; equally important for most teachers is their role in developing the full human potential of every one of their students. The freedom to pursue such a vision of combined professional purpose is essential to effective teaching and learning.

Teachers with exceptional students in their classes have extra difficulty in this pursuit. Part of the difficulty is having to, and wanting to, and trying to, find the time and opportunity and skill to respond to needs that appear to go beyond the normal demands one might reasonably anticipate in a classroom. Experience has taught that no matter how extensive the support available, students with special needs invariably require something extra from the teacher. And while teachers are generally willing and able to do that something extra, a difficulty arises in the attempts to do so without denying the rest of the students the equal treatment they deserve.

Finding this balance is extremely difficult, and the fact that so many teachers are successful much of the time is a tribute to the profession. However to find the balance, a teacher needs the freedom to make decisions, and this freedom is often obstructed by traditional educational practice. Schools are run bureaucratically, with all the pluses and

from an address by Evelyn T., school board chair, and member of the Cree nation, to an audience of teachers in Edmonton

"...We have come a long way in understanding each other's funny ways. Pretty well everyone of my generation realizes now that when a white person shakes hands so vigorously it only means you're being friendly, not that you're looking for a fight! And I think, on the other hand, you now know that when our children avoid looking you straight in the eye, it means they are being polite, not that they're guilty of something.

But one thing we still have to work on — both of us — is our different attitudes to silence. My people revere silence. That's reasonable, you know, in a hunting tradition. Noise — *talking* — means failure to a hunter. Schools though, are full of talk. They thrive on it. And sometimes, because our children don't seem to take part, they seem different – exceptional. Now really, whose problem is this? ..."

minuses that bureaucracy implies. Because special education is relatively new, and because it seems to attract a disproportionate amount of legalism, and because its implementation frequently incorporates a wider range of professionals and a greater degree of administrative activity than regular education, the bureaucracy tends to be thicker, and often more regulatory and precise. The result is that teachers are often denied the autonomy to make decisions that realistically, can only be made ad hoc and on-site. The mere existence of the bureaucracy, no matter how enlightened its application, can deny teachers the flexibility and spontaneity (and most often, simple common sense) so vital to fulfilling their role professionally.

The issue is often exacerbated by the not-yet-completely-dead medical model tradition, wherein the teacher, despite his or her position on the front lines, is denied expert status and must frequently yield to decisions that are made far away from the classroom. Further delicacy arises in the more recent phenomenon of intensive, day-to-day parental involvement. Although initial experience suggests that the benefits are significant, close parental involvement, even in the most accommodating situations, holds the potential for stress, especially in the case of parents who advocate vigorously.

Taken together, or even separately, these are pressures which may deny a classroom teacher the level of responsibility necessary to be effective. It is an issue that has not yet worked its way through the special education experience, and one on which the progress of the past twenty-five years could well founder, for after the last bell of technical advance or service delivery or change in policy has been rung, it is only in classroom implementation where success or failure is realized. And classroom implementation is in the hands of the teacher.

For Discussion: The Case of Arnold

As the result of birth trauma (anoxia), Arnold is intellectually slower than most seven year olds. He speaks with a lisp that seems very resistant to speech therapy. And as if life had not already dealt Arnold enough poor cards, he has somewhat distorted facial features owing to an accident in babyhood (a fall down porch steps onto a sidewalk).

Despite all of this, Arnold is infinitely good-natured. He never complains; he always cooperates with his teachers and his classmates; and he cheerfully attempts every task put before him, although he usually fails to complete it, or to do it properly.

Arnold's speech and appearance provoke teasing and cruel mockery particularly from older boys. However the staff's, and the administration's, fondness for this likeable little boy has led them to crack down extraordinarily hard on any hazing, so that it has decreased considerably. In Arnold's own class he has many friends.

Arnold's parents are loving, and like him, easy going and cheerful. They both work in a local assembly plant and both respond dutifully to any requests from the school. They are quite sanguine about Arnold and his future, a stance that his teacher in grade two does not share.

Arnold has made no progress since early grade one. He is in the remedial reading group, still draws (poorly) his stories and waits for someone to write the narration he provides, and his basic arithmetic skills are uncertain. The teacher, the principal, and the primary consultant are reluctantly beginning to agree that Arnold is not achieving as well as he might in his present situation.

One response being considered is to transfer Arnold to a special class, part time, where he might be able to get more intensive instruction. There is such a class available but it is in another school and everyone is loathe to see Arnold leave. Another possibility is to have a teaching assistant assigned to Arnold's class for half the day, to provide the extra attention he — and several other students — need. In order to do this however, board policy requires that there be at least one student in the class formally identified as mentally handicapped. Although there is already one student in the class who meets all the criteria for that identification, her parents have steadfastly fought against any such formal classification. Arnold's parents, on the other hand, have no objection to his being identified that way.

The Economics of Special Education

Nothing exposes the political and moral tenderness of special education more than money. It takes no great insight to realize that the costs of educating an exceptional student generally exceed those of educating one who is not. (A study by the Rand Corporation [Kakalik et al., 1981] suggests that the cost is increased by a factor of six in the case of a blind student for example, by three in a student identified behavioural, and by about two in the case of one who is learning disabled.) Generally, these costs arise mostly from the number and type of personnel required for special education and from the amount of specialized technology used.

When the costs of public education are under attack — which seems to be most of the time — it takes equally minimal insight to realize that special education is a readily available target if only because it is so visibly expensive, and because its outcomes are often so uncertain. The latter issue becomes even more sensitive and profoundly delicate when cost-benefit analysis is applied. That is: just what is the return to society for the money spent trying to educate someone whose exceptionality for example, is so pronounced that he

---

Timothy W. versus Rochester, New Hampshire

Timothy was born with severe handicaps. He is cortically blind, quadriplegic, makes no sounds and has seizure disorders. The Rochester, New Hampshire school district applied for a hearing to be excused from an obligation to educate Timothy on the grounds that he could not benefit. The hearing officer denied the application but the decision was reversed by the federal district court in 1988. In 1989, the Court of Appeal overturned the federal court decision, following which the U.S. Supreme Court declined to hear further appeals. Timothy therefore became an educational — and necessarily, custodial — responsibility for the Rochester district. It is a small jurisdiction, with a correspondingly small tax base, and school officials indicated that because of the obligations to Timothy, they would have to realign priorities for the entire district.

---

or she will always need some kind of custodial care? The issue becomes still more controversial when it is overlaid with the accusation that the expense may well reduce the opportunity for those who do have the potential, not only to return a benefit to society but to keep the whole system going in the first place.

Even though the posing of questions like these seems to deny the very soul of our culture and the essence of what we like to think of as our civilizing spirit, they are impossible to ignore, especially in periods of economic downturn. On the other hand, they are also natural and honest questions. After a quarter century in which special education grew from almost nothing into an integral part of education in general, the field seems to have reached a point of maturity at which it must pause and reassess itself in this way.

That process, for most school jurisdictions and for much of professional practice, is well launched. For educators, the issue is not one of whether to educate exceptional students, for the overwhelming majority would fight to the last breath for the right of *all* students to be educated. Rather, the issue is how to do it in the best and most effective (including costs) way. Clearly this is one of the challenges of the next quarter century.

4

Service Delivery:
The Placements • The Personnel • The Process

The Placements

When factors like legislation, official policy, authorized practice — and politics — are set aside, special education is essentially a three stage procedure:

1. Determining that a student has special needs;

2. Delivering the program and instruction and support that will meet those needs;

3. Evaluating the student's progress.

Needless to say, because Canada's education systems are publicly supported and bureaucratically organized, and because special education is a field where extremely diverse opinions prevail and advocacy plays a large role, it is not surprising that the three stages above seem remarkably uncomplicated in comparison to what actually goes on day by day. Nevertheless, the sequence summarizes precisely what needs to be done in the delivery of special education service: determine the need, deliver the appropriate response, and then evaluate the results. One of the first — and most contentious — matters to resolve, is just where to do this.

A description of what have been typical placements or settings follows here.

Regular Classroom

In this setting, the exceptional student's education is delivered by the regular classroom teacher with whatever resources would normally be in that classroom in any case. Very often in this setting and situation, what is special about the student's education is a straightforward adjustment or modification of his or her program to accommodate special needs of one kind or another. A reasonable example would be the situation of a student who has spina bifida and does not walk. If this student has learned to manage his own condition, as most do, he will participate in every aspect of the regular classroom in an entirely normal way. But for certain parts of his program like physical education, the teacher may make accommodations for him. Or should he need extra time for, say, personal hygiene, the teacher would again make accommodations.

Regular Classroom With Support

In this situation, extra support in a variety of forms is delivered in the classroom to either student, or teacher, or both. For example, in the case of say, a deaf student, the extra support may range from special technical equipment to the presence of a signing interpreter. At the same time, a teacher or consultant with specialized knowledge about deafness may work with the classroom teacher in anything from program preparation to in-service training.

A most effective and certainly very popular form of direct in-classroom assistance is the educational or teaching assistant, or classroom aide.

Part-Time Special Class (Resource Room)

For part of their program, some exceptional students are deemed to need a more intense, individualized learning experience, one that can best be delivered in a setting that is less distracting or competitive than the regular classroom. This special setting is usually known as a 'resource room', a facility where, ideally, specialized personnel work in close concert with the teacher of the students' regular class to deliver the modified learning experience necessary. Important to this setting is the fact that exceptional students participate in it only part time, even if they do so on a regular basis, and then they return to the regular classroom as a matter of course. A fairly typical example of a student who uses this type of placement is one with a learning disability for whom reading and writing pose extra difficulty. Often, the structure and opportunity for practice and repetition and one-on-one coaching, strategies that usually benefit the learning disabled as well as others with special needs, can be very effectively delivered in this type of resource setting.

For Discussion: The Case of Tara and Deenie

Until six months ago, Tara and Deenie were residents in adjacent rooms of 'R' Wing in a large government-run facility devoted to the care of young people (until age 21) with severe, multiple disabilities. Although there is a school in the facility, staffed by teachers seconded from surrounding communities, the principal purpose of the facility is custodial and it makes no pretence to be otherwise. 'R' Wing is deliberately identified, for all its residents, in addition to their individual special needs, have very high risk respiratory problems.

As part of an integration-into-the community program, combined with an attempt to down-size the facility, Deenie was returned to her foster family home and community high school, full time, with extensive support. The school is fully inclusive, with excellent resource support (Deenie has a full time health aide) but no segregated facilities. All students are fully integrated, all the time.

Deenie's special needs are fairly extensive. Although she is mobile, she stays in a wheelchair because of asthma so severe that the slightest effort seems to bring on an attack. So far the asthma has been entirely unresponsive to medication. Deenie has normal vision but is hard of hearing and wears a hearing aid. Her latest assessment indicated an I.Q. test score of 55. She does not speak, but perseverates in the production of a variety of sounds, often quite loud.

Deenie is seventeen. Her self-care skills are quite well developed but she habitually soils herself if stressed.

After six months in the community, Deenie returned to 'R' Wing. Both the school and her foster parents agreed that she had regressed significantly, and that the frequency and severity of the asthma attacks warranted the return. However, this decision has had an effect on Tara's case. Tara was to be integrated into the same school as Deenie at the beginning of the following school term but her situation is now being reconsidered.

Tara is sixteen. Because of a spinal problem she is mostly immobile, and has limited control over her body. She requires diapering and must be aspirated at least every two hours. Tara is legally blind, profoundly deaf, and makes no sounds. However, it is clear from her facial expressions that she delights in the presence of other people. There have been no attempts to assess her intellectual potential. Tara's waking time is spent in a wheelchair or on a custom-made, skateboard-style platform which can be raised and lowered.

There is considerable concern, given the experience with Deenie, whether services can be delivered effectively — even safely — to a student like Tara, in a high school. Her parents, with the vigorous support of the teaching staff at the facility, insist that Tara's case is an entirely different one from Deenie's.

Full Time Special Class

In order to generate a very specific kind of learning experience it may be deemed appropriate that an exceptional student be placed full time in a special setting. These settings, often called 'self-contained' classrooms, are usually found in regular community schools. Ideally, exceptional students who take their entire program in such classes, participate in all other aspects of the school in the same way as other students. Students identified as gifted are often found in such settings where it may be simpler to arrange the kinds of experiences that will challenge them in the best and most effective way.

Special Day or Residential School

Still other students — usually quite a small number — may have a complexity of needs that require unique responses, some of them in many cases, being entirely separate from their educational needs. In these situations, a very special setting is often necessary to access a variety of specialized support, expertise, and in some cases, care. Examples of such settings vary from schools maintained in hospitals, for students under long term care to schools devoted to very special needs such as Canada's residential schools for the deaf.

Most of the time, these schools are established and run under direct provincial authority, or by organizations (such as the Atlantic Provinces Special Education Authority, APSEA) established under provincial authority. It has become quite unusual now for individual school districts in Canada to maintain special schools.

Range-of-Settings Model? or Integration Model?

Many jurisdictions in Canada have used variations of the Range-of-Settings Model (see Figure 4-A) as their philosophical basis for arranging special education placements. The distinguishing feature of this model, often called 'Cascade', a schema first suggested by Reynolds (1962) and adapted by Deno (1970) is that a range of different settings for exceptional students is available on a formal, more or less permanent basis. The settings, or learning environments, are progressively more specialized, and students therefore, if it is deemed necessary and beneficial, may be formally placed in these alternative settings on a short or longer term basis. An important philosophical principle inherent in the model is that as much as possible, exceptional students be placed in the regular classroom, and that alternative placements always be regarded as temporary.

The Range-of-Settings Model

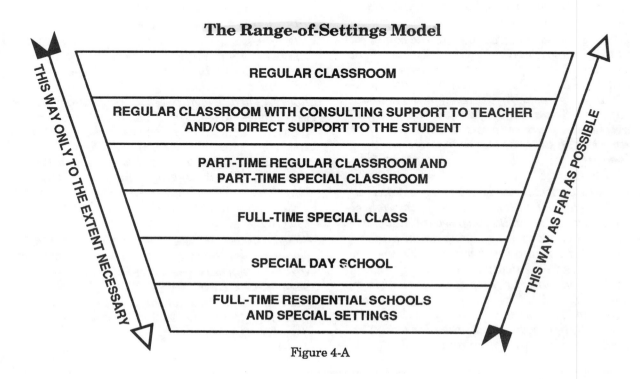

Figure 4-A

Throughout a jurisdiction the entire range of settings is almost always set up on a geography-cum-needs basis. For example, in the case of a very specialized setting, one that is organized to deal with, say, extremely unusual behaviour, a jurisdiction might arrange that in a geographical area containing several schools, only one would offer this special environment on behalf of all. Another school then, might be the only one with a special setting, along with appropriate technology and personnel, for blind students. And so on. Within the geographical area, each school would likely have its own "resource room" or similar, moderately specialized setting for part or full time placements.

Placement arrangements built on the inherent principle of integration tend to be quite flexible and quite ad hoc (see Figure 4-B). Very often, arrangements are created — and collapsed — entirely according to needs of the moment. In fact, there is probably good reason to conclude that placement arrangements are generally so individual, and so tailored on a by-case basis, that there really is no such thing as an integration model at all.

A Descriptive Scheme for Integration

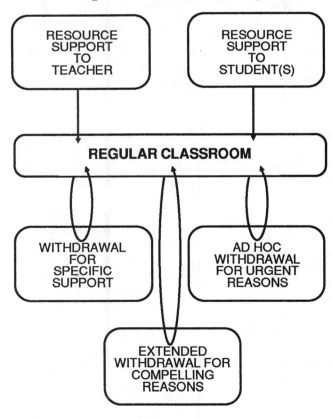

Figure 4-B

It is important to recognize that most systems which have integration as the underpinning philosophy, nevertheless do make at least minimal use of alternative settings. A jurisdiction which has every single one of its exceptional students in regular settings, full time, is rare. However, the fundamental principle of integration is not diluted: an exceptional student, no matter where her special education service is delivered, is considered a full time student in her regular classroom. She is never 'placed' elsewhere.

The Personnel

The number and type of personnel involved in the delivery of service to an exceptional student is usually a factor of just how extensive that student's needs happen to be. Of course, the service can only be delivered if the necessary personnel are available, if the system is organized to flow the service to the need, and if the ever-so-crucial element of *cooperation* prevails. Fortunately, the combination of professionalism among educators and members of related fields, and the natural disposition to ameliorate the situation of students with special needs, means that most of the time, the right things happen.

The list of personnel — of *service providers* — who work with exceptional students in an exceptional setting can be as varied as there are variations among students. By far the most heavily involved personnel in literally every educational situation are combinations of the following:

- classroom teacher
- teaching assistant
- resource teacher
- special consultant

with input from:
- parents
- advisory groups
- advocacy groups
- social agencies

Other personnel, usually employed by a community services agency, or who have independent practices, typically become involved with exceptional students in cases where special needs require a particular expertise. These include members of such fields as psychiatry, psychology, psychometry, social work, health, speech, physical and occupational therapy.

Some boards of education, particularly larger ones, employ members of these professions directly. This is most frequently the case with professionals in the speech area, and with what has come to be called 'psycho-educational services' (or a variation thereof) generally consisting of professionals who specialize in assessment and counselling. The latter are usually more heavily involved at the assessment and program planning stages, although to an extent, they will also become involved in ongoing delivery of service in situations where exceptional behaviour, for example, is a factor.

Deploying The Personnel

Within a single school, or within a single jurisdiction, an abiding concern of administrators is to get the appropriate resources (i.e., the personnel) into the appropriate settings as efficiently and effectively as possible, all with a view to cost, cooperation and availability. To accomplish this, schools and boards generally organize deployment models, or service models: schemas for managing the various elements in delivering service. For once it has been decided that a student is exceptional and is to receive special education support there are certain management factors that cannot be ignored, such as

☐ What personnel are involved in providing support?

☐ How much support will be available?

☐ Who determines the amount of support?

☐ How long will the support continue?

☐ Where does the support take place?

☐ Who has primary responsibility for the student?

☐ When and with what frequency will the case be reviewed?

A typical example of a service model that attempts to address all these factors appears in Figure 4-C (next page).

In this particular arrangement, the school has available a qualified special education teacher (called *Resource Teacher*); a *Rotary Assignment Teacher* who may or may not have special education qualifications, but whose timetable has been arranged so that she will be available as assigned by the principal; and a *Special Needs Instructor*. This last position is filled by an itinerant teacher with very specialized qualifications (e.g., manual communication) and who has responsibility in several schools.

Note that this design in 4-C anticipates the availability of *teaching assistants* in the school, and also makes full use of a *school team*. A school team is a committee of staff members whose purpose is to assist in the delivery of special education service. (See page 32 for more.)

School-Based vs District-Based Deployment?

An increasingly popular approach in Canada now is to turn over management of resources to individual schools. Whereas in district-wide management of service delivery, resources are allocated across an entire jurisdiction (theoretically according to need and availability, but in practice, usually according to a formula) a school-based delivery system is one which uses available resources according to its own, site-determined priorities.

Both styles have merit. The district-wide system because of its wider purview and financial capability can usually tap into a deeper pool of expertise, and allocate it fairly. School-based management however, because it circumvents time-consuming bureaucracy, can bring service to bear more quickly and flexibly, along with a greater likelihood of informal but immediate cooperation and approval from parents.

"I can't thank our school team enough. I mean — they rescued me in my first year!

Nothing that big. Simple things. But it's the simple things that either save you or drive you insane! For example this boy M____. I knew ahead of time that he had some behaviour problems but I still got off on the wrong foot. Did everything wrong with him. Yet in just one meeting with the team I learned what others did that worked. I got to exchange ideas about management. I think most important, I learned I wasn't alone. The team kept M____ and me from becoming enemies. Not that we're buddies now, but we get along and his behaviour is not a problem — for me or for him. The team did that."

—Franco B.

Service Delivery Model For Students with Special Needs

Student Placements →	Regular Classroom ↓	Regular Classroom with Resource Support ↓	Regular Classroom with Resource Support and Withdrawal ↓	Regular Classroom with Withdrawal ↓
Who provides support? →	Resource teacher, principal	Resource teacher, rotary assignment teacher, special needs instructor, teaching assistant	Resource teacher, rotary assignment teacher, special needs instructor, teaching assistant	Rotary assignment teacher, resource teacher, principal, vice-principal, coordinator
Who has responsibility for the support? →	Regular teacher	Shared and flexible among regular teacher, resource teacher, rotary assignment teacher, special needs instructor or teaching assistant	Shared and flexible among regular teacher, resource teacher, rotary assignment teacher, special needs instructor or teaching assistant	Principal, vice-principal, coordinator, resource teacher, or rotary assignment teacher may be solely responsible for withdrawal instruction
Where does the support take place? →	Regular classroom	Regular classroom	Both in and outside the regular classroom	Outside the regular classroom
How much support may be available? →		One hour to a full day every day	One hour to a full day every day	20 minutes to 3 hours daily
Who determines the amount of support? →	Principal in consultation with school team →	→	→	→
How long does the support continue? →	Principal in consultation with school team	Reviewed at least twice annually →	→	→

Figure 4-C

Many districts are now finding a compromise in a marriage of the two approaches (as in Figure 4-C) while at the same time accommodating a thrust toward fuller integration. Experience in special education continues to confirm that the majority of exceptional students' needs require immediate, flexible, varied responses that can best be arranged when there is local control. As well, under these conditions of service delivery it is much easier for a school to reflect whatever the community attitude may be to integration. At the same time, special needs that require expert response — blindness for example, or cases of unique physical need — which tend to be more costly to meet, but are also relatively more rare, can continue to be managed in a district-centred delivery system if necessary.

This combination, integrating board and school service delivery, seems not only fiscally reasonable and responsible, but also practically, addresses the issues of immediacy, flexibility, and optimum use of resources.

The School Team

One of the most significant developments of the late 1980's and early 90's grew from the maturing of special education practice. After two decades of more or less reflexively deferring decisions and delivery to specialists, teachers and administrators came to realize that the mystery of educating the vast majority of students with special needs is not all that different from the mystery of educating any student, and that most educational matters which at first glance imply an elaborate response, can actually be addressed 'in-house'. No one denies that expertise continues to be important, and there is no question that dealing with certain types of exceptionality such as, say, hearing or blindness, often requires specialization of some kind. Nevertheless, the needs of most exceptional students can usually be met through a healthy application of common sense, the kind of approach that all effective teachers use in all of educational practice.

At the same time, teachers have found that cases of special need are almost always more effectively addressed when they are the focus of broad concern, of general cooperation and support, rather than the sole responsibility of a single individual. In many schools, this awareness has now come to be reflected in a more or less formal arrangement known as the School Assistance Team, or the In-School Team or Teacher Support Team or School-Based Support Team or similar title.

The School Team Concept

Described in its simplest terms, a support or assistance team is a committee of staff members whose purpose is to consult with individual teachers who request assistance regarding students perceived as having special needs. The team neither precludes nor replaces formal special education nor diminishes it in any way. Rather, it supports special education, and helps it function more effectively in a school, and more efficiently (as in the model described in Figure 4-C).

In many schools, the team is a forum of first resort to which teachers and parents may bring concerns about the special needs of particular students, without formally invoking special education procedures. This practice not only tends to keep students in the mainstream, but also, by offering this pre-referral opportunity, a team helps to free its school's special education personnel to bring resources to bear where needs are greatest. A team can also enhance service delivery simply by offering broader involvement. Perhaps most important — to teachers and students equally — a team can be a vital instigator of professionalism: the kind of drive that leads a staff to seek solutions.

The Team Concept in Practice

Although procedures vary from to school to school, teams more or less follow a structure that has these features:

i) The team is permanent; i.e., established at least for the school year.

ii) It is composed principally of regular classroom teachers.

iii) Most teams have at least one member who is involved with delivery of special education service in the school (and where the population warrants, an ESL teacher).

iv) The team meets in time set aside for the purpose by the administration.

v) An individual student's needs are brought forward by his regular classroom teacher, who for that 'case' is a member of the team.

vi) After the student's teacher presents the situation, the team proposes teaching strategies, suggests resources, presents alternatives; i.e., consults professionally and collegially.

vii) Followup and review are always built in.

viii) Unresponsive or intractable or extremely delicate situations, or those requiring wider jurisdictional involvement, go forward to administration for more formal disposition. (In most cases, the team stays involved especially if the situation is one in which a whole-school involvement can be helpful — which is often the case.)

A Successful Team at Work

(The following describes an actual team that has operated very successfully for several years in a Canadian school.)

Formal Policies and Procedures:

a) Meetings are weekly and are regularly scheduled. (Thus the team is perceived to be an integral *and* normal part of the school's operation.)

b) No meeting lasts longer than 45 minutes. Team members leave their classes 20 minutes before the lunch hour — the principal's arrangement — and if necessary, spend 25 minutes of their lunch time in the meeting.

c) Every member has an agenda in hand 24 hours ahead of time, including a copy of the referral description from the referring teacher when a 'case' is being brought forward. (See next page.)

d) Only the team leader keeps records. Others *may* do so.

e) The team has five members: leader, three regular staff, one special education teacher. All five, including the leader, are appointed by the school's administration committee.

f) The referring teacher becomes a member of the team for the student he or she presents.

g) The team is not authorized to grant special education assistance or withdrawals or other special support, but may make recommendations in this direction.

h) All students believed by regular classroom teachers to have special needs must come before the school team as a first step (except for those who are already identified as exceptional, and are receiving special education services, but teachers bring these cases forward prior to a formal review, or when it is apparent that modification of program or placement is necessary).

i) Early in *every* school year a formal workshop is held with the entire staff on the nature of the team and its function.

Informal Practices:

a) Verbal economy is practiced.

b) The referring teacher does not review at the meeting. The team is expected to have read the referral description in advance.

c) Referring teachers are encouraged to limit the presenting problems to one, two, or at the very most three.

d) There is no written policy regarding the involvement of parents, but they are informed of meetings and may attend and participate if they choose.

e) The referring teacher is asked to suggest the time when review and followup will be discussed.

f) At least once in *every* school year, the team networks formally with teams from other schools or engages in some form of professional development.

Formal Practices:
Step one:

Presenting teacher completes a referral description and submits it to the team leader (five copies). The referral form is *one page only* and requests only the following:

i) student's current placement and birth date;

ii) description of the presenting problem;

iii) description of the remediating strategies attempted thus far.

Step Two:

Team meets and attempts to develop a strategic plan with the referring teacher.

Step Three:

At a meeting date suggested by the referring teacher, the team reviews results. These are reported verbally by the referring teacher.

At Step Three, the team evaluates results and decides whether to continue, to modify, or perhaps to advise the referring teacher that it would be in the student's best interests to request more intensive — and formal — special education service. If the latter decision is taken, then the school board's established procedures must be followed, and the student's 'case' is no longer the direct concern of the team.

Why This Team Succeeds:

At the school described here, the view is unanimous that the team concept is now an integral part of the system. Its success, the school feels,

```
+---------------------------------------------------------------+
|                    School Team Referral*                       |
|                                                                |
|  Referring Teacher: _____  Date: _____    |
|  Accepted for Discussion by Team: _____  Date: _____    |
|  Date for Team Meeting: _____                      |
|  +-------------------+  +-----------------+  +---------------+  |
|  |  Student's Name   |  |    Placement    |  |    d. o. b.   |  |
|  +-------------------+  +-----------------+  +---------------+  |
|                                                                |
|  Presenting Problem: (If more than one problem, use back of    |
|  this form and present Part A and Part B)                      |
|  A: _____         |
|  _____          |
|  _____          |
|  _____          |
|                                                                |
|  Responsive Strategies Attempted Thus Far:                     |
|  B: _____         |
|  _____          |
|  _____          |
|  _____          |
|                                                                |
|  Recommendation By Team: _____        |
|  _____          |
|  _____          |
|  _____          |
|                                                                |
|  Date for Review: _____  Forward to S.E.Committee:         |
|                                        Yes [ ]    No [ ]        |
+---------------------------------------------------------------+
```

*form used by team described on previous page. The form appears here, one half size.

is in its simplicity, its non-bureaucratic procedures, its support from administration and staff, the sense of professionalism it evokes, and most important, in the number of students it has helped.

The Multidisciplinary Team

For particularly demanding exceptional cases, some districts choose to deal with service delivery by first convening a *multidisciplinary team*. Usually, such a team will be made up of educators along with a number of professionals from areas outside education itself. The situation, for example, of an exceptional student with multiple needs such as a severe mental handicap and physical disabilities, along with serious emotional adjustment difficulties, may well require the services of a variety of personnel. For this student, a multidisciplinary team may be brought together once or twice on a more or less ad hoc basis, usually at the initial stages when the student's placement and programming arebeing established. Ongoing

delivery of service then becomes the responsibility of only certain members of the team.

An area of difficulty with the multidisciplinary team approach in educational settings is management and organization. Since the approach is used almost exclusively in cases of extensive need, there is sometimes disagreement over priority in meeting the needs (education? social? physical well-being?). Also, the mere task of bringing together a team of otherwise occupied, diverse professionals is awkward and time-consuming, and usually requires the authority (i.e., for budget, for freeing personnel from other obligations, etc.) of someone in an upper-level administrative role. As well, because there is such wide involvement, ultimate responsibility for the student — even legal responsibility — may become an issue.

Difficulties like these often force serious consideration of a quite restricted placement (like special day school or residential facility) simply because the situation is easier to manage in such a setting.

The Process

Although the process of identifying a student as exceptional and then delivering the service in the appropriate setting would seem, on the surface, to be a relatively straightforward one, the process can turn out to be quite complex in practice. There is no blame to attach for this; rather, the complexity is a result of a combination of wide-ranging circumstances. What a parent perceives as a student's needs for example, may not be in agreement with what the school sees, and some kind of compromise must be worked out therefore. Sometimes the necessary — or the desireable — support is not available, or not available in the student's neighbourhood school. The number and degree of a student's needs can shape the referral process. Provincial and federal laws, passed for purposes wider than just education, sometimes have a profound impact on what educators are permitted to do. Budgets are invariably a consideration. All these factors —and more— bend the process away from the straightforward path that appears to logically present itself.

Fortunately, experience has taught educators and parents how to deal with the referral process quite effectively for the most part. A significant lesson that comes from experience is an awareness of the need for collaboration (hence the trend toward extensive consultation with parents for example, and the use of school teams to help solve problems in-house). Another lesson has been to keep the process as simple and unbureaucratic — and thereby flexible and modifiable — as possible.

For Discussion: The Case of Amanda

Like many nine year olds at the beginning of the fourth grade, Amanda was given to doodling on much of her work and throughout her notebooks. During the previous year when she was in grade three, her teacher then had reflected on the fact that Amanda's doodling was just a bit excessive. He was quite accustomed to this 'art work' on most of his students' writing assignments and on other work, but Amanda always seemed to have the most: sometimes at the expense of what had been assigned.

When he passed this observation on to the grade four teacher, he found she had already noted the practice and felt it was increasing. Now, at the end of the fall term, matters have become more serious.

Amanda is now producing "wigglies". This is her name for the little creatures that she draws on all her notebooks. In fact, about half the time they are all that appear in her notebooks. To a large extent Amanda has simply stopped working. She draws wigglies on the chalkboard, in her daily journal, and on the classroom textbooks. The grade four teacher's uneasiness about this behaviour is reinforced significantly by the accompanying behaviour Amanda presents. She has become a passive refuser.

She will not respond to any request, but instead draws wigglies, no matter what the subject or assignment. Nothing whatever seems to interest her. To make matters worse — at least for the teacher — Amanda has become passively defiant. Her response to both encouragement and imperative is:

"I don't want to. And you can't make me."

Amanda's school record thus far is generally one of average to slightly above average success. She appears to be in good health. There are no reported difficulties or crises or changes in her family. Her mother reports an increase in Amanda's passivity at home, but not to any worrisome extent — at least to her. The grade four teacher however, feels she cannot treat the situation lightly, if only because Amanda's passive refusing is beginning to have a contaminating effect on other students in the class, particularly the ones who are achieving at lower levels. The teacher therefore, with the principal's encouragement has brought the situation of Amanda before the school team.

Both principal and teacher hope that the team may be able to identify some strategies to bring Amanda back onside, or at the very least to give the grade four teacher some moral support for a decision of her own. One decision that is causing a slight problem is whether or not to invite Amanda's mother to the team meeting.

Meanwhile Amanda continues to produce wigglies.

Referral Process: *Most* Situations

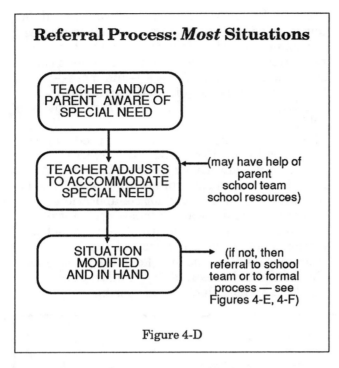

Figure 4-D

The three diagramatic descriptions on this page show typical referral paths in the majority of Canada's provinces and territories. Although jurisdictions will vary in the degree of formality, the amount of bureaucratic procedure, and in the level of direct administrative involvement, most cases of special need are expedited in one of these three ways.

Referral Process: *Some* Situations

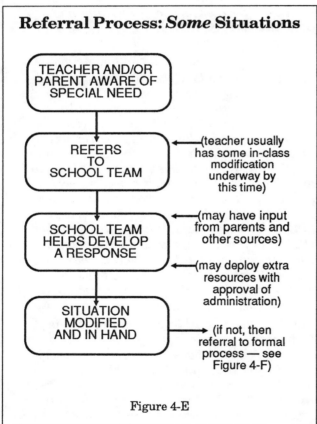

Figure 4-E

Referral Process: *Few* Situations

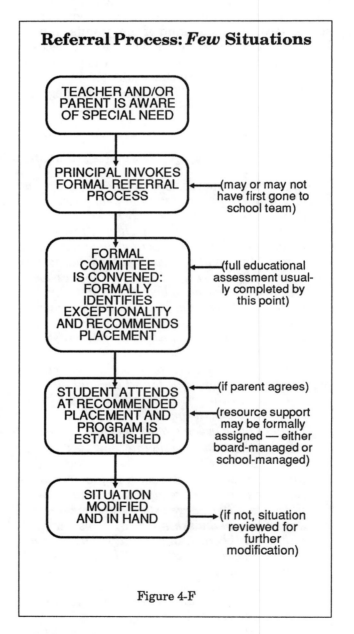

Figure 4-F

5

Using an Individual Education Plan (IEP) and a Tracking System

Since an underlying premise of special education is that the pace and style and capacity of some students' learning is so different that special approaches are required, it makes sense to free those students, at least to a degree, from the obligations imposed by a school's grade-wide or subject-wide demands, in favour of a program that is individualized to meet their special needs. Yet such a liberation can be uncomfortable for the teacher of an integrated class, for it begs the question: what then *should* this exceptional student's program be?. An Individual Education Plan (IEP) becomes the answer. An IEP establishes learning and behaviour objectives for the exceptional student, along with a description of how they will be achieved (or, at least, attempted) and a focus for ongoing evaluation. The regular curriculum may not be the core program in precisely the same way it is for others in the student's class, but adaptations of it, or replacements, or specially designed components, all detailed in the student's written plan, now fill that role. The IEP then, becomes both the student's *and* the teacher's program.

In addition to describing a program for the student, and giving the teacher a specific focus, the IEP serves a number of other purposes, one of the most obvious of which is the maintenance of a record of the student's case. It also provides a mechanism for monitoring progress, and offers a reference point for future reviews and more formal evaluations.

Properly used, it will coordinate the activities of support personnel with those established by the classroom teacher, and will preclude confusion, duplication, or unintentionally conflicting approaches. Of more subtle significance, but equally important, is the fact that a plan formalizes an exceptional student's situation. With a plan in place and on record, an exceptional student is far less likely to fall through the cracks.

Contents of a Typical IEP

(See also Figures 5-A, and 5-B)
An IEP will usually contain the following items:

☐ *basic demographic data* (name, d.o.b., placement);

☐ *names of key personnel involved*;

☐ *important dates*;

☐ *learning and behaviour objectives*. In practice, these are written in a variety of ways, from very formal, expressed-in-terms-of-behaviour-outcome, to quite informal descriptions. Experience has generally taught that leaning to the side of informality permits more flexibility and modification in mid-plan, and also ensures that the plan will be more readily and faithfully used;

☐ *key strategies* (but not all) to be tried, and materials or special devices, if applicable. Through experience, teachers have found that this list is, in part, symbolic. Only the "key" strategies are written down;

☐ *space for evaluations* (most often, by the teacher or assistant).

The amount of information in a plan varies from school to school and from board to board. Some IEPs may include description of support services if these are involved; others may even include more formal data such as assessment results. Some IEPs, but not all, will always include space for evaluation and comment; however, many teachers find it helpful to have a separate tracking system to follow the student's progress (See *Tracking Progress* in this chapter). Larger boards usually require that a standard format be followed for IEPs, so that the amount and type of information is controlled (or viewed from another perspective: so that the inclusion of appropriate information is assured.)

It is important to recognize that an IEP does not cover every moment and every activity of a student's day. Teachers and educational assistants in an integrated class simply do not have the time to manage an exceptional student's case in that way and still fulfill their obligations to the class as a whole. Besides which, an overly detailed, minutely controlled plan would contradict the very principle of integration. What an IEP does is provide consistency, continuity, and clarity of purpose in each exceptional student's situation. It supports the teacher's professionalism and allows it room to be exercised.

Sample IEP: The Case of Arveena (page 39)

The IEP here (Figure 5-A) is relatively informal, and is reasonably typical for a school or board that tries to minimize paperwork for teachers. This plan will be used as the basis for Arveena's program for two months, after which time the plan will be formally reviewed. Usually, this means a review with the school team, or perhaps with the principal and Arveena's parents. The contents of this plan are the result of cooperative effort by Arveena's teacher and the school's special education teacher, after a productive school team meeting. At the time of review, a new plan will be

drawn up for another period. Likely, this one will contain the same goals as the previous plan, with some modifications if appropriate. Unproductive strategies will be discarded; successful ones confirmed, and new ones added. Unless Arveena's parents object, plan #3 will be filed with other information about her.

(Arveena is seven. Her speech is very difficult to understand. Her words are rarely more than two syllables, and she rarely uses more than one or two word sentences. She also has trouble following instructions of more than a sentence or two. Arveena is extremely shy, does not involve herself with the other students, and appears to be very lethargic and clumsy. There continues to be suspicion that she may have suffered a brain injury at some point. In class, if she is allowed to, Arveena will sit on the edge of activities, especially physical ones, and avoid any involvement. She has been identified as severely learning disabled.)

Sample IEP: The Case of Lucas (page 40)

This example (Figure 5-B) is considerably more formal than that used for Arveena's program (Figure 5-A). Clearly, the plan is an approved form sanctioned for use within the school. It is set up for a longer period too (a complete semester). Plans of this type are more typical of secondary school. There are more personnel to coordinate in an integrated secondary school situation, and considerably more need, therefore, for wider cooperation. Usually, a plan like this will be the responsibility of *one* of the student's teachers; in this case — a typical one — it is one of the school's special education teachers, who teaches a course that Lucas is taking: English Strategies.

(A committee unanimously identified Lucas 'behavioural', although various teachers have argued that a more appropriate identification would be mental handicap or possibly, learning disability. The boy is sixteen. He has a tortured history of detentions, and suspensions, and for periods in grades seven and eight, received home instruction. Lucas has great difficulty controlling his frustrations. He is in an integrated grade nine class but has no friends. Peers avoid him. His IEP, designed by M.P. in consultation with each of his teachers this semester, is committed to helping him self-manage so that other parts of his life will normalize.)

Individual Education Plan

Student __Arveena P.__ d.o.b. __2 Mar', xx__ Current Placement __Gr. 2__ Plan # __3__ Date Begun __15 Oct.__

Review Date __15 Dec.__ Teacher __Jane K.__ Other Personnel __XXX   XXX   XXX   XXX__

Identified Exceptional? Yes ✓ No ☐ Home Telephone No. __X X X__

GOALS	PROGRAM STRATEGIES	TEACHER EVALUATION
I. Increase communication in both speech and language (receptive and expressive).	1. Provide more opportunity for natural communication. a) increase amount of free play time. b) when talking to her, ask open ended questions. 2. Add more drama and puppet work* to the curriculum. a) act out stories that have been read to the class. b) have her write or dictate new stories that could be acted out. *Making puppets will also aid in her fine motor development. (See Goal II.) 3. Sing more songs during the daily routine. a) "The Other Day I Saw a Bear" — (good for receptive language). b) "Three Little Pigeons" — (fine motor). c) songs that have a lot of repetition.	19 Oct. I - still uses single words or elliptical phrases ("go bath room") - sang a complete song for the first time II - very successful built a lego tower unassisted III - very reluctant (may be shyness rather than physical)
II. Increase level of motor skills.	1. Use more manipulation and construction materials. a) encourage her to use small blocks and lego in free play. i) Have her retell stories using small blocks (e.g., "Goldilocks and the Three Bears"). b) art. i) use manipulative materials (e.g., finger paint, clay, plasticine). ii) complete activities that use scissors.	26 Oct. I - said "may I go to the bath-room"! Constructed a puppet with popsicle sticks and glue (assisted by Dino) - told a story about her puppet in group. Lasted 25 seconds! Longest communication yet! II - see above, re puppet
III. Increase opportunity for physical exercise.	1. Attend regular recess periods. 2. Have her partner with one other student, once a week, to lead in class calisthenics. 3. Encourage her to become involved in a physical activity.	III - still resists strongly

Figure 5-A

School District #XX — Individual Education Plan

Student: __Lucas A.__ D.O.B. __Aug. 9 'XX__ Current Placement: __Grade 9__

School Year: __XX__ Date Plan Began: __Sep. 10 'XX__ Proposed Date of Review: __Jan. 20 'XX__

Special Ed Teacher: __M.P.__ Other Personnel: __A.V., S.R., C.W.__ Most Recent Review: __June 20 'XX__

Distribution: __OSR, Sp. Ed. Dept., Parents__

SPECIAL NEEDS	OBJECTIVES	DISTRICT SERVICES		EVALUATION	
		Personnel/Eqpt.	Instruction	Commentary	Init. & Date
1. finds it hard to curb compulsive reactions	will await turn during instruction	all regular teachers as above	-stand near Lucas at times of change in class, -use "just-a-minute-and-I'll-help" _signal_ as agreed, -use rewards for cumulative periods of self-restraint.	Outbursts have decreased slightly. Need more consistent approach by all teachers. / Responding well to reinforcement.	24 Sept. M.P. / 1 Oct. M.P.
2. Uses aggression to deal with problems, esp. frequent failures	will use negotiation and assisted intervention	all teachers _and_ behaviour consultant	-allow more time to complete work, -provide more assistance, -reinforce completions and cooperation with praise.	Allowing more time proving very effective	15 Oct. M.P.
3. Reads at 4-5 grades below age-appropriate	will increase reading level by one-two grades.	Sp.Ed. (English) Teacher (M.P.) _and_ volunteer	Reading Recovery Program.	No formal evaluation yet. L. is enthusiastic about the program	15 Oct. M.P.

Figure 5-B

Who Usually Prepares the IEP?

The designer and writer of an IEP may be a special education teacher, or a team of teachers, or the student's regular classroom teacher(s). Generally, the writer is the teacher principally responsible for the student, in consultation with several others. In elementary schools, that writer is usually the student's regular classroom teacher; in secondary schools, where the student is integrated on a rotary timetable, principal responsibility for the IEP usually is taken on by one of the teachers in the student's rotary scheme.

Using a Tracking System

Some teachers find it worth while to add a component to an IEP which evaluates, and which creates opportunity for reinforcement and further instruction at the same time. This is a kind of tracking system and progress chart in which *both* the teacher and the exceptional student participate. Figures 5-C and 5-D, are examples. They are tracking systems used with two different students, Dharma and Leona.

Dharma is an almost-eight year old with a mental handicap. He has been quite successful, through "learned helplessness" — simply sitting in an entirely placid and non-participating way — in making everyone else in the class, including the teacher and the assistant, do everything for him. His IEP is devoted almost entirely to goals and strategies emphasizing self-management and involvement. Dharma's role in the tracking system is to colour in the rectangles from the bottom of the rocket upward, as he makes progess in this direction. (See Figure 5-C.) In practice, what happens is that the teacher or teaching assistant sits down with him, usually at the end of the day, and leads a brief discussion about his conduct that day. The discussion centres around the extent to which he has acted for himself. Then Dharma colours in as many rectangles as, by agreement or, in the opinion of the adult, he has earned. (Given Dharma's handicap, this dialogue was very much controlled by the adult at first, with the longer term objective of motivating Dharma to contribute.) The teacher or assistant then makes commentary in the right hand column at her discretion.

What is accomplished by a tracking-cum-progress system like this is the same as with a standard IEP form, except that it is enhanced by the student's participation. Teachers especially, recognize the all important boost to a student's momentum that this kind of active, visual record achieves.

Figure 5-D, the tracking system for Leona is more sophisticated because she is older. Leona is 15 in grade nine and her difficulties are complex. She is believed to be gifted, but her behaviour completely masks any achievement. Whether the constant acting-out comes about out of general frustration and impatience and what she perceives to be lack of challenge, or whether it arises out of a very unfortunate home life, no one knows. In any case, the goals of Leona's IEP are to get her first of all, to come to class, and secondly to attend to academic work and thereby feed her considerable talent, and to get her to behave more responsibly.

Because Leona is in a semestered secondary school, enrolled in four courses, her progress is tracked over the four classes. How this chart works is thus pretty much self-evident. In practice, at the end of each of the four classes, the teacher and Leona meet briefly and each enters the appropriate information. The design in Figure 5-D covers five school days. One of Leona's teachers is her mentor and oversees the tracking system, but to succeed, it requires the active cooperation of the other three, especially at first.

Why Tracking Systems Are Successful

☐ Because students like and appreciate them. (The "real" Leona was responsible for taking her own chart from class to class. At first, she refused, referring to it as her "shit list", so it was taken around by the mentor teacher. All teachers cooperated fully, and agreed to deliberately look for positives and enter them on the chart, in her presence, whether she participated or not. At the beginning of the second week, Leona indicated, on her own, that she would take responsibility for the chart henceforth. Dharma, after eleven days, carried his completely filled-in rocket to the principal's office unaccompanied. His very first such trip.)

☐ Because teachers like and appreciate them. Tracking systems like this enable the teacher to do evaluations, and at the same

Figure 5-C

Dharma S.	Teacher Comments : Date
Dharma Blasts Off! (rocket illustration with dated boxes: Oct. 13 / Oct. 13, Oct. 12 / Oct. 13, Oct. 11 / Oct. 12, Oct. 9 / Oct. 10, Oct. 8 / Oct. 8, Oct. 5 / Oct. 5, Oct. 3 / Oct. 4, Oct. 1 / Oct. 2; "Dharma" on the base; note "Hand over hand printing →")	**Oct. 13** Best yet. 2½ pages of phonics. Three complete activities at counting centre. Helped Louis get dressed for recess! **Oct. 12** Big change! Finished yesterday's work. Completed ~~two~~ pages of phonics. Stayed at counting centre for 20 mins. Now asking for rocket! **Oct. 11** Not a terribly good day. Did not complete work. Wandered from centre to centre. **Oct. 9** Completed 1½ pages of sound/letter match. **Oct. 8** Dressed himself for recess. Asked to be chip monitor. **Oct. 5** Asked for rocket! Explained how it works to Jean (T.A.)! **Oct. 2** Completed a full page of sound/letter match. FIRST TIME! **Oct. 1** I think Dharma understands the idea. Slow beginning.

Leona D.

Date 2 Dec

Leona's View	Teacher Comment
	Did not disturb anyone today RF
	ANSWERED A GENERAL ISSUE QUESTION MOST INTELLIGENTLY BL
	absent JA
	Deer before in B140 JP

Date 3 Dec

Leona's View	Teacher Comment
	Worked very well at beginning of class RF
Class was OK for a change	GENERALLY A GOOD DAY BL
	absent JA
Don't push me	excellent piece of creative writing JP

Date 6 Dec

Leona's View	Teacher Comment
OK for me too	an excellent day. RF
Let's do this	TOOK LEADERSHIP ROLE IN GROUP ACTIVITY. BL
Try to make it interesting	present, must do make up JA
Not bad actually	creative writing is going very well JP

Date 7 Dec

Leona's View	Teacher Comment
They better do what I say!	Leona will be chairing ISU project RF
This is really OK	GROUP ACTIVITY CONTINUES. EXCELLENT PARTICIPATION BL
I am fine with it	makeup proceeding JA
	absent JP

Date 8 Dec

Leona's View	Teacher Comment
We need a better textbook	ISU proceeding very satisfactory RF
Get the others to work too.	SHAPING UP TO BE A REALLY GOOD WEEK BL
This could be OK. Maybe	working very well JA
I had a reason yesterday. This class is OK	ready for major writing project JP

Figure 5-D

time, reinforce the student, as well as turn over to him, some of the responsibility for his own development.

☐ Tracking systems can be very individualized to the student and her situation (which makes room for the teacher's creativity). They are more flexible than the evaluation component on the IEP itself. Teachers inherently, are believers in the principle of "catch a kid doing something good!" and a progress chart makes that easier.

☐ Above all, tracking systems are an extension of the IEP. They make a student's individualized program more complete by providing a regular, recorded reinforcement of development.

For Discussion: The Case of Lek

During the eighteen months he spent in a hospital in Yorkshire, Lek learned to speak English quite well. Prior to that time he spoke a patois of French, Magyar and what was believed to be a Carpathian dialect. Staff at the hospital estimated his age at the time to be three or four years. He is believed to be an orphan, but this too is uncertain. Lek — which may or may not be his correct name — was one of four very young children discovered by Red Cross relief workers in a Romanian village during the uprising against the regime of Nicolai Ceaucescu.

The other three children did not survive. Lek spent two years in England, most of that time under fairly intensive medical care. He was severely malnourished when found by the relief workers, and also required surgery to correct hip dysplasia. Lek also suffered from rickets and will likely bear the effects for life with slightly deformed bones in his legs and arms. After two years in England, the boy was adopted by a Canadian family. Within two months of coming to Canada (in June) Lek began his Canadian schooling and was placed in the first grade of his neighbourhood elementary.

Despite such a dramatic episode in his early life, Lek does not appear to have suffered too many ill effects, at least superficially and for the present. The slight bone deformities do not hamper his movements significantly — he wears leg braces at night and will do so for another year at least — certainly his enthusiasm for games and sports and all athletic activities is unbounded. Lek also appears to be an average to above average learner. He is an emerging reader, an exceptional artist for one so young, and while he does not particularly enjoy math activities, he completes them correctly, if reluctantly.

What has brought Lek to the attention of the School Support Team is his explosive temper and extremely limited patience. Both inside and outside the classroom, Lek reacts instantly to the least frustration, or what he perceives to be a slight or an insult. The behaviour appears both in academics and on the playground. If he doesn't "get" something right away in an academic activity, he will rip up the material and stand with clenched fists and red face until an adult intervenes. On the playground this intervention is even more necessary, for Lek, if thwarted, lashes out with his fists.

What has moved his teacher to seek some advice and help is that this behaviour has intensified and now seems to be occurring without provocation. Lek hits his classmates — or kicks or pulls hair; he has begun to spit on them as well — without warning and without apparent reason, or at least any immediately apparent reason. When his teacher discusses the behaviour with him, Lek cannot explain why he does these things.

In his favour, the teacher says, Lek often bursts into tears when she speaks to him about what he has done. To the teacher, this remorse is genuine; what she wants is some means for helping Lek to get control of himself.

6

Students With Learning Disabilities

Prevailing Misconceptions About Learning Disabilities

1. There is no supportable connection between learning disabilities and neurological dysfunction.

A once popular term for learning disability was *minimal brain dysfunction* (MBD)*. The term grew out of brain injury research in the early part of the twentieth century and was used to describe a condition in which an individual was not a normal learner, yet presented no apparent sensory or intellectual differences that would account for that fact. It was assumed therefore that the cause lay in some neurological abnormality too subtle to be detected, hence *minimal*. When the term MBD was generally discarded in favour of *learning disabilities*, the notion of neurological abnormality as an explanation for the condition seemed to disappear with it. More recently however, neuro-anatomical research has suggested a fairly certain connection between learning disability and anomalous structures in the brain.

2. Dyslexia and learning disability are the same thing.

People who have dyslexia appear to have fundamental difficulties with integrating the

sight, sound, and meaning of print, despite apparently normal intellectual ability and sensory capacity. In this sense, dyslexia is not unlike some kinds of learning disability. However dyslexia is but one form of learning disability and confusion arises when the two terms are used interchangeably. In the first place, there are significant numbers of learning disabled students who do not have this difficulty at all with print. Secondly, the term dyslexia itself seems to have credibility largely because of tradition. Although the term and the condition it supposedly identifies, have been around for a long time and have attracted committed supporters, more recent and very intensive research suggests that dyslexics are no different from ordinary, garden variety poor readers, either in their difficulties or in the remediation to which they best respond.**

3. Poor eye-hand coordination is a sign of learning disability.

At an early point in the learning disabilities field, it was believed that the difficulties faced by the learning disabled were the product of poor perceptual integration: viz., poor eye-hand coordination; impaired ability to reproduce on paper a figure presented visually; poor body awareness; confusion of left-right; confusion of the self in space, etc. The term *perceptually handicapped* became a popular one. Although

---

*or "minimal brain damage/injury"

**For an excellent review see Siegel, 1992.

some learning disabled students may have these perceptual difficulties, there is no absolute connection between perceptual handicap and learning disability. Many people who have perceptual difficulties have no difficulty learning, no difficulty with reading, writing, and language use, and are certainly not learning disabled. On the other hand, many students who find academic learning enormously difficult, are wonderfully coordinated and have no difficulty discriminating among shapes, or reproducing figures visually represented.

4. Learning disabled students have highly developed/poorly developed memory capacity.

In terms of general memory, students with learning disabilities are no different from everyone else. However, they seem to have significant difficulty transferring information from short-term to long-term memory. The learning disabled often comprehend today's lesson today, but tomorrow may not remember it in part or at all.

5. Learning disabled students are highly intelligent.

There is little evidence to suggest that learning disabled people have a higher intelligence than the normal population. In fact, the weight of evidence suggests that on I.Q. tests at least, the learning disabled score across the same range as the rest of the population, but with what seems to be a tendency to fall in the average to below-average categories.

6. Learning disabled students are more likely to become delinquent or criminal.

Despite the origin of this claim in the early 1960s, a clear link has never been established, largely because of the difficulty in defining learning disability for research purposes. Murphy's (1986) review for example, found that incidence figures varied from 4 to 36 percent! Other studies find no connection at all. A Canadian study (Crealock, 1986) found that 20 to 30 percent of young offenders have *academic* problems.

7. Left-handed students are more likely to be learning disabled.

Students who are left-handed are often over-represented in special education classes for the learning disabled, but no hard data exist to show that left-handedness is a predictor or indicator of learning disability.

8. Hyperactive (A.D.H.D.) students are learning disabled.

The term *hyperactivity* or *hyperkinesis* has generally been replaced by *attention deficit hyperactivity disorder* (A.D.H.D.) to describe a condition in which students present consistently counter-productive, inattentive behaviour (see page 58). Although it follows that students who have difficulty sustaining attention, or who make decisions too rapidly, often on inadequate data, would also have learning problems, there is limited hard evidence to establish that students identified A.D.H.D. become that way because of a learning disability. Likewise, the negative behaviour often seen in learning disabled students is not necessarily A.D.H.D. behaviour. Often it is avoidance behaviour or the result of frustration.

9. Students with learning disabilities are speech and language disabled too.

Although it is not uncommon for learning disabled students to have a speech or language disorder, the connection is not absolute. There is considerable overlap however, between learning disabilities and language problems.*

10. There are tests which detect the presence of a learning disability.

Despite the claims of test publishers and the reputation — unjustified, as it turns out — of some tests, there is no clear evidence at all, to substantiate the notion that a test exists which can detect a learning disability in the same way that a hearing test for example, can specify the nature and seriousness of a hearing loss.

11. Hereditary factors have no bearing on learning disabilities.

Research on this matter is sparse, but the information currently available hints that there is likely a pattern of learning disabilities in families.

*A brief section on speech and language disorders follows at the end of this chapter.

For Discussion: The Case of Claudio

An inordinate amount of time has already been spent on Claudio's case by the school's support services. He has been the subject of assessments, and meetings, and most recently case conferences (three) since he was in Grade two. He is presently fifteen.

Claudio is handsome, charming, and very talkative. He is a social leader with a seeming confidence that belies his age and his grade in a large secondary school. He is currently running for Grade Nine Representative on the Student Council and is expected to win hands down, in large measure because of his speech to the grade nine assembly where he appeared to present off-the-cuff. Certainly, he had no notes.

The challenge of Claudio is that he does no schoolwork. He has no notes (it is now October); he rarely if ever, brings a pen or a textbook to class; and in those classes where considerable time is devoted to on-task activity — particularly math and geography in this school — Claudio tries to fast-talk his way around the task by the need to attend to other urgent obligations. (His parents do not speak English and since he is the eldest of three, it is true that he must be the frontman in dealing with bureaucracy, etc.)

The latest case conference, held in Grade 8, identified Claudio as learning disabled, and recommended placement in Grade nine where he enrolled in a variety of regular classes. His situation is coming up for review now, and although there has been some impetus from staff to push for a transfer of Claudio to a self-contained class, the administration has decreed that Claudio is: "A responsibility of this school" and that "we will meet the challenge in the regular class environment."

Accordingly, a meeting of Claudio's teachers is being held to determine on what points they can agree to make a concerted, coordinated, and consistent effort to turn this student, who seems bright enough, into one who also produces.

Further notes:

(1) Assessments completed earlier generally agree that Claudio is indeed learning disabled, and that processing written language is for him an enormously difficult task. The latest assessment emphasized that note-taking, organization and completion of assignments, and homework, are his most pressing remedial needs.

(2) Claudio's timetable has one free period per day, which might be utilized in the school's Special Education department. Worthy of note however, is the principal's refusal to let Claudio, and cases like his, be dumped here.

(3) Claudio's favourite adult, and mentor, is his auto shop teacher.

What Kind of Exceptionality Is a Learning Disability?

Students with exceptionalities are often grouped together according to their primary need, sometimes for administrative purposes, sometimes to facilitate instruction, often for research purposes — there are many reasons for grouping. Whether or not the practice is ultimately beneficial or ultimately insidious, the fact is that most exceptional students who are hard of hearing for example, or physically disabled, despite their differences as individuals, usually share one characteristic that is sufficiently marked to include them in the group or category. Not so with the learning disabled. This is the most elusive of all areas in special education.

The only criterion that all learning disabled students seem to share can be at best loosely described as a difficulty in learning, in dealing with information, particularly language-based information, despite apparent freedom from any intellectual or sensory handicap. They may be disorganized, distractible, overactive, resistant to changing counter-productive behaviours, unable to focus attention, forgetful, and disoriented — among other things. One student may manifest all of these characteristics; another student, while functioning at the same low academic level, may manifest only one of them. And either student may demonstrate some of these characteristics on one day, and on another day, show absolutely none of them. Or all of them!

A learning disability is not a discrete, measurable entity. In fact there is a school of thought which argues that the disability does not exist at all, that it is an escape for middle and upper class white children who might otherwise have to be labelled slow or even behavioural. Nevertheless, on an empirical basis alone, it is impossible to deny the existence of a large group of students who share what seem to be consistently inefficient strategies for assimilating, organizing, retaining and producing information. Extremely intense activity in special education over the past twenty-five years has led to the irrefutable conclusion that learning disabilities do exist, that they are responsible for very serious academic problems and sometimes social problems as well, and that they are strikingly resistant to educational intervention.

Characteristics of Learning Disabilities

Processing Language

As might be expected, a seeming inability in most learning disabled students to process language fully and accurately, is a most serious issue. At the *receiving* stage (when the student is hearing language or attempting to read it) or at the *sending* stage (speaking or writing), or at the *elaboration* stage (when the student attempts to integrate some language he's just heard with information he already holds), a learning disabled student often has real problems. For some students it's only at one of the stages; for others, difficulty arises at two or all three stages. For example, a younger student may not be able to process an incoming set of instructions like: "Use your red crayon to colour the robins, and then your yellow one to draw a line under the 'r-r-r-r' sound." He will *hear* the instruction all right, but all the linguistic information: robins, crayons, red, yellow, 'r-r-r-r' sound, not to mention the activity, may be too much to process. He may miss the instruction altogether, or miss a piece of it, or confuse red and yellow, or interchange pieces of information. The result will likely be a poor performance or a non-performance.

An older student may have an equally difficult time with something like this from, say, a geography teacher: "If you refer to your maps of West Africa, you'll notice a good example of how Africa became politically fragmented by

decolonialization in the way Gambia is literally inserted into Senegal. And then further down the coast you'll see even more examples with Guinea-Bissau, Guinea, Togo, and Benin all sitting side by side." The older student may have more sophisticated language ability than the one colouring robins, but then he is expected to deal with more sophisticated language, and relatively, is going to have just as much or even more trouble.

Variations in Ability

What makes this language processing deficiency so insidious is that it is so variable. If there are three students in the geography class who have learning disabilities, one of them might be entirely confused by the very concept of "decolonialization" and miss everything else as a result. A second, unless there is a map right before him will be overwhelmed by all the verbal details of the countries mentioned. The third may understand the point perfectly, and even be able to hypothesize on it, but three days later on the examination, she may be entirely unable to put together the language that will explain what she thinks.

The Problem of the English Language

The subtleties of English itself pose a huge barrier for the learning disabled. A teacher for example, who stands beside a student and says, "I don't see your answer" may mean a number of things depending on the context of the statement. It may mean the answer is simply not visibly apparent. Or it may mean the answer was not completed, or possibly that the teacher does not understand the answer or does not agree with it. Because some learning disabled students not only have difficulty with language, but even further difficulty in reading between the lines of communication situations and social contexts, they may respond incorrectly to "I don't see your answer" or, respond undiplomatically, or just not at all.

Language that attempts to capture time and sequence is another of the many stumbling blocks, in part because the language itself can be very complicated, and in part because chronology and sequence are problems all on their own. For example, in the sentence "Only after it first sprouts blossoms, can the tree bear fruit", the words and the syntax used to describe the sequence, set up real complication. The phrase " only after" is at the beginning of

Some Day-to-Day School Problems of the Learning Disabled

Difficulty with Alphabet/Penmanship

• may confuse letters in writing and in recitation
• mixes upper and lower case letters
• mixes manuscript and cursive styles, or will continue to use manuscript long after age and grade peers use cursive
• frequently distorts letter size and shape
• attempts at continuous text are scratchy, barely legible
• often mirrors or reverses letters
• awkward, even unnatural movement of the pen or pencil

Difficulty Remembering

• forgets, misplaces things
• needs constant reminding (and often has successfully trained family/teacher/friends to do this)

Difficulty in Copying/Note-Making

• very careless, often reproduces inaccurately
• loses place often
• far-point copying very slow and inaccurate
• overprints, telescopes, omits
• may have difficulty reproducing a shape from memory
• ignores sub-headings and organization cues

Problems in Arithmetic

• reverses numbers (as well as letters)
• careless about columnar structure
• may not remember multiplication tables
• carries or borrows wrong digit
• skips or omits steps in problem solving

Problems in Reading

• loses place regularly
• makes many flying guesses
• does not "attack" a new or strange word, but tends to gaze at the teacher, or use other avoidance techniques
• ignores punctuation and other cues
• makes up words, telescopes
• reverses and transposes
• loses meaning of a sentence from beginning to end
• gets events out of sequence
• infers content that is not there
• forgets details

Slow Work Speed

• very often does not finish
• works slower than age and grade peers
• frustrated under time pressure

Problems with Time and Sequence

• poor notion of chronological order, sometimes confused about days of week, etc.
• tends not to see time in discrete units
• confuses a set of instructions, so that they are followed out of sequence (or partially ignored)
• often has difficulty starting a piece of work (doesn't know where, or how, or at what point)

Confusion in Spelling

• uses phonetic or invented spelling long past the age when more attention to correctness is expected
• does not seem to retain a basic stock of spelling words

the sentence. Yet it sets up a condition and presents a time frame for the rest of the sentence which then describes what in effect must happen *before* "only after "! Efficient language users can usually comprehend such a sentence. Students with learning disabilities often do not.

Still another barrier exists in the pronoun "it". Not only must "it" be held in short term memory until its referent ("tree") surfaces, the listener/reader must perceive that "it" refers to "tree" and not some other idea! (Research shows that the difficulty with pronouns normally experienced by young language learners, aged four and five, is experienced by the learning disabled, well into their teenage and adult years.)

Difficulties like those above are compounded by learning disabled students' problems in relating one sentence to others in a passage, or in relating passages to passages, or even stories to stories, whether written or spoken.

Are We on the Same Wave Length?

One of the more unsettling aspects of the problem in processing language, for teachers, parents, and certainly for the students themselves, is the frustration of discovering that a communication which appeared at the time to be successful, has been partly or even completely misunderstood or misinterpreted. (Admittedly, this is a common trait in all children, especially adolescents, but what distinguishes the learning disabled is the consistency with which this occurs.)

The pattern of the difficulty recurs again and again, something like this: because teachers, parents, and again the students themselves, often engage in a communication fully recognizing that the potential for confusion is high, all parties often take extra care to be sure they are 'on the same wave length', and that the communication has meshed in a way that what was *sent* is also what has been *received*. It is not difficult therefore to imagine the stress that results when what appeared to have been a more or less successful interchange, in retrospect is revealed to have been two separate tracks of communication that overlapped from time to time but never bonded into that stage of information interchange we like to call *understanding*.

The implications of this problem for life in general, and for the classroom especially, are very significant. Whether it occurs solely because of faulty language processing or because of memory problems has yet to be clearly established. All that is known for sure is that it happens. Often.

Problems Remembering

An apparently poor memory for learning and for new information is another characteristic that distinguishes many students with a learning disability. They may indeed, at the moment, learn a technique or an idea, or acquire information, or memorize a sequence or a formula during a classroom lesson, at the same pace and in the same depth as their non-learning disabled colleagues. But unlike the latter, they will have difficulty retrieving it next day.

Accounting for this supposed memory problem has generated considerable speculation. There are those who argue that this forgetting occurs because the students cannot transfer learning and information from short term to long term memory, or at least, cannot do so easily. For others it is strictly a result of poor language processing: not a case of simple forgetting but of not getting a correct grasp of the material in the first place. (More recently, there has been argument, particularly from audiologists, that the faulty processing results from imperfections in the central auditory nerve.)

None of the explanations is entirely satisfactory. If the students cannot transfer from short to long term memory, then why can teachers and parents cite examples of phenomenal long term memory retention in learning disabled students? If the central auditory nerve is the culprit, why does the forgetting occur just as frequently with written language? And if language processing problems are the sole cause, why do learning disabled students so often make the same *social mistakes* time after time? (Learning disabled students frequently have difficult peer relations because of a seeming inability to benefit from social experience. In situations where language has a minor role, if any, a learning disabled student will continue to make the same gaffe, seemingly not remembering what happened when he did so the previous time.)

Whatever the cause, it is essential to be aware that learning disabled students may well not have retained what everyone else thinks they have — or should have. It inevitably shapes how we relate to them.

Poor Executive Function

Usually a learning disabled student has great difficulty taking on a project or even a simple assignment, and organizing it through to completion. He — or she* — finds it extremely difficult to begin, to know *how* to begin and *where* to begin. Finding information — the research component — is as problematic as is dealing with the information if it is found. The student

*The tendency toward the masculine pronoun in this chapter is not merely the product of tradition and ease of writing, but because boys usually outnumber girls in LD cases 3-4 to 1.

will almost invariably fail to complete an assignment without some very specific direction, not because he is avoiding or rejecting it (although by adolescence, avoidance does tend to be habituated) but because he simply does not know how to go about pulling it together. He needs executive help. (Parents particularly, are often frustrated observers of this characteristic in day-to-day living. Such matters as organizing one's own room, or hockey equipment, or toys, or hobby materials are managerial challenges for learning disabled children that go beyond "just being a kid".)

For Discussion: The Case of Ted

Ted is eleven years old, in grade five. He has been in his present school since the beginning of grade three. Prior to that time he had been enrolled in four different schools because his family moved back and forth twice, between southern Ontario and British Columbia.

When Ted came to the school in grade three he was identified as learning disabled. The placement decision was part-time special class: mornings in a self-contained class called "developmentally delayed" (PTR of 10:1 with a teaching assistant) and afternoons in the regular grade three. A Review in the spring of grade three decided on one hour per day of withdrawal to the special education teacher. The Review in the spring of grade four recommended total integration for grade five with regular weekly visits from the school's reading specialist.

Ted's present academic performance is below standard for grade five. A recent test of reading placed his comprehension level at grade 3.2 and vocabulary at 2.8. Math skills are generally at the grade four to five level, although the teacher reports that the introduction of fractions has caused Ted great difficulty.

Even an untrained observer would notice Ted in this grade five classroom. When students are working in groups, Ted is invariably on the perimeter of his group, often focussed on something another group is doing. In gym, he is the one with shoelaces dragging (or missing altogether). At recess — he usually plays with much younger

children — Ted is always the last to go outside because he cannot find hat or boots or even coat. During silent reading time, Ted lies stomach-down on the bean bags in the 'Reading Corner' with his book on the floor. Observation reveals that the book is either upside down or open to the page that he was reading the day before. One of Ted's classmates once accounted for her unwillingness to work with him on a cooperative project by saying "He never knows what he has to do. And he doesn't care either."

Finally, a paragraph from the Special Education teacher's evaluation summary (end of grade 4) describes Ted's learning style thus:

"Ted finds it difficult to concentrate for long periods without relief. He does not tend to structure things sequentially, and when presented with a sequenced task will often approach items out of order. Ted will frequently miss or simply ignore details, and must be encouraged to appreciate the value of completing things. Unless directed to remain on task, Ted will drift easily and miss things. He will not be concerned about missing. If Ted is asked to do assignments requiring extended planning, research and reporting, he will need help."

Ted's grade five teacher will be presenting his case to the school special education team next week so that a decision can be made on whether to send daily resource help to her class, or to withdraw Ted for two hours a day to a resource room.

Difficulties With Sequence and Order

Learning disabled students miss steps in a sequence, get them out of sequence, reverse the sequence, and as often as not, may simply ignore a sequence. Research has not been able to demonstrate clearly whether this is a cognitive or an affective characteristic but the weight of empirical evidence is in favour of the former interpretation.

Satisfaction With a Peripheral Understanding

An adolescent taking a credit in chemistry, when asked what is Boyles Law, might typically answer "Oh it's about pressure and that." The likelihood is he knows more: probably a definition of Boyles Law, perhaps even an understanding of how to apply it in a problem. If this adolescent is learning disabled the answer "Pressure and that" may well constitute the sum total of his knowledge of the law. Yet he will quite likely believe he has a thorough grasp of it, and proceed comfortably in that self-assurance until confronted by a request to apply Boyles Law to a problem. This is the same student who in grade two wrote three lines in his journal while the rest of the class averaged twenty. And who likely responded indignantly to a comment about such a slim output with something like "I *did* my journal." or "That's all I have to say!"

The key feature of this element in the student's way of dealing with the world is his satisfaction with a vague, incomplete, peripheral piece of work, and his conviction that it is adequate. This is a crucial behaviour for teachers to recognize. It's not defiance; it is not shirking; and it is not an utter lack of ability. It is a misinterpretation of what constitutes completeness.

> **On Having LD: The Words of Vinny T.**
>
> "I'll never forget the day after Hallowe'en in grade five. Mrs. Korol came into class and said, 'Well, how was Hallowe'en?'
>
> I was in the first seat and she was looking at me. I said 'I'm fine. How are you?'
>
> And all the kids laughed. It seemed like they would never stop laughing. That was the hardest thing in school. Being laughed at. I don't know why I answered that way. Maybe I thought Mrs. Korol said 'How are you?' Maybe I just understood 'How'. I'm not sure if I misunderstood her question. I'm not even sure if I understood it but then my answer came out wrong.
>
> It's so simple: 'How was Hallowe'en?' How can you possibly screw that up? But I did. And they all laughed. They always laughed."

Poor Time Management

It is not surprising that a student who rarely forward plans, and even more rarely accommodates his activity to due dates and timetables, is frequently late, or in the wrong place, or in conflict with some time-specific requirement, or is just chronically off-task. Many learning disabled students seem to be unaware of time, or at least of time as a concept organized into sequentially discrete units. This page in the LD catalogue accounts for a significant portion of their trouble in school. Because schools are so time-driven, so inflexibly organized into chronological chunks — sequenced, hierarchical, chronological chunks — the student often feels entirely out of place. School bewilders him not just because of its emphasis on language (and its commensurate de-emphasis of non-language elements where he often shines) but also because of its apparent obsession with time in specified units. Regrettably, the outside world is equally passionate about time, and learning to deal with that fact is a necessary prerequisite in all of education. It is not unusual for a student with learning disabilities to perform better, both generally and academically, in an environment where he is liberated somewhat from the demands of time.

Inconsistent and Episodic

What is at once tantalizing and frustrating for anyone who tries to view the field of learning disabilities objectively (viz., teachers, parents, academics, medical professionals, et al.) is the knowledge that a learning disabled student's profile is never the same day after day, and that a single characteristic of learning disability is never universal. A student with this disability may regularly write "on" for "no" and "b" for "d", yet in the same sentence use all four elements correctly. He may use "on" for "no" consistently for three weeks, and then suddenly and spontaneously use them correctly while simultaneously begin writing "was" for "saw", even though those had been correctly used hitherto.

This is the adolescent who cannot remember a single irregular verb in French, or the formula for calculating the area of a circle, or the definition of alliteration, but who on a warm Saturday can strip down, clean, repair, and completely reassemble a dirt bike. This is the child who bumps into everyone in the queue, whose shoes are untied and whose shirttail hangs out, but who is the first in his age group to earn Red Cross badges for swimming excellence.

This is the student who forgets where he put his clothes, his books, and his lunch, who confuses his telephone number and his address, but can recite without error, a T.V. ad or the lyrics of a rock song.

It is an acknowledged fact by all associated with the learning disabled that no one student will be the same as another, and that no one student's own pattern will ever be consistent and regular. This phenomenon, among other things, makes students almost completely resistant to positive identification by formal standardized tests. It bears equally important weight for the classroom teacher who must be ever prepared to adjust to the episodic nature of a learning disabled student's performance. And of course for parents, it is yet one more arrow in the quiver of confusion.

Difficulty Paying Attention

That learning disabled students do not attend as well in class as their more academically successful colleagues is a given. What is less clear

---

For Discussion: The Case of Raj

Like two of his grade one classmates, Raj is a "December baby", and will not celebrate his sixth birthday for three more weeks. Unlike the other two however, Raj seems to be making no progress whatever in learning to read. Despite both a junior and a senior kindergarten experience where reading readiness and language development were strongly emphasized, Raj still does not recognize very many words, or even letters of the alphabet. He has not made much connection either between letters and sounds, even though he has had daily phonics instruction for three months now.

Raj reads a very few words with confidence (e.g., the, cat, is, hat) but his teacher is unconvinced that this is anything more than reflexive because of the amount of practice he gets. He does not seem to be able to print the words independently, or even copy them. However, he can trace them, albeit slowly and laboriously. The case is only a bit better for printing single letters. These he can copy freehand from models, but the efforts are usually recognizable only about half the time. During any of these activities Raj will stay on-task only with encouragement.

The class has had extensive daily work on the alphabet but on a recent informal assessment, Raj was able to name only twelve letters and give the principal phonetic sound of only eight. (Four of these eight he could not name.) During the same assessment, Raj was able to point to only six letters when letter-names were given him orally. These apparent deficiencies in Raj's ability seem all the more serious because everyone else in the class is "letter-competent"; in fact, most of his classmates are now moving toward independence in reading.

What perplexes the adults working with Raj is that he invariably has a complete grasp of any story when it is read to him, and he always contributes intelligently to discussions. He also seems to have a much better grasp of numbers than letters.

The issues currently being discussed by the adults responsible for Raj are these:

Should a more intense phonics program be implemented on the premise that he is likely learning disabled? Or, should Raj be exposed to more stories (i.e., read to, via "talking book", etc.) on the premise that he is still maturing? Another issue is where either of the two choices above can be best carried out. Should he be sent to a resource room daily for extra work? (He is eligible. On the other hand, his class has a very accomplished assistant, full time.)

is the cause. Do they fail to attend because years of confusion have taught the value of avoidance? Or is this habit innate? The response to this question is a continuing debate in the field. Whether the characteristic is inherent or learned, the simple fact is that most learning disabled students do not concentrate in school (and often at home) in sufficient depth or for sufficient time to learn or acquire new information or receive instruction effectively. This attention deficit is expressed in forms that vary from simple daydreaming to pervasive, counter-productive physical activity. Obviously, there is a commensurate range of challenge for the teacher.

Very Low Self-Esteem

Although there may be argument over whether other traits of the learning disabled are inherent or not, this one, clearly, is acquired. And the cause, at least as far as school is concerned, is fairly obvious. In a system, in a tradition that not only rewards but celebrates academic achievement, it is easy to understand that a student who consistently, often dramatically, fails to achieve at anywhere near the expected standards, will develop serious doubts about his whole persona.

What makes this characteristic so damaging is that it feeds a continuous loop. A student with a learning disability who has become accustomed to low achievement, also becomes accustomed to putting out minimal effort on the quite understandable premise that there is no point if there is no payoff. Therefore the achievement level decreases even further, both because it may have been affected in the first place by the learning disability, but also by lack of effort. As a result, neither teacher nor parent, nor the student gets to see how good the results really could be. Even worse, both sides become so accustomed to poor achievement that on the rare occasions of success they often look first for the fluke that brought it about!

The next link in this chain is invariably behavioural. Students develop personas to divert attention from their disability and their failure and to attract attention to other matters. The class clown, the victim, the super-competent, the I-don't-care, the bad-guy — these are all popular masks that learning disabled students wear.

Some Issues in the Field

■ A satisfactory official definition of learning disabilities, one that is universally accepted, continues to elude the field. When the term learning disabilities was first established in 1963, its popularity was broad and immediate. The term was non-pejorative and all-encompassing. It avoided altogether, implications of low intellect and ineptitude, and successfully subsumed a variety of unsatisfactory descriptors like *dyslexia, perceptual handicap, minimally brain-injured, maturational lag,* even *slow learner.* The dark side however, is that the term is loose enough to permit a variety of interpretations, and it has defied attempts at successful definition.

In most definitions (practically every large jurisdiction has its own) the following major ideas are common.

i) There is significant to serious academic retardation (2 years+ discrepancy between measured performance and age norms).

ii) The individual has shown an uneven pattern of development that continues through adolescence and adulthood.

iii) There may or may not be brain dysfunction or central nervous system disorder.

iv) The learning problems are not due to environmental disadvantage, physical problems, or mental handicap.

■ There continues to be strong contention that learning disability as a concept has no separate integrity because it overlaps so many other concepts of learning difficulty, and for that reason may be said not to exist in any real way, except as a polite, convenient invention to explain the slower or unwilling learner. (There is some question as to whether certain neurological conditions are reflected in learning disabilities. About a third of the students diagnosed with Tourette syndrome, for example, typically show LD characteristics.) The accusation is understandable because so many of the characteristics of a learning disabled student can be found in practically anyone from time to time. The key phrase however, is *from time to time.* Although all of us misunderstand, sequence poorly, get confused, or fail to organize intelligently, from time to time, we do not do so with the unremitting consistency demonstrated by those who have a learning disability. Nor usually, do we exhibit as many characteristics as frequently. A student with a learning disability is one who presents a cluster of characteristics regularly over time. Any teacher or parent who has a basis for comparison with students who do not exhibit these characteristics in the same way, has no doubt about the existence of learning disability.

Still, there can be potential danger in the identification *learning disabled*, particularly if it is applied hastily. For example, the frequent social failures of many learning disabled students, and their early difficulties in learning to read and write is often described as immature behaviour — sometimes as *maturational lag*. This is indeed the case; some learning disabled students do conduct themselves immaturely. But so do other students who are not learning disabled. Only after extensive observation, and with great care, can a student be identified with confidence. As well, the episodic nature of learning disability makes regular review a priority.*

■ Assessing the learning disabled has long been a thorny issue. Although no formal standardized test has yet been developed to clearly show the presence of a learning disability, formal tests continue to be used for the purpose. One tradition has been to use the *Wechsler Intelligence Scale for Children* (now in third edition). This tradition holds that a major difference between the Performance Scale score and the Verbal Scale score with the latter being relatively lower, suggests the presence of a learning disability. Unfortunately the validity of the practice has not held up under rigorous examination.

Another practice has been to use standardized achievement tests to verify a discrepancy between actual achievement by a student and what would be expected according to her age and grade. However this does little more than confirm what everyone knew in the first place.

Still other tests which claim to identify the presence and nature of a learning disability, such as the *Illinois Test of Psycholinguistic*

Abilities (1968) and the *Slingerland Screening Tests* (1970) have very little support in the professional reviews.

Given the broad spectrum of characteristics in learning disability, its episodic nature and its variations in intensity, the failure of formal tests to provide a confident identification is not surprising. Experience in the field has demonstrated however, that informed, objective observations from teachers, other professionals, and parents, balanced against a knowledge of what constitutes this exceptionality in the first place, can establish the presence or absence of a learning disability with considerable certainty, and may in fact be the only way to do it.

■ Although the data on the value of integrating learning disabled adolescents are as equivocal as most data on the subject, there is a significant body of research which suggests that learning disabled adolescents particularly, make better academic gains in self-contained classes. To that end, advocates like the Learning Disabilities Association (LDA) are generally supportive of the idea that schools should maintain the option of self-contained resource placement for some students. The trend in the school system, however, is toward integration, so much so that given the prevalence of learning disabilities, teachers of regular classes can be certain of having one or more — usually more — such students in their classes.

■ A prevailing confusion is that learning disabled students are uncoordinated and have a poor sense of spatial relations, along with poor visual and auditory discrimination. The deficit is — or was — often referred to as *perceptual handicap*. Particularly in the early years of the field it was customary to test and train a student's ability to discriminate among shapes, and sometimes among letters of the alphabet. As well, it was common practice to test a student's ability to discriminate among words that sounded similar, e.g., "cow-now; loan-loam". (This may well account for the early interest in the field by optometrists and audiologists although in the early days, everyone but the neighbourhood blacksmith had a theory and a remedy!)

The belief no doubt sprang from the evidence offered in the writing of the severely learning disabled.

* An issue that causes embarrassment and irritation for those intimately involved with learning disabilities as a major branch of special education is the apparent vulnerability of the field to theory and practice that is not supported by research, empiricism or even common sense. For a description of some of these, see Appendix C.

Here are some examples from students for whom writing class, note-taking, or any writing at all was an exercise in agony.

Wally (aged 7) Grade two (Wally could write his first name in September)

Mike (aged 12) Grade five

My three cats were on the roof. They looked like a mother and three kittens. I took them into the home for some food. Then out popped ...(Story ends.)

Brian (aged 16) in Grade nine English class

I was walking through the forest. And I heard a noise and I followed it. And I saw a flying saucer. They had heads like a dog's face and they had eight heads but a grizzly bear ran to kill the monster from outer space, but one of the creatures killed the grizzly bear. The bear tried to duck and one of the creatures . .

These pieces show why the idea of *perceptual handicap* developed, and why it continues to retain some momentum. Yet it is simplistic to attribute the quality of this writing solely to some kind of visual or auditory discrimination deficit or weakness in visual-motor integration. For one thing, if that alone were the cause, then spelling and syntax would not be the large factors they obviously are. Nor do all learning disabled write this way. Wally, Mike and Brian are a minority — albeit a significant one. (It's worth noting that Brian by age 16 was quite an accomplished snooker player. Mike's hobby was building prefabricated models in plastic — usually cars — with intricate detail. Both activities require considerable visual discriminatory and integration skill.)

The simple fact is that learning disabled students seem to be able to discriminate visually and auditorially as well as anyone. Where their difficulty arises is in *processing* the visual, auditory, and lexical aspects of language meaningfully. The student usually has no difficulty in visually discriminating the letter A from a picture of a teepee, or the sound of "book" from the sound of "hook". Where he will manifest difficulty, is in recognizing the letter A as such, and giving its name (or recalling the word teepee and saying it). It is not distinguishing between the sounds of "book" and "hook" that is hard; it is recognizing the words and the meanings; or, giving the right answers even if he knows them.

The learning disabled student may also manifest difficulty in *producing* the letter A on paper (or the words "book" or "hook"). He may draw a teepee, but it may be disproportionate. On the other hand, he may be able to draw a beautiful teepee but when instructed to add a campfire at the left and a horse on the right, will have to guess at these juxtapositions. The writing by Wally, Brian and Mike is a product of this processing difficulty, in addition to — in their cases — severe problems in spatial relations and poor coordination.

■ Many students, particularly younger ones, find it extremely difficult to pay attention, and manifest a consistently high level of physical activity in situations where it is inappropriate, coupled with an apparent inability to inhibit the activity upon request. These students usually have a low frustration tolerance, and are very distractible and emotionally labile (i.e., show extreme or inappropriate response to stimulation). The condition has been called hyperactivity, hyperkinesis, attention deficit disorder (ADD), and then finally (in 1987) attention deficit hyperactivity disorder (ADHD) (See next page.) Whether or not it is appropriate or accurate, ADHD is generally considered to be a part of the learning disability field. This may be because many learning disabled students manifest some, if not all of the symptoms of ADHD, especially attention deficit.

ADHD is difficult to deal with. It is a problem practically: children who present the condition are difficult to educate (not to mention raise). It is a problem clinically: professionals sometimes find it difficult to establish that symptoms are indeed genuinely present rather than temporary.* It is further, a problem academically: namely, is the condition really a learning disability, or is it a behaviour problem, or is it an adjunct to a learning disability, or is it a behaviour problem which causes some children to appear learning disabled? Or does the frustration of a learning disability cause some children to appear hyperactive? The fact that there are no clear and unanimous responses to these questions is itself an issue.

Although the development of ADHD as a diagnostic concept does not offer teachers, parents, classroom assistants and other front-line personnel any immediate, practical solutions, it has made a significant contribution toward clarification and general understanding so that more effective classroom responses can be determined. For one thing, it has led to a consensus among professionals that the primary symptom of concern — and therefore treatment — should be the attention deficit factor, over the physical activity. For another, the clarification has led to some useful research. Cotugno, (1987) for example, has shown that compared to controls, students with ADHD have more difficulty regulating their motor tempos especially when it is necessary to pause; that they are narrower in their scanning of a field of visual information, slower in attending selectively, more distracted in the face of contradictory information and external distractions, and that they take longer when field articulation is called for. This type of information certainly does not tell teachers what to do, but it can be very useful when they reflect on what it is they might

*Reeve (1990) showed that incidence rates for the condition stabilized at 3-5% of the population after the diagnostic criteria for ADHD became established.

A.D.H.D.

In September 1987, the revised third edition of the Diagnostic and Statistical Manual (DSM-III-R) published by the American Psychiatric Association, replaced Attention Deficit Disorder (ADD) with a new diagnostic label: Attention Deficit Hyperactivity Disorder (A.D.H.D.). This was done on the premise that the ADD label is too loose, too easily misunderstood, and too frequently misapplied to children whose behaviour problems stem from other causes (e.g., unrecognized gifted children, those with social learning disabilities, the emotionally deprived, etc.). The criteria for an A.D.H.D. diagnosis place more emphasis on the hyperactivity itself and reserve it for individuals who before the age of seven, and for more than six months, have exhibited at least eight of the following fourteen symptoms:

(i) often fidgets or squirms in seat; exhibits restlessness,

(ii) has difficulty staying in seat when required,

(iii) is easily distracted by extraneous stimuli,

(iv) has difficulty awaiting turn,

(v) often blurts a response before a question is completed,

(vi) has problems following through and fulfilling instructions,

(vii) has difficulty playing quietly,

(viii) frequently drops one uncompleted activity for another,

(ix) has problems staying on task,

(x) often interrupts or intrudes,

(xi) often does not appear to be listening,

(xii) often talks excessively,

(xiii) often loses necessary items,

(xiv) often exposes self to dangerous activity without apparent consideration of consequences.

The DSM-III-R insists that other developmental disorders be ruled out before a diagnosis of A.D.H.D. is applied, and assumes that a complete history is taken.

(See also **Managing Behaviour with Medication** and **Classroom Strategies for Students with Attention Problems** in Chapter 7. Note that the APA has stated that the upcoming DSM-IV will present new descriptions of attention deficit.)

adjust in their presentation style in order to be more effective in the instruction and management of the students. Above all, it suggests the importance of a carefully structured learning experience for students with ADHD, whether or not they are also learning disabled.

Strategies for the Classroom

(1) *Empathy and understanding* are prerequisite qualities in any person hoping to offer instruction to the learning disabled (although this point is likely redundant to an effective teacher). Once one "gets inside" the particular nature of the learning disabled students, making the necessary steps of accommodation follows naturally. A teacher must set up a warm, supportive climate, without pandering to, or making excuses for, or drawing unnecessary attention to the students' particular needs. The older the students are, the more difficult this task tends to be, for they will likely have well-established and annoying avoidance behaviours, developed with years of practice. Yet, unless a teacher has an appreciation of what his or her students are contending with, and unless there is some sensitivity toward that, all efforts will eventually degenerate into despair and conflict. An environment of mutual trust is crucial for teaching all students with exceptionalities, but for the learning disabled there is an added, subtle layer, for these students usually do not appear at first to be handicapped in any way; in fact they often seem as though they should be especially successful. But they are not, and most of the time, they do not understand why, any more than the adults in their lives do. Such is the insidious nature of a learning disability. It is why empathy and understanding on the part of the teacher are so important.

(2) *Positive, frequent feedback* as quickly as possible, especially on academic matters, is crucial. This helps practically, by keeping the student on task, and more abstractly, by reinforcing momentum, the component so necessary for continuing academic success and achievement.

Naturally, it also promotes the self esteem that is so vital if learning disabled students are to put forth a best effort. The academic feature here is very important: a teacher who can arrange for academic success in a student with learning disabilities, often does far more for that student's ego than she could by deliberately invoking a warm, fuzzy, but non-academic strategy for the simple reason that academics are what school is all about. It is a safe bet that, if the learning disabled student has a low self-esteem, it got that way in large part because of academic failure, so it follows that meaningful and lasting repair has to come about via the same route. Fortunately, this kind of feedback does not have to be dramatic (although an occasional "celebration" can work wonders). Simple attention to even modest achievement is often all that is necessary to develop self-esteem.

(3) *A consistent, systematic approach* will help the learning disabled student eventually learn to interpret and accommodate expectations. Part of this approach necessarily, will be a firm insistence on on-task behaviour and thoroughness. Perhaps a more encompassing term would be structure. The very nature of the learning disabled student's day-to-day cognitive function means that not only classroom instruction but such apparently simple things as classroom regulations and expectations must be clearly outlined, with the parameters firmly established. Teachers must remember that a learning disabled student not only does not learn or manage himself as effectively as he might, he usually does not know how to. If his teacher establishes the boundaries and points out the steps, both self-management and learning become easier. (And once a structure is established, it is also easier for the teacher to be empathetic and supportive because an operating context has been established which both parties understand.)

(4) Learning disabled students usually benefit from as much *graphic and visual support* as possible in a lesson. Use of the blackboard, overhead transparencies, pictures, maps, and other concrete supports, helps them to understand. In fact, many successful teachers assert that it is impossible to teach otherwise. A positive note here is that while graphic and visual support are essential for the learning disabled, they are also helpful techniques for all students.

(5) *Help in sequencing* is important. Teachers must emphasize steps and stages in the proper order as a lesson progresses. The same applies to all assignments, projects, homework or any other item that requires independent and individual completion. Without guidance in where to begin, and what organization to follow, the learning disabled student will become confused and likely as not tune out or give up. This is especially significant with a regular activity like homework.

(6) *Help in dealing with print* is important for many, although not all learning disabled students. Because reading, as well as producing legible and coherent text can be a difficult and time-consuming procedure, a teacher's role therefore, must not only include the assistance necessary by way of direct instruction and by providing opportunity for practice, but must also include recognition of how difficult a challenge print offers for these students and how much longer than other students it will take for them to deal with it.

(7) It will usually be necessary for the teacher to help the learning disabled student *be aware of time* and time constraints. These students often do not forward plan, and it may well take their entire school careers before they learn the responsibilities inherent in due dates, appointments and scheduling. At the same time, it is important for the teacher to recognize that most of the time, learning disabled students do eventually acquire these skills, however imperfectly, and for that reason it is is essential that their teachers persist. (Both parents and teachers attest that this issue is one of the most frustrating, and one that offers the strongest temptation to simply give up.)

(8) For lack of a more professional-sounding phrase, "*staying-on-top of things*" may be an apt way of describing all those apparently superficial but in reality, fundamental behaviours, that a teacher must exercise. Drawing the student's attention to signal words, counselling about sequence and about time, reminding him to bring and take, cueing things by saying "Watch for the change here." and "This is important." — all these seemingly small things go together to help the student cope with daily life in the classroom.

(9) *Making allowances* for those skills which the learning disabled never ever seem to master, is another part of the teacher's role. Correct spelling, for example, is an expectation many almost never meet, and to pursue it relentlessly is counter-productive. It is far more effective both in short and long term to teach them how to *use a dictionary*. Similarly, since they never seem to master the memorization of multiplication tables, it makes sense to forgo the memorization requirement. Other matters, simple on the surface to most of us, frequently escape the learning disabled with ease. Multiple choice questions for example, so time-honoured and so commonly used, often have a subtlety that totally confounds them. So does convoluted syntax. An attempt to persuade, for example, by saying "Inasmuch as the field day is on Monday and the movie on Wednesday, wouldn't you be better to get the project done this week?" will not succeed like this will: "Finish the project this week, because next week we have a field day and a movie. There will be no time to do it next week".

(10) Empirical evidence suggests that sheer *drill and repetition* together constitute a reliable strategy for learning disabled students. By going over and over and over a task — often the very same task — the combination of skills and insights necessary to produce it effectively seem finally to root in long term memory. The work of Brian and Mike and Wally shown below is evidence of this method. One can see major improvement over their efforts of before. (See also 'Neurological Impress Method' [NIM] in Chapter 8.)

(11) *Simplifying the environment* — within the bounds of practical common sense — can be effective (thereby supporting the notion that a separate resource room setting at least part of the time, can be beneficial). Very often such simple accommodations as removing unnecessary distractions, or providing a seating arrangement in which distractions are minimized, can make a difference.

12. Finally, as evanescent as *hope and optimism*, may seem, they are the glue that holds the relationship of teacher and student together. Without them there would not be the extra steps, the extra efforts, the one-more-times that lead to the breakthroughs, although breakthroughs as such are more rare than common. What is more typical is plodding progress. But then progress of any kind is important.

Wally,
at the end of October, Grade two

Birthday Party
We have a birthday cake
and we have 7 Up pop
We go swimming.

Mike
(six weeks after the "three cats" passage)

Describe your favourite dinosaur.

My favourite ~~dinosaur~~ is the "Tyrannosaurus rex. He is big and bad. He Has sharp tees.

teeth   teeth
bad   bad

"My favourite dinosaur is the Tyrannosaurus rex.
He is big and bad. He has sharp teeth."

Brian
(three months after the "creature" passage, in response to a question about losing someone else's schoolwork)

5 #l wud rieft sond anothr rope out soo woulps be wod not be with and l wod him the giv it one at school and morbjing too him foar losing it opotogis

"I would write another copy out so as he would not be without one and I
would give it to him in the morning at school and apologize to him for losing it."

Speech and Language Disorders

Speech and language disorders have traditionally been the responsibility of specialists in the speech and language field, and generally in Canada, this continues to be the case. In part because speech and language therapy and remediation was solidly established in schools well before special education became more or less universal, this particular area of support tends to continue to be somewhat of a separate unit in most jurisdictions, even though, administratively, it is often grouped with special education or with psycho-educational services. Speech and language specialists work cooperatively with special educators and regular classroom teachers, but because the principal responsibility lies largely outside the domain of special education, at least in practice, what follows here is only a brief overview, offered for information purposes.

Speech disorders are problems in conveying the utterances necessary to communicate orally, the sounds that are encoded and decoded in communication between people.

Language disorders are problems associated with the inability to derive meaning from what one hears, or the inability to express ideas in words or other elements of an arbitrary symbol system that is used according to semantic and grammatical rules.

A fairly commonly occurring example of a speech disorder, and one that continues to be mysterious, is *stuttering*: interruptions in the rhythm and fluency of normal speech. An example of a language disorder is *aphasia* (complete) or *dysphasia* (partial). With this condition, the individual is unable to understand or to formulate language (often the result of brain damage caused by stroke or trauma or congenital defect).

Although most children with language disorders have speech disorders as well, it is entirely possible for the two conditions to exist separately. And, although speech and language disorders are often present in individuals with other exceptionalities, they are also present in people who are otherwise normal physically, emotionally and cognitively.

Prevalence data for speech and language disorders are tenuous at best, in part because of confusing reporting schemata, but as well because of disagreements as to what constitutes an absolute disorder as opposed to a temporary, and remediable difference. Also, speech and language specialists are often described as having inordinately high standards regarding the determination of what is normal and what is not, with the result that fairly high numbers tend to be identified. Generally, jurisdictions in Canada report 3-5% of the school population as receiving "speech help".

Speech and language personnel usually fill a role which includes assessment of students with disorders, active therapy and remediation with these students on a regularly scheduled basis, and recommendations to the regular classroom teacher of daily procedures for speech and language improvement. While the numbers in their respective case loads may be weighted toward the students with mild disorders who are in integrated classes, many speech and language personnel spend a significant amount of their time with special classes where problems are quite severe even though populations are small. In Canada, the prevailing modus operandi for regular classroom and even special education teachers is to yield responsibility for assessment and programming of exceptionalities in speech and language, to the specialists.

Types of Speech Disorder

Phonological disorders are shortcomings in phoneme production. They are considered to be disorders when the phonemes sound wrong to people who are attempting to listen. Phonological disorders include distortions, consistent omission of sounds (such as "l" or "st") and substitutions ("l" is fairly frequent; e.g., "widdle wed wowipop" for "little red lollipop"). Unfortunately in younger children this is often seen as 'cute', and is reinforced by adult imitation.

Voice disorders include problems in pitch, quality and volume which hamper communication or are displeasing to a listener. There is also a wide variety of disorders associated with *orofacial defects* the most commonly known being clefts of the prepalate and palate.

Disorders of speech flow include disruptions in the rate, rhythm and fluency of speech. Stuttering is perhaps the primary example.

Types of Language Disorder

Because language disorders are less accessible to exact definition than speech, their description as well as their limits are more imprecise. Disorders in language, i.e., inability or impairment to derive meaning from speech, or to produce it meaningfully, are usually classified according to their causes or by association with other disorders. Congenital deafness, brain damage or childhood psychosis will often lead to a disorder classification known as *No Verbal Language*, applied to children who have not shown understanding or spontaneous use of language by age 3. *Qualitatively Different Language* describes a significant reduction in communicative ability because the language used is so variant from the norm. *Delayed Language Development* is self-explanatory. It is sometimes a product of deprivation, or at times an outcome of hearing loss or mental handicap. *Interrupted Language Development* is usually the result of trauma, and is an acquired disorder.

The Teacher's Responsibility

As indicated previously, the teacher's role is usually governed by advice provided by a specialist in speech and language, and will be particular to the needs of each child. The more severe the case, the more likely the teacher will be part of a team, and will be fulfilling responsibility for part of a program developed by someone else. However, since nothing in practice is as straightforward as it appears in theory, it will still be incumbent upon regular classroom and special education teachers to provide leadership in several ways. These would include providing many extended opportunities for the student to talk; making the classroom an enjoyable place for him or her to work on speech and language, and by modelling an appropriate response to abnormal, difficult-to-understand language for the student's age-peers to follow.

In short, the teacher's role with speech and language disorders is similar to what he or she fills with all students: to be a compassionate professional who takes responsibility for developing the whole individual. An essential difference in the speech and language area lies largely in the tradition that considerable expert help is usually available.

7

Students With Behaviour Disorders

Prevailing Misconceptions About Behaviour Disorders

1. There is a higher incidence of behaviour disorders in school among students from homes of lower socio-economic status.

Data suggest that students from lower SES homes may be more frequently reported as behaviour disordered. There is argument however, that this frequency is owing more to differences in social values and social structure than to real disorders.

2. A permissive atmosphere that allows students to develop understanding and acceptance of the self, is the most effective way to change inappropriate behaviour.

Evidence suggests that a highly structured, ordered, and predictable environment provokes the greatest change in students with a behaviour disorder.

3. Behaviour disorders generally are patterns of conduct which express aggression and frustration.

There is no doubt that outward-directed behaviour is noticeable and it may well be disordered. However, symptoms of behaviour disorder can also be expressed by reticence and

withdrawal. A principal difference is that the latter behavior is not as easily noticed, particularly in large classroom groupings.

4. Very often a behaviour disorder indicates a student who is bright but frustrated.

It happens, but generally, this is not the case. Assessment of intelligence is often difficult with behaviour disordered students. Available data suggest a correlation between behaviour disorders and average to low I.Q. test scores, with the more severe cases even lower.

5. Only mental health professionals are properly equipped to help students with a behaviour disorder.

Many people who have little or no professional training can be very helpful to these students.

6. Behaviour is almost always an external manifestation of something deep-rooted in a student's psyche.

There is no sound evidence that all the causes of behaviour are rooted deep in a student's psyche, or even necessarily connected to emotional disturbance. Especially in school, inappropriate behaviour is often spontaneous and temporary.

7. Behaviour disorders respect neither age nor sex among school students.

Most studies show boys in the clear majority over girls in numbers of identified cases. The ratio varies from 3.5-5 to 1. Incidence rates are highest in the upper grades of elementary school and first grades of secondary school, and lowest in the primary grades.

What is a Behaviour Disorder?

In spite of the fact that attitudes to behaviour vary by individual, by incident, by culture, by social class, by value system, by almost any measure conceivable, there is a surprising degree of consensus over what constitutes disordered behaviour. To most people, disordered behaviour is behaviour that varies markedly and chronically from accepted norms. In a general way then, the notion is quite widely accepted and understood, much in the same way that a general notion of *normal* behaviour is widely accepted and understood.

It is from this point that differences develop. In the same way that normal behaviour is an open-ended construct — within limits — disordered behaviour is too. Therefore, in order to create a common ground of understanding, professionals concerned with behaviour disorders, particularly mental health professionals, have attempted to classify behaviour disorders. Unfortunately the consensus in these classifications varies from limited to non-existent. Interestingly, professionals in education seem to have less difficulty with this issue, probably because they have a more unified perspective. Immediately following is a brief description of the more popular views held by mental health professionals, and of the general view held by educators.

Describing Behaviour Disorders (Mental Health View)

One method used by mental health professionals is **classification by severity** of the condition. Usually this involves identifying the student's behaviour as 'mild, moderate, severe, or profound'. In this schema, the description does not attempt to describe etiology, but simply ranks the behaviour on a scale of intensity.

Another descriptive classification system is called **dimensional classification**. This schema describes behaviour by type or what it calls 'clusters of behaviour'. Although the descriptions are more specific than in the scale of intensity system, they harbour potential for confusion. The clusters include *aggressive*, a classification that lists such obvious characteristics as 'fighting' and 'destructive behaviour' (but also lists 'hyperactivity', 'poor relationships', and 'academic lag, especially reading'); *anxious and withdrawn*, which lists characteristics like 'fearful, shy, and depressed' (but also lists 'short attention span' and 'poor self-esteem that affects interpersonal relationships'); *immature*, which lists 'messy', 'passive', and 'clumsy' (along with 'short attention span' and 'socially inadequate'); *socialized aggressive*, which lists characteristics like 'delinquent activity', 'substance abuse', 'truancy', and 'sexual precocity'.

Still another schema is the **clinical classification** provided by the American Psychiatric Association. This one offers five principal categories that attempt to reflect etiology. The five are *intellectual* (inappropriate behaviour as a result of mental handicap); *behavioural*, (attention deficit and conduct disorders); *emotional* (anxiety and other disorders); *physical*, (allergies, etc.); *developmental* (including pervasive developmental disorders and specific developmental disorders).

Describing Behaviour Disorders (Educators' View)

Most teachers, teaching assistants, child care workers and others on the front lines of education and treatment of students with behaviour disorders, although they accept the value of classifications for mental health purposes, do not find them very practical for immediate educational purposes, if only because classifications do not necessarily imply a treatment or an educational response. Therefore, while the types of classification used by mental health professionals may well be used from time to time by educators, especially for administrative purposes, or in cases where the multidisciplinary team approach is being used, the tendency in education is to approach the notion of behaviour disorder very broadly.

When educators identify a student as having a behaviour disorder, they generally do so on the basis that the student

☐ deviates in a significant manner from the behaviour that is normally expected in the situation;

☐ breaks social or cultural norms that are usually quite well established for the age level;

☐ shows a tendency toward compulsive and impulsive behaviour that negatively affects learning;

☐ has poor interpersonal relationships, and low self-esteem;

☐ demonstrates very low academic achievement for reasons that can best be explained by his or her conduct;

☐ manifests any or all of the above characteristics regularly and consistently over a period of time such that special education is likely required.

In evaluating whether or not a student might be behaviour disordered, an assessment team will almost always consider exclusionary factors as well: whether or not the behaviour can be traced to specific sensory, social or health-related causes. Nevertheless, even if a student's inappropriate behaviour can be explained as a direct outcome of some specific, explainable factor, he or she might still be identified as behaviour disordered, for the simple reason that no matter what the cause, it is still the behaviour — the effect — that the educators must deal with.

Causes of Behaviour Disorders

Biological

The majority of students who have behaviour disorders appear to be physically healthy. Nevertheless, theory and research in the latter years of the twentieth century now suggest possible links between biological makeup and behaviour. Sometimes the connection is clearly, if also distressingly, apparent. Children born with fetal alcohol syndrome or fetal alcohol effects are a case in point. The causes of autism have become an area of extensive research — and speculation — inasmuch as biology is concerned. (See Garreau et al., 1984). Research in

genetics is provoking a continuing reassessment of disorders like schizophrenia. In short, biology is now being considered in cases of behaviour disorder, almost as a matter of course.

Allergies are also being re-evaluated as possible causes of disordered behaviour. While the physical effects of allergies on some students have long been acknowledged, a more recent conception of allergies incorporates the thesis that allergenic reactions can generate learning and behaviour problems far deeper and more subtle than the very obvious physical reactions. A widely accepted notion now, is 'total load': the idea that an individual has a capacity to tolerate only so much substance in the environment, and in some individuals, say, a student in a classroom, a combination of stale air, chalk dust, moulds and fungi in the carpet, and perfume or shaving lotion on the teacher, may exceed that student's tolerance (total load) and cause an allergenic reaction expressed both in a physical way (e.g., a rash or watery eyes or sneezing) and in his or her behaviour. According to Rapp (1991), a somewhat controversial figure in the field, these reactions are often far more profound than may be immediately apparent.

Speech and Language

There is a higher prevalence of behaviour disorders among students with speech and language impairments than is found in the general population. Cohen et al. (1993) for example, in a study of young psychiatric outpatients, found a significantly higher number of language impairments in the outpatients than had been suspected at intake. While there is some debate in the field over whether language impairment is a cause or an effect of behaviour disorder, it seems logical to conclude that a student who has difficulty expressing his needs — or his frustrations — may choose to act them out.

Psychological

In the Home

Explanations for behaviour that are found in psychology will vary by perspective (e.g., a psychoanalyst will see things differently from a behaviourist) and by setting (e.g., the home, the community, the school, etc.). For educators, two very powerful influences on a child's behaviour are the home and the school itself.

A child's relationship with her parents is crucial to development, particularly in the early years. Empirical evidence, supported by research, has consistently shown that the style of child-rearing used by parents will have an impact on the behaviour of their children. In homes, for example, where discipline is inconsistent and sometimes harsh, and where there is little reinforcement for affection, children often learn to be aggressive. Yet, it is important to recognize that this is not the case every time, as it was popular to believe earlier in the twentieth century. Patterson (1982) among others, showed that it may well be a two-way street, with parents responding to the behaviour originated by the child. Unfortunately for teachers, assistants, and others working directly with the child, the cause of the disordered behaviour is less of an immediate issue than the effects, and is in any case, something they are somewhat powerless to modify: one reason why the multi-disciplinary team, which usually has a member working with the family, can be effective.

In the School

While some professionals have said that schools are the major cause of behaviour disorders, there is no clear evidence to support this. Still, Thomas et al. (1968), among others, have shown that deviant behaviour patterns have actually intensified as teachers have tried to help students. Since schools are where students spend a major portion of their wakeful day, it is logical to conclude that what goes on in the classroom, under the direction of the adults there, can have a major influence on a child's behaviour. The relationship therefore, between the child and her teacher, between the child and peers, and between the child and the school at large, can have a significant impact. A key issue for school personnel is to give this impact an appropriate and sensible weight, for just as children must share some responsibilty for their behaviour in the home, so must they in school. Many an attempt by school personnel to resolve a behaviour situation has undermined itself by too obsessive a concern with the dynamism of intra-school relationships. (Walker, 1979.)

"Trying to determine in what proportion a student's behaviour pattern is attributable to [various sources] is an impossible and unnecessary task. Deviant child behaviour can be changed very effectively without knowing the original causes for its acquisition and development." —H.M. Walker

Assessment of Behaviour Disorders

Identification of a student with behaviour disorders usually begins with a feeling in the mind of a teacher or parent that something is not right. As subjective as this might seem, and despite the concern that classroom teachers, especially teachers of a regular classroom, tend to identify a very high proportion of students as behaviour disordered (Rich, 1982), informal screening by teachers and teaching assistants has been established as a fairly reliable first measure (Edelbrock and Achenbach, 1984).

In most jurisdictions in Canada, what follows formally after this initial phase is usually governed by a district's particular plans and procedures for behaviour disordered students. These would include the types of assessment used (which in turn may also be governed by the availability and the expertise of personnel) and the conceptual model for dealing with behaviour disorders.

Typically, to provide a somewhat more objective overview of the student in question, the teacher, and teaching assistant, and often the parents and possibly a social worker or other community service worker, will be asked to complete a behaviour checklist or rating scale.

A declining practice in the assessment of behaviour disorders, although it is still used in some jurisdictions that favor the psycho-dynamic approach, is the administration of projective tests.* These instruments purport to reveal the intra-psychic life of the subject, but have come under fairly heavy criticism not just for their questionable validity and potential for entirely subjective interpretation, but also because an evaluation of this type can tap only an extremely limited sample of the subject's life.

Since there is fairly convincing evidence (Koppitz, 1980) that students who have serious behaviour problems in the later grades often had difficulties in kindergarten, there is

* For a fuller explanation of rating scales and projective tests, see Chapter 13 — Assessment in Special Education.

usually some pressure to identify behaviour disorders early. This is not always possible, however, since disorders often do not emerge until the later grades when personal responsibilities and social and academic demands increase in complexity.

For Discussion:
The Case of Lakeesha

In the classroom and in the school yard, Lakeesha has explosive tantrums on a regular basis. Usually she lies on the floor and kicks and screams in a way that is impossible to ignore. They can be triggered by anything: a change in activity, the end of recess (or the beginning), the desire for a toy which someone else is using. She also bites, pulls hair, scratches, and throws things. (Her favorites are the plastic dishes in the play house.)

When a tantrum subsides, she will spend some time sucking her thumb and rocking back and forth.

Lakeesha will be six years old in three months. She is presently in a regular primary class although a committee will reconvene next week to decide whether or not she should be placed in a self-contained class for students with behaviour disorders. Although the committee recommended Lakeesha be placed in this primary class, it identified her as "behavioural", an unusual step for a primary grade student. The decision will be entirely the school's since Lakeesha's mother seems to have abdicated responsibility for anything but minimal care. She is a very unassertive person and seems totally bewildered by her daughter.

The primary teacher is experienced. She has a very competent full-time assistant. There are also parent volunteers, but some have stopped coming because of Lakeesha. (Others are very regular, principally — in the words of one — "to protect my own kid!")

One of the interesting issues the committee will discuss is that it originally felt that Lakeesha needed the role models she would encounter in this regular primary class.

Some Issues in the Field

■ An enduring concern has been simply what to call this exceptionality. Among the more popular identifiers, some of which are still current, are: *socially maladjusted, emotionally disturbed, mentally ill, predelinquent, delinquent, emotionally handicapped, socially handicapped,* and of course, most frequently used in education: *behaviour disordered.*

In the past, these identifiers appeared at what seemed to be the discretion of whoever was writing on the subject. *Emotionally disturbed,* for example, first appeared (without precise definition) at the beginning of this century. Other terms have cropped up at other times. Education has not always been helpful either, for one jurisdiction will choose whatever term suits it, often without reference to any other jurisdiction, so that across Canada there can be found a variety of descriptors all more or less the same in intent but sometimes markedly different in substance.

The term *behaviour disordered* has acquired a steadily strengthening credibility among educators because it is conceptually inclusive of a variety of problems that warrant professional attention; it is less negative and stigmatizing than many of the other terms in use; and it tends to circumvent the suggestion of legal identification. Above all it is sufficiently comprehensive to have wide applicability in education.

■ It follows that if the names for an exceptionality are at once elastic and capricious, describing it would be just as problematic, and indeed in this case it is. Definitions are vulnerable to their authors' theoretical perspective: behavioural? psychodynamic?; to their discipline: teacher? psychiatrist? lawyer?; and to their purpose for writing a definition: for research? for education? The effect of these differences is a serious block to practical communication, especially in light of the fact that a multi-disciplinary approach is often necessary, especially in the more serious cases.

■ An area of more recent concern is the discrepancy between the percentage of the school population that is behaviour disordered and the percentage that is actually being served. A Canada-wide study by Dworet and Rathgeber (1990) found that not only are the needs of large numbers of behaviour disordered students going unserved, this population is getting even less attention than it did in 1981! Kauffman (1989) in a summary of a range of studies, concluded that over two per cent of the school population exhibits disordered behaviour. Yet data show that typically, under one per cent is being served. This issue has serious, long-range implications. According to Wagner (1989), nearly 50% of students identified *seriously emotionally disturbed* (SED) are arrested within two years of leaving school. Whether or not SED as used in Wagner's study would be similar to 'behaviour disorder' as typically understood in Canada is moot. But the data are cause for serious reflection.

■ There is some evidence that schools illuminate behaviour as unacceptable because they have unrealistic and unnatural standards. Some theorists refer to this as *iatrogenic disorder*: i.e., the behaviour arises as a consequence of the way the student is treated and not out of a natural predisposition at all. Other theorists advance the idea of *psychonoxious* behaviours or attention-getting styles that over time accumulate a large pool of resentment in peers and teachers so that the student in question is treated as behaviour disordered whether he or she actually is so or not. Interestingly, research (Algozzine, 1980) shows that regular classroom teachers find unacceptable behaviours more distressing than special education teachers do. Taken together, these facts argue that schools must engage in some evaluation of their standards and their systems when examining students' behaviour.

Classroom Strategies for Students with Attention Problems

Environment: Seat the student away from distracting stimuli like doorways and other traffic areas. Try to seat him so that stimulating peers are not in his natural line of sight; if possible, surround him with stable peer models. Provide a special, stimulus-reduced study area. Encourage parents to do the same. (Experiment with the effect of natural vs. fluorescent light. It *may* be a factor.)

While Instructing: Be simple and concise. Offer one instruction or task at a time. Limit your use of subordinate clauses. Welcome questions of clarification. Make the student feel secure. Stay nearby until she starts the work. While instructing a large group, stand near her often. If school policy permits, and if you and the student are comfortable with it, use frequent, BRIEF, physical contact (like a hand on the shoulder).

Managing The Day: Prepare him for shifts in topic, setting, schedule, etc. (Again, be physically nearby when these are about to happen.) Meet him and spend a few, positive, one-on-one seconds at crucial points (e.g., when he returns from somewhere, like lunch). When in-class work is assigned (homework too) help him get started, and then at first, check back frequently. Help the student organize and maintain (retain?) his work output so that he develops a visible, concrete, and cumulative record of achievement. Maybe try a daily assignment book.

Other Support: Enforce your classroom rules and procedures consistently. (And have only a very few!) Always give enough time. DO NOT debate or argue; you can't win. Reinforce "good" chunks of time with just-for-her, positive eye contact/expressions. Use antiseptic bouncing; i.e., when she is stirred up, send her on an important errand out of the room, or, provide an important-task-that-needs-doing-now.

Think Momentum: Not motivation but *momentum*. A teacher who motivates is always pushing from behind. Eventually, she wears out — or runs out of patience, ideas, or most likely, desire. On the other hand, a teacher who tries to build momentum in her students, who works at developing in the student, a sense of responsibility for his own fate (and his own behaviour) and a sense of desire within, will not only last longer herself, but make a far greater impact on the student. One way to do this is to help the student focus and manage his own behaviour by establishing a contract or agreement that aims at two, and only two, behaviours so that the objectives are clear (and realistically attainable) and the hope of success thereby increased. Reinforce these with a progress record in chart or other form so that you and the student can point to accumulating proof of improvement.

For Discussion: The Case of Julio

At a case conference a social worker described Julio as "a powder keg with a short fuse". He is a handsome sixteen year old and very athletic, but won't participate in school sports. He rarely goes to class, but comes to school almost every day. More often than not, when he does attend class, he does no work (he brings no books or writing materials in any case) is rudely inattentive, stirs up deliberate disruptions, and tries to distract other students in a way that suggests he doesn't want them to learn either. Most of the time Julio abruptly leaves class after a few minutes, a step that teachers generally ignore with relief.

The school seems helpless to control Julio, or to remove him. Twice he has been seen extorting money from younger students, but in both incidents the victims refused to 'testify'. On one occasion, Julio is alleged to have taken a swing at a teacher, but the incident was blurred by the teacher's own provocative role. Julio has a reputation as a lady killer, an image he promotes with his dress, his style and his speech. Most students avoid him, but he has a small, tight circle that he dominates. There is one known incident of a drug-related arrest, but because of the Young Offenders Act, the school has no details.

There have been two parents' meetings. The first was unsuccessful because neither father nor mother speaks English very well. At the second meeting, the parish priest attended as interpreter. The result was disappointing in that both parents seem to reject entirely, the notion that Julio could be doing anything wrong.

A month ago, Julio's teachers unanimously petitioned the principal to " do something" about him. Julio is aware of this and told the principal that he would respond to any suspension or expulsion by going to the Human Rights Commission. The principal is doubtful that the Commission would involve itself in this case, and doubts it would even respond. But she does recognize that for the sake of everyone it is indeed important to "do something".

■ Particularly among adolescents, students from low income families report a greater number and variety of penalties for their behaviour. Moreover, certain behaviours by these students are more likely to be regarded as disordered, whereas similar behaviours by students from high-income families are more likely to be seen as legitimate responses to some stimulus. A study by Brantlinger (1991) suggests that this phenomenon may be owing to inequities in the school conditions for lower income students. Her study was conducted in the U.S., however. In Canada, there is ample reason to argue that poor school conditions for lower SES areas, are not typical, and that in fact extensive resources are committed to preventing such inequities. Nevertheless, this is not to deny that different *attitudes* toward the behaviour of students from lower social classes may well prevail here.

■ Once identified in the behavioural category, exceptional students often find their history hard to escape. The stigma of behaviour disorder creates a lasting impression; it affects the opinion of teachers and peers, and it contaminates the environment for the student in question. He or she, unfortunately, then lives in an atmosphere where expectations often govern the way others respond. Thus administrators are often reluctant to apply a behavioural label, with the further consequence that even more genuine cases of behaviour disorder may elude appropriate intervention.

■ Legal requirements regularly complicate the education of a behaviour disordered student who has become involved in crime. One of the more significant issues is the disruption of a student's education if he or she is moved through a variety of settings while a case is being decided and a sentence is being served. It is not unusual for an adolescent particularly, to experience a variety of custodial settings through both the court hearing procedures and subsequent serving of a sentence. These settings will invariably have different educational approaches — if any — and usually, little effort is made to coordinate them. A recent addition to the delicacy of the legal issue has been the rigorous privacy stipulations of the Young Offenders Act which in some cases preclude a teacher's being informed of circumstances surrounding a student's involvement in crime, or even of being informed about a transgression at all. While this law may have no immediate bearing on educational planning, it may require the withholding of information that in some cases could be important not just to the student's program, but also to the well-being of the teacher and other members of the class.

Models of Treatment and Educational Implications

There is a broad spectrum of remedial and treatment approaches to behaviour disorder at both the academic and practical levels. Theorists, most especially since the triggering work of Sigmund Freud, debate intensely from what they individually regard as unified perspectives. Academics tend to be *psychodynamics* or *behaviourists* or *environmentalists*, etc. Classroom teachers and teaching assistants who study behaviour theory often find it difficult to be so faithful to a single academic perspective when they apply it in the cold (or hot!) reality of the classroom. Therefore, while academics tend to attach themselves to a set of opinions or theoretical perspective and do research or offer lectures from that viewpoint, educators tend to be quite a bit more eclectic.

❖ There seems to be agreement among those who approach behaviour as a science that there are four main camps of analysis. One of these, the *psychodynamic perspective* is a declining force among educators (but continues to attract a lot of attention in television shows and popular literature). This perspective views behaviour disorders as being within the individual. In the classroom when this treatment approach is taken, the teacher is part of a mental health team that seeks to develop a warm supportive atmosphere in which the student will hopefully overcome his or her inner turmoil. Greater emphasis by far is placed on acceptance and toleration than on direct instruction and acquisition of academic skills. A variation of this style is called the *psychoeducational approach*, in which more effort is directed to practical classroom outcomes. One of the reasons for the decline of the psychodynamic approach is that its advocates have limited hard evidence that it improves either behaviour or academic achievement.

❖ The *biophysical perspective* emphasizes organic origins of behaviour, postulating a direct relationship between such things as physical defects, illnesses, diet, and allergies, and an individual's behaviour. Advocates of this view have generated a multiplicity of causation theories each with a responsive therapy. Some examples include megavitamin therapy, diet control, symptom control medication, removal of offending substances (like carpets) etc. In the classroom this perspective is often combined with a structured, behaviour-based approach that emphasizes routine, daily scheduling, frequent repetition of tasks presented in careful sequence, and the elimination of environmental stimuli that are perceived to be extraneous.

❖ Supporters of the *environmental perspective* offer the view that individuals are a particular collective in a particular space and time, and as such, must be regarded as the product of an ecological unit made up of themselves, their family, school, neighbourhood, and community. Educational response to behaviour disorder therefore must necessarily involve the whole of the ecological unit.

Where this theory is followed in educational practice, teachers are expected to instruct the student in social and interpersonal environment skills. At the same time, attempts are made to modify the school's environment to meet the needs of the individual. Family counselling, and in some cases, counselling of the student's classmates may be part of the program. The key element is to create in all parts of the unit, an awareness of its reciprocal relationships, and an impetus toward monitoring these relationships to the ultimate benefit of the behaviour disordered student.

❖ Often regarded as the dominant theory in the field is the *behavioural perspective,* which is not so concerned with deep-rooted causes but rather, follows the assumption that all behaviour is observable and modifiable by principles of reinforcement. (The assumed dominance of this perspective is at least partly owing to the vast amount of published material it spawns, much of it from American colleges and universities where the theory does indeed dominate. The Canadian view, and especially Canadian educational practice, does not favour behaviourism as heavily.) Educators who adhere to the behavioural approach believe that behaviour is controlled by impinging stimuli and that it is possible to: i) create behaviours that presently do not exist; ii) maintain and generalize behaviours already established; iii) eliminate inappropriate behaviours. What happens practically, is that first, a desireable behaviour or set of behaviours is established. Then, using a potent reinforcer at the appropriate time, the teachers and teaching assistants intervene when these behaviours appear. Educators who use behaviour modification — and many do to a degree, even those who would deny being behaviourist — regard every student as a candidate for learning, irrespective of whatever psychopathology may be at the root of behaviour.

❖ As mentioned previously, the number of educators who follow a single theory religiously, is quite smaller than the number who combine a variety of approaches and apply them on a by-case basis. All teachers of all students, not just the behaviour disordered, espouse the value of a warm, supportive atmosphere. All teachers recognize the interplay of environmental stimuli and are aware of the importance of these phenomena in both learning and social development. Classroom personnel universally modify behaviour in their students but only

some will call it behaviour modification. And the view of each student as a dynamic, individual entity is at the very heart of teaching as a profession.

Taken together, the practices followed by most educators most of the time, could best be collected under the expression: flexible common sense. While the term may not have definitive intellectual reverberations in the field of behaviour theory, it describes pretty much the route that is followed in the classroom.

Managing Behaviour with Medication

The use of drugs to affect hyperactive behaviour has been a subject of very sharp debate since the late 1960's. The principal drug used is Ritalin (methylphenidate hydrochloride) although Dexadrine (dextroamphetamine) and Cylert (magnesium pemoline) are also prescribed.

For Discussion: The Case of Moonshadow

The commune where Moonshadow lives has been in constant struggle with government authorities over a number of issues, including Moonshadow's education. Although she is now nine years old, Moonshadow did not attend school until ordered by the court two months ago.

At first, Moonshadow would not participate in any class activity or communicate with any other children. The teacher, recognizing the degree of change for her, did not press at first, but after Moonshadow made no move of her own in over five weeks, the teacher tried a more pro-active approach. Moonshadow resisted strongly. She would hover on the edge of things from time to time, with what could reasonably be interpreted as curiosity; yet whenever the teacher tried to induce her to participate — gently, firmly, by any manner of persuasion — Moonshadow would scream and run in circles, dipping and diving with arms extended.

The other children were amused at first, then tolerant. Now they shun her. After extensive effort, the teacher found that he had

no better strategy than simply to leave her alone, so that for the next month or so, Moonshadow lived her own life in the class.

Now, a new and urgent problem has arisen. For the past week, at least three or four times a day, Moonshadow has sat in lotus fashion in the middle of the room loudly chanting what the teacher believes to be her mantra. It is not an entirely new behaviour. In September she had done this — quietly — in response to stress. Now it is very regular and very loud. Yesterday, in response to a plea from the teacher, the principal attempted to pick up and carry Moonshadow from the room, whereupon, in the principal's words, "she went berzerk". The other children in the class, not to mention their parents, are very upset.

This school has a segregated behaviour class run by an exceptionally able teacher with a string of successes in seemingly intractable cases. However the principal fears that placing Moonshadow there will destroy the significant gains made by the children in that class.

The negative arguments generally coalesce around the very use of drugs, but Ritalin in particular has been controversial, probably because it seems to be the most widely prescribed. It is actually a stimulant drug (as is Dexadrine) which in *some* hyperactive children* apparently enables the child to control inappropriate behaviour. Criticism centres around the physical side effects of the drug (irritability, drowsiness, sleeplessness, facial tics, loss of appetite, etc.) and around the possible psychological effect of dependency. Although Ritalin is not a narcotic, its detractors say that it produces dependency, and may cause the child — and others — to believe that intellectual achievements are owing to the ingestion of the drug and not to natural intellectual growth.

Supporters of the use of medication, especially Ritalin, argue that it stabilizes hyperactivity, allowing the child to learn and to form social relationships hitherto impossible to achieve.

Both sides agree that the side effects may be potentially serious (The claims for Cylert are that it is not as prone to these effects) and also agree that irrespective of the ethics involved in the actual use of these drugs, the potential for abuse — and the actual abuse — is significant. Those who support the use of medication emphasize that both administration of a drug and the dosage must be monitored carefully and the necessary adjustments made, if there are to be any positive outcomes. Neither side of the dispute has been able to establish definitively whether learning is enhanced or artificial under the drug regimen. This particular aspect of the debate is the subject of continuing research with many contradictory results.

In 1993, Swanson et al. in an extensive overview of the literature on stimulant medication, concluded that, in children to whom it is administered, one can expect temporary management of diagnostic symptoms (like impulsivity) and temporary improvement of associated features (like aggression). The reviewers went on to say that what should *not* be expected from stimulant medication is a major effect on skills or higher order processes, or improvement in long term adjustment.

Teachers of students taking prescribed stimulant drugs need to be sensitive to the debate, and need to be especially sensitive to the ramifications involved in having these students in their classes.

*Early claims were that 80% of these children were helped. Present figures move in the 50-60% range.

Strategies for the Classroom

It is axiomatic among teachers who work in special education that there is no instructional panacea, no pedagogical magic for any exceptionality. In the case of the behaviour disordered this axiom has an especially intense and often uncomfortable ring of truth. Despite the most careful planning possible, despite the most rigorous attention to therapeutic and instructional practice, the results of a teaching-learning situation in these cases can be an utter failure. On the other hand it can turn out to be entirely successful — but more by chance than design. Then there are the situations that show immediate improvement, only to deteriorate with equally dramatic speed. Or the situations where improvement is evident on one day and gone the next.

Instruction of students identified as behaviour disordered requires patience, resilience, and a never-ending willingness to try again. Usually these are the natural characteristics of a teacher who operates under the principle previously described as *flexible common sense*. Empirical evidence supports the value of this approach, and suggests that in spite of all the problems in educating students with a behaviour disorder, there is reason to believe it can benefit them in both specific and general ways. What follows are some of its features.

At the Prevention Level

1. Establishing a realistic, *consistent* learning environment is a crucial first step. There should be a minimum number of rules, positively stated, and these should be made clear early on, and followed carefully and equitably. For the teacher who is comfortable with it, he or she may wish to involve the students in the formulation of the rules. (It is essential, however, that rules — their establishment, their content, and adherence to them — not become the most important element in the classroom. Learning is.)

2. Except for students who have a genuine psychosis, a positive, reinforcing teaching style is almost always successful. "Catch a kid doing something good" is not just a catch phrase.

For Discussion: The Case of Jordie

At first glance it is tempting to accept the frustrated opinion of one of Jordie's former teachers that he is "just an airhead". But a second glance reveals that this grade six boy's problems are more complex than that. And sadder too.

Jordie is an outcast. He has no friends, male or female, in grade six. No one wants to associate with him on the playground and everyone vigorously resists being paired or grouped with him in class. Not that the students can really be blamed for this response. Jordie does just about everything possible — whether out of malice aforethought (which seems unlikely) or out of sheer lack of self-control (which is far more probable) — to alienate his classmates.

To begin with, Jordie is in constant motion. This varies from repetitive jiggling, foot-tapping, finger-drumming and arm flapping while he is seated, to purposeless pacing and general wandering. Jordie is not just out of his seat a lot, he always seems to be precisely in the midst of someone else's or some other group's affairs. Nor does he linger on the periphery in these situations; instead, he insinuates himself right into the middle of their activities and discussions, disrupting, annoying, even accidentally destroying. The kinesthetic behaviour is matched by verbal behaviour. Jordie talks out loud to anyone and no one. All the time. He also has the unhappy facility of going too far. Jordie never knows when to back away on his own. He seems to have no concept at all of social retreat or interchange.

As might be expected, Jordie's achievement suffers in kind. He rarely completes anything unless the teacher or assistant monitors carefully; in any case he loses it right away. Jordie also borrows things — without asking — and neglects to return them.

In his own words, Jordie desperately wants to be "a nice guy". He always obeys requests from adults. When his classmates tell him to go away — usually quite sharply — he never argues. Jordie seems to want to do what is right but apparently cannot.

3. Positive, receptive behaviour on the part of the teacher and teaching assistant is important. If students learn they have an adult who is open, who listens, who will discuss their concerns (ideally *later*, in private) they will often learn to curb impulses and govern their own behaviour.

4. Communication in several directions is necessary. To be successful, a teacher must have open lines with parents, with administration, and with support personnel. It is not unusual for this responsibility to devolve upon the teacher entirely; nevertheless unless these lines are used, and hopefully, used to guarantee universal cooperation, the chance for both behavioural and academic remediation diminishes.

5. Except for the very severely behaviour disordered (where uncertainty will inevitably reign) the premier classroom focus should be on education. Even if the development of social skills is a vital feature of a student's educational plan, the perception of the student should always be that he or she is "here for education". A student with behaviour disorder already feels distinguished, singled out. To devote the major part of a program to the development of social skills in a transparent, obvious way, only reinforces the distinction. Social skill development can continue to be the principal objective, but its realization should be achieved not just by direct social skill instruction itself, but by learning it during the process of studying what all the other kids are studying.

This focus will tend to blur in direct ratio to the restrictiveness of the student's setting, for it is a natural inclination to reduce academics in favour of socialization the farther one gets from a regular classroom.

6. A teacher's or an assistant's personal conduct may often be the single most valuable factor in preventing and ultimately eliminating disordered behaviour in the classroom. Ideally, adults are role models who don't respond defensively to challenge, who have the skills to divert a troublesome situation until stability is restored (and then deal with it) and who employ fair and realistic consequences in a consistent way. These are also the people who get to class ahead of time, who are present and visible and interacting: role models of adulthood that communicate to the (behaviour disordered) student that the world does have some sense to it.

Naturally, things do not always work out this way. Yet this type of conduct must be a goal if prevention of disordered behaviour is to be achieved.

At the Supportive Level

1. Daily instruction and classroom management styles will be shaped by behaviour disorders in students whether the teacher is organized or not! But it is better to be organized.

(a) The physical arrangement of the room, especially in elementary grades, should allow for a quiet work/study area which can become a private retreat for discussion if necessary. Seating arrangements — *changes* in the seating arrangements can be either harmful or beneficial. Teachers should never bring these about without pre-planning.

(b) Routines make more sense (to all students) if they are indeed routines, and are followed consistently.

(c) Because the student with a behaviour disorder is often bewildered by change, shifts, and steps of a sequence, it is usually advisable to help him through these. If possible, for example, a teacher can give general class instructions while in close proximity to the student, in order to be immediately available to guide, or if necessary, to prevent.

2. Very often, students exhibiting behaviour disorder are cognitively deficient. They seem to lack organization and executive function, and are unlikely to acquire it spontaneously in a classroom. An essential part of the teacher's role therefore is helping the student to organize for successful achievement. By setting out a project or major assignment for the whole class, and then by helping the students to plan, organize, and execute the requirements, the teacher or assistant (sometimes peer tutor) will not only be teaching cognitive skills, but will be creating an opportunity for achievement and academic success. There is no stronger elixir than success.

3. For students in whom a lack of commitment and a profound unwillingness to defer gratification are powerful forces, it follows that setting long term behavioural or academic goals, either with them or for them, may not be very productive. On the other hand, setting short term, achievable goals in which students can see the possibility of achievement, and can attain the achievement and can enjoy it, all within a comprehensible — for them — time frame, is an ideal approach. Students must be able to see the light at the end of the tunnel before they go into it.

4. There is a range of supportive strategies available to the classroom teacher which he or she may develop, or tap into, according to the needs of the individual student and the intuitive and sensitive strengths of the teacher. Some teachers can release tension through humour. Others are very adept at finding reinforcers which will shape a student's behaviour to appropriate ends. Some are comfortable with "Grandma's Rule" ('First you do what I want, then ...') and use it effectively. Some establish formal behavioural contracts, complete with specific terms and rewards. Others use a form of behavioural task analysis called *chaining,* wherein an activity like entering the classroom and opening a notebook is broken down into a chain of behaviours, each guided, evaluated, and appropriately rewarded.

In practice, the more unusual or dramatic or even esoteric a technique may seem, the more unlikely it is to be found in the regular classroom setting. Highly specialized methods, those that would exist outside the canon of *flexible common sense* have greater applicability in more specialized, restrictive settings, first because the clientele in these settings are more likely to require dramatic approaches, and secondly, because the teachers in these settings would more likely have the support personnel, the environment, and the kind of pupil-teacher ratio that would make these strategies feasible. By far the largest number of students with behaviour disorder are found in the regular classroom however, and it is these more than any other who respond to flexible common sense.

Finally it may seem obvious that teachers working with behaviour disorders, should themselves be people who are emotionally stable and in sound mental health. Yet, according to Roy, in *Canada's Mental Health* 1981, #29 (16-18) a distressing number of Canadian teachers have mental health problems of their own. This finding implies a major responsibility on the part of administrators in the placement of students. It also follows that teachers who work with behaviour disorders should, for practical reasons, make periodic intra-career changes for the sake of their own health, and ultimately that of their students.

8

Students With Mental Handicaps

Choosing a descriptive term for this area of special education is a delicate matter. A variety of terms have been suggested in the past few years, and some advocates have argued against the use of any term at all. Still, to have a useful academic discussion, it is helpful to have vocabulary which identifies a significant characteristic that affects the education and life style of some students. *Special Education in Canadian Schools* chooses to use 'mentally handicapped'. It is our position that 'mentally handicapped' is a phrase that educators and parents can use sensibly and beneficially with no pejorative effects.

Prevailing Misconceptions About Mental Handicaps

1. There are limitations on what a person can learn.

There is no hard evidence to confirm the existence of a ceiling of learning or of a limit to an individual's developmental capacity. Learning and development can be life long for everyone.

2. Students with a mental handicap always learn more and learn better when they are integrated with regular students.

It is not possible to lump all mentally handicapped students into a learning environment classification. If these students learn much like everyone else, as the evidence suggests, it must be granted that — just as with everyone else — no one environment is consistently and universally superior.

3. A low I.Q. test score is usually evidence of at least borderline mental handicap, and means the subject's adaptive skills are below normal.

An I.Q. test may be an indicator of mental ability, particularly as it pertains to academic or school matters. However an individual's adaptive skills can be largely independent of his I.Q. test score, because they are often more a factor of training, motivation, and social environment.

4. Mentally handicapped people develop in different learning stages than non-handicapped people.

They develop through the same stages but usually do so at a slower rate and often with smaller gains.

5. Students with Down syndrome are invariably pleasant and compliant.

Many individuals with Down syndrome are pleasant, compliant and happy, but like all people with or without a disability, they experience emotional stresses and react accordingly.

6. Certain racial groups have a higher incidence of mental handicaps.

This particular misconception has developed in part because a severe, genetically based condition, Tay-Sachs disease, occurs almost exclusively among Eastern European Jews. However, other causes are no more frequent among Eastern European Jews than among other racial groups, nor do other causes have the peculiar racial exclusivity of Tay-Sachs disease.

7. Mentally handicapped students look different.

Certain groups of students, including many with Down syndrome, do appear physically different from their peers, but the vast majority of mentally handicapped students look just like any other students.

Definition And Classification

Like blindness, deafness, and physical disability, a mental handicap is recognized as an identifiable, exceptional condition, but unlike the others, it has no universally accepted, standardized definition. One reason is that various disciplines — education, medicine, psychology, for example — all approach this exceptionality from their own perspectives. Another reason is that the public perception of a mental handicap is constantly changing. The once common view of this exceptionality as a genetically determined, developmentally terminal condition (reflected in classifications like 'idiot', 'imbecile' and 'moron') has been replaced by a much more flexible view that acknowledges the dynamic interplay between an individual's natural abilities and the environment.

The most widely accepted definition in use today is that proposed by the American Association on Mental Retardation (AAMR) formerly known as the American Association on Mental Deficiency. While the parameters of the definition are under constant review, there seems to be stable acceptance that a mental handicap is defined by the presence of three interrelated factors:

☐ sub-average intellectual functioning, resulting in or associated with

☐ problems in adaptive behaviour,

☐ manifested during the developmental period.

Sub-average Intellectual Functioning

This part of the definition is usually addressed by the use of I.Q. test scores to indicate different levels of intellectual function. Whereas it was once common practice to use a single number as a plateau or cutoff point, the AAMR recommendation now offers the following ranges of test scores.

I.Q. test score range

50-55 to approx. 70:	likely indicates a mild mental handicap
35-40 to 50-55:	moderate mental handicap
20-25 to 35-40:	severe mental handicap
below 20-25:	profound mental handicap

The use of *ranges* of scores rather than absolute numbers is important for it implies flexibility, and acknowledges the possible imperfections in I.Q. tests for identifying the presence of a mental handicap. The AAMR's recommendation of the scores above also reflects an evolution in attitude. Prior to 1973, the association recommended a cutoff I.Q. score of 85, only one standard deviation below the mean, or norm, of 100 to define a mental handicap. The change to approximately 70, or *two* standard deviations below the mean, indicates a recognition of the importance of adaptive behaviour relative to so-called measured intelligence.

Adaptive Behaviour

Generally, adaptive behaviour refers to how well an individual is able to meet — *to adapt to* — demands made by the environment. It is a dynamic construct, necessarily affected by cultural norms and age-related expectations. The inclusion of this factor in the definition is an important step away from the use of I.Q. score results as the sole criterion for definition. The fact is that many students who obtain a low

I.Q. test score can live and learn quite well in a variety of environments.

Developmental Period

According to the AAMR, this is the period from conception to an individual's eighteenth birthday.

Classification in Education

There are considerable variations in the jurisdictions across Canada. Some districts use no classifications at all. Usually, these jurisdictions describe themselves as inclusive ones that integrate all students at all levels. Others, whether or not they have an inclusive policy, or a variation of this, use the mild-moderate-severe-profound ranges of the AAMR. Still others use variations of the three descriptors below that suggest attainable levels of performance for educational purposes. These descriptors continue in wide use, and have in fact been used for years in Canadian definitions of exceptionalities.

☐ Educable: Capable of basic academic subjects up to advanced elementary levels. General achievement ranges from second to fifth grade. (This classification is usually determined by an I.Q. score of 50-75.)

☐ Trainable: Capable of attaining self-help skills, self-protection, and social adjustment. Very limited achievement in areas considered academic. Will likely be able to succeed in employment under supervision. (Classification usually determined by an I.Q. score of 25-49.)

☐ Custodial: With intensive and extensive training may learn some basic self-help and communicative skills. Will almost certainly require regular supervision and support. (Classification by I.Q. score of below 25.)

Some Issues in the Field

■ Identification. An abiding concern among educators, health professionals, and particularly advocates and parents, is what to call a mental handicap — or whether to call it anything at all! Part of the tension arises out of the desire of administrators, researchers, clinicians and academics to have a practical and efficient means of identifying a consonant group for their various purposes. The wish is to have a neutral, scientific, and widely accepted term. Balanced against this is the far less scientific but equally important desire of parents and advocates to expunge terminology from the field for the simple reason that descriptive terms for

For Discussion: The Case of Alf

Alf has been attending regular schools since age nine, prior to which he attended a special school. He has Down syndrome, and presents some of the fairly typical manifestations. Height and weight are slightly above average for the age (16). He has some fairly serious respiratory difficulties and misses quite a bit of school because of colds (and on two occasions, pneumonia). At age four, Alf had major heart surgery to correct a defect.

Alf has been in high school now for four weeks. He is pleasant, accommodating, and cooperative, although several notations in his file refer to his explosive temper. (One comment describes a day three years ago when Alf overturned desks and broke a window during a fit of temper.) The committee which recommended he be placed in grade nine had initially recommended a self-contained class for language arts and math

studies, but his parents appealed this placement and were prepared to go to higher authority to have Alf placed in fully integrated programs with no withdrawal support. The school district has acquiesced and Alf is now fully integrated.

In all academic areas, Alf seems to function about 3-4 grade levels below that of his classmates. Although his teachers have made adjustments to accommodate this reality, another problem has cropped up. Because Alf is so far behind his classmates academically, they associate with him only on a very limited basis in class, and ignore him completely out of class. This is an outcome directly opposite to the parents' goal in arguing for full integration. The parents — and teachers — have observed that Alf is losing his temper more frequently of late.

this exceptionality, no matter how carefully they are chosen, invariably seem to imply limitations, and very rapidly are adopted for pejorative use in popular parlance.

There appears to be no simple way out of this dilemma. Terminology is not just useful to professionals, it is part and parcel of scientific, educational practice. Yet what terms are appropriate, and how can they be kept from degenerating into insult? No serious professional today would dream of using discarded terms like 'feeble-minded', a once popular scientific term, but so much of the new, semantically gentler terminology seems only to generate its own black humor (such as developed with the use of various 'challenged' descriptors from the late 1980s). This is made especially ironic in light of the fact that 'mentally retarded', the long-accepted term, seemed to have successfully shed its pejorative connotations as society at large developed a more enlightened and balanced view of intelligence, ability, and individual worth. Yet advocates were generally successful in arguing for its removal from the special education lexicon.

The situation may resolve itself at some point in the future, for more and more, students with a mental handicap are seen, not as different at all, but as people with abilities and disabilities and likes and dislikes and all the attributes that contribute to the uniqueness of all persons. But for the present at least, as long as the vast majority of a population, in school and elsewhere, continues to rise to the academic and social demands made of them, in a way that contrasts with a small group who do not do as well for apparently intellectual reasons, it seems difficult to conceive of that group not being noticed for their distinctiveness. For this reason alone, the human tendency in all cultures to apply a descriptor to a special group is almost sure to prevail. Perhaps the best to hope for, is that the descriptor will be used in an entirely neutral, functional context.

■ Normalization. The argument that people with a mental handicap should be seen for their similarities to rather than their differences from the population at large, and that they should be allowed to thrive in the larger society to the maximum possible extent, has implications that morally, ethically, and academically, are very provocative. In the nineteenth century, the gradual development of institutions to care for the mentally handicapped was regarded as a major step forward in the attitude toward exceptional people. And no doubt it was, for institutions which offered care when the alternative was often abandonment, reflected a degree of social and moral responsibility hitherto unknown. But institutions have a potentially insidious nature. For reasons of economy, ease of management, and sometimes ignorance, the residents of an institution are often kept in an environment that is impoverished in terms of stimulation and opportunity. Given what special educators now know about human development, it is apparent that many of the behaviours historically associated with a mental handicap are consequences of institutional life, or perhaps more specifically, lack of stimulation and direct instruction.

The overwhelming impetus in the field therefore, has been toward de-institutionalization, and integration with mainstreamed society. The impetus has been driven more by support and counsel groups than by governments and educators, but the response of the latter two groups although late, has been very positive. The reality today therefore, is that very large numbers of mentally handicapped people are living in the mainstream, many of them on their own, or with some supervision, many with gainful employment, and acquiring and enjoying the benefits of education.

■ Integration. The de-institutionalization-cum-integration movement is clearly one of the most high profile issues in the field, in large part because of conflict that seems to arise out of the impatience of its supporters, and the guarded hesitancy of parts of the larger society. At the most liberal end of the integration spectrum are those who argue that all persons should be fully integrated into society — and most especially into schools — immediately. These supporters tend to see the matter in absolute terms and would brook no modification of a person's environment whatever. Their view is that total integration at once is the only possible position that a society can morally, ethically — and, in Canada, *legally** — adopt.

The intensity with which this position is presented often forces an adversarial context, particularly when educators respond that integration is a relative matter, and that for some students, a modified school environment may

*Legal action on behalf of persons with retardation continues to be put forth using the Charter of Rights and in some cases, human rights legislation for support. As yet, the courts have not taken a clear, consistent position.

be more beneficial. It is not that the educators reject integration but rather that some prefer cautious integration, arguing that students should be considered on an individual basis, that not all cases are ideal for total integration immediately, and that the consequences of forced, immediate integration can be potentially disastrous for everyone involved. But often, instead of being able to recommend this position, these educators are made to defend it, and find themselves using arguments — and taking positions as a result — that can be interpreted as pro-segregation, whether or not this is indeed what they believe. The risk for students with mental handicaps in this controversy, is that the significant maturing of society's attitude, especially in the past few decades, may be put in jeopardy by hasty decisions, emotion, polemics and blanket policies.

What makes this especially distressing to classroom teachers and parents is that empirical evidence shows that generally, children who begin their school lives in integrated classrooms treat that environment as natural. And most of the time, this integration is successful and continues to succeed for all children as they grow. Where success is not as universal is in those situations where the integration does not start until later grades, and where it is arbitrary. (Some interesting research on the issue is in Snyder et al., 1977, Peterson & Harolick, 1987, and Zigmond & Baker, 1990.)

For Discussion: The Case of Sarah

Sarah is in grade six. This is her third year at ABC elementary school. She is believed to be thirteen years old. There are no records available prior to a time nine years ago when she was found at a roadside by the police. The Family and Juvenile Court ruled that she was abandoned, and made her a ward of the Children's Aid. During the nine year period, Sarah has been with six sets of foster parents, the most recent one for 30 months.

Two of Sarah's previous teachers contend that she has significant potential as a student, and that her lack of success in school is more a product of her behaviour and of the way she has been treated. Some of her behaviours include perseveration. She sucks her thumb while patting her head and rocking; she eats a great deal, almost uncontrollably, and is very overweight. When she is distressed, and sometimes for no apparent reason at all, she runs around in circles and if restrained will spin around top-like. These behaviours have decreased significantly in the last year however, and occur only at moments of stress.

A recent school team meeting established that Sarah can recite the alphabet when prompted but does not recognize, or at least not give the correct response to individual letters when they are presented randomly. She recognizes her own first name in print about 50% of the time but not her last name. On the other hand she responds when her last name is called but not her first name!

(There is another Sarah in the class.) Sarah had a last name given her by CAS but for over a year now has been called by the surname of her current foster parents.

She prints most of the alphabet but only with dot to dot stimuli to assist her. Sarah counts easily to twenty-five, but does not associate the process with actually counting things. She will count 1-2-3-4-5, for example, but does not seem to be able to count 5 things on her desk.

At present Sarah is integrated in a regular grade six class, and is withdrawn to a resource room for intensive remedial work, one hour per day. However a change has been proposed. The school board has offered to provide a full time teaching assistant to Sarah's classroom. To invoke the funding for this, it will be necessary to officially identify Sarah in the school records as mentally handicapped. If the teaching assistant becomes involved, Sarah will no longer be withdrawn to the resource room.

There is one more concern. Although Sarah has known most of her class for the past two years and was quite naturally accepted and taken in socially, her teacher reports that of late, the students in the class seem to be staying away from her. The teacher theorizes that this may be coincident with a new dynamic she has perceived in the class: namely that most of the class has suddenly developed an intense interest in the opposite sex. Sarah has not.

■ **Major/minor role for teachers.** The heat of the argument over the speed and extent of integration is often felt most by teachers who, ironically, have remarkably little opportunity to rule on the matter, despite the fact that theirs is the most crucial role in whether or not integration succeeds. Teachers must accept the integration policies of their school boards, and these policies vary. Some jurisdictions for example, offer a variety of placements from complete integration to partially self-contained and fully self-contained classes. Other jurisdictions have a policy of total integration. However, whatever the policy, it is a certainty for teachers that they will likely have mentally handicapped students in their regular classes, part or all of the time. Herein lies an issue over which integration may one day founder. Despite the fact that the classroom teacher's role in the success or failure of integration is so central, it is a curious anomaly not just in Canada, but in North America generally, that strikingly little opinion is sought from them on matters of integration policy. Other than the students themselves, they are the key to the matter of integration; yet they often have the least input. As educational budgets shrink — now an accepted phenomenon — and support in its various forms declines in the regular classroom, the voices of teachers may well be heard in a way that will not augur well for integration.

■ **Time to learn.** Early theory held that a mental handicap implied an absolute limit to potential. This notion was handily reinforced by supposed empirical evidence (especially bizarre behaviours which often turned out to be institutional behaviours) and by notions of incurability. Particularly since the success of the normalization movement, it has become evident that with stimulation, support, and direct instruction, there is literally no limit to students' learning capacity. However, the process for some takes longer. Mentally handicapped students are learners but they are slower learners. This fact should not make much difference in a modern education context, especially in light of individualized learning principles. However, the time factor becomes an issue because many jurisdictions make school enrolment terminal (usually tied to chronological ages of students) either through funding limitations or simply by decree. While continuing

education programs go a long way toward circumventing this problem, it is still an issue that has not yet been satisfactorily resolved by school boards and governments.

■ **Employment and vocational training.** Some mentally handicapped adults have paid employment in industries known by such descriptions as 'sheltered workshops', where they are paid for relatively simplistic and repetitive industrial tasks. On one side of this issue is the thought that these individuals are given opportunity to contribute to their own support by gainful activity that is within their capacity under supervision. On the other side, there is opinion that such employment is exploitation, and simply an unsubtle extension of institutionalization. The issue is an awkward and difficult one to resolve in a free economy, and proponents of both sides are able to refer to many practical examples that support their respective arguments. For educators the disagreement is uncomfortable, since they must resolve for themselves the importance of this potential employment when determining learning objectives for their students.

■ **Modern medicine.** Techniques in medical science have introduced whole new areas of uneasiness and controversy. The process of amniocentesis for example, makes it possible to determine whether or not a child, in utero, has a chromosomal abnormality which would indicate a condition like Down syndrome. Regrettably, this analysis may provoke in turn a debate for or against a therapeutic abortion; it does not, at least so far, offer any technique which would alter the abnormality.

Another technique, developed in Europe, involves surgery that may alleviate the respiratory complications often suffered by children with Down syndrome. It has become fairly common practice to include facial surgery in the procedure — some argue it is necessary — in order to enhance speech abilities, and to alter the mongoloidal appearance of the children so that they will look "normal". Its advocates support it largely on the premise that the children if they appear normal, will respond as normal, or be treated more normally, and grow into a better life as a result. Its detractors hold that normal appearance will raise false and unattainable expectations.

Causes of Mental Handicap: Implications for Educators

For educators, knowing the cause of a particular student's mental handicap satisfies both intellectual curiosity and a teacher's natural desire to know as much as possible about an exceptional student in order to support him effectively. However, the value to educators of knowing the causes of mental handicaps is somewhat diminished by three factors.

❖ 1) The corpus of scientific knowledge is both extensive and bewildering, even to members of the medical profession. Causes range from trauma (such as anoxia at birth) through chromosomal abnormality (e.g., Down syndrome, tuberous sclerosis, Klinefelter's syndrome) to metabolic (e.g., phenylketonuria, Prader-Willi syndrome) and infectious/toxic in the pregnant mother (e.g., rubella, syphilis, alcohol, cocaine). As well, more than one name is used for some conditions (e.g., *epiloia* for tuberous sclerosis), and very often the conditions are very poorly or incompletely described, or presented in language that is comprehensible only to the thoroughly initiated. Most important, it is almost always impossible to infer any practical educational response from a description of cause; even worse, it is not unknown for a child's case to be given up as educationally hopeless on the basis of a scientific description of cause, and for this reason, some educators argue that descriptions of cause should be tendered only for very compelling reasons.

❖ 2) It is usually only with the moderate through profound classifications (which constitute the lowest numbers) that fairly clear cause can be established. In any case, the physiological factors in moderate through profound mental handicaps are pretty much irreversible, and unless immediate issues of health and safety are involved, these factors are generally irrelevant for decisions involving educational placement, curriculum, and style of instruction.

❖ 3) For a significant percentage of the students, particularly those in the mild classification, or those only suspected of a mental handicap, it is often very difficult if not impossible to determine whether they are genuinely

---

The Words of Davey and Dennis

DAVEY: In our home I can eat when I want to. We could never do that in the institution. We had to eat when they said so. And we always had peas. I hate peas!

DENNIS: I like chocolate cake!

INTERVIEWER: Have you got chocolate cake in your home?

DENNIS: Yes! We make it. Sheena makes it.

DAVEY: Sheena comes in every day. She's our social worker. She comes at night because we all work in the day. It's so nice.

DENNIS: I have a hamster too!

INTERVIEWER: You have a hamster?

DENNIS: I have a hamster. At (institution) they took my hamster. It was only little. They took it. Mrs. M.____ took it. She said I couldn't have it.

DAVEY: Dennis was very upset.

DENNIS: My sister gave it to me. She's dead, my sister. She had cancer. I never saw her again. Mrs. M.____ took my hamster.

DAVEY: At our home we can have things. I have a Wayne Gretzky book. You should see it. I cut out all the stuff in the newspaper about Wayne Gretzky and put it in my book.

INTERVIEWER: How long were you in (institution)?

DAVEY: Twenty-one years. I was nine when my parents put me there. I don't blame them. I was bad. I set fires. But I used to get so mad, and I didn't know why and I couldn't tell nobody. I don't get mad anymore. If I do I talk to Sheena. I don't get mad because I can do things I want to do. I go to movies. We play cards. And I go to bed when I want to.

INTERVIEWER: How long were you there, Dennis?

DENNIS: Twenty-one years. I was there twenty-one years.

DAVEY: No, Dennis. It was fifteen. That's OK. Dennis has a little trouble with numbers but he's getting better. He's only been at our home for a little while. He'll learn . . .

(Davey had been in an independent-living group home for seven years at the time of the interview; Dennis for six months. The institution both refer to has been closed.)

---

slower intellectually, or whether their performance is a temporary outcome of limited learning opportunities, or repression, or poor nutrition, or other external conditions. Of all the causes of mental handicaps, this one can be very important to education, since if deprivation in one form or another is in fact a cause of retarded performance, it at least is potentially reversible.

Educational Implications of Mental Handicaps

The developmental effects of mental handicaps usually revolve around slower attainment of normal life achievements.

Physical

Developmental milestones tend to be attained later than what is age-expected, up to nine months or a year longer for example, to learn to walk, eat, toilet, etc. There is also a tendency to perform below expected age-related standards in motor areas, and frequently, characteristics in height, weight and skeletal development are noted that seem to be more extreme for the age norms.

Persons in the moderate classification often show even more complex physical difficulties, tending to be markedly less able motorically. Very often severe mental handicaps are part of a multiple set of disabilities with the consequence that physical matters like locomotion and other simple activities are an issue.

Learning and Memory

Problems here, as with other areas, become more marked and more easily observable from 'mild' to 'severe', but with almost all students with a mental handicap, learning and memory problems are usually significant. Specific areas of difficulty include ability to pay attention, verbal communication, motivation, ability to generalize, and the ability to understand similarities and differences.

Students with a mental handicap typically have difficulty with short term memory. They also do not tend to use memory strategies spontaneously, although they can learn to use mnemonic strategies if explicitly trained to do so. However, it is important to realize that once a thing is learned and filed in long term memory, they will recall it as well as anyone else when conditions are appropriate.

The combination of apparent lack of motivation, tendency to be off-task, and poor short term memory often leads the students to become passive and to surrender control to an outward locus such as teacher, parent or peer. A not infrequent occurrence is *learned helplessness* wherein the student generally gives up trying and allows a significant adult to manage everything for him. Viewed from the other side, so to speak, the student sometimes manages to effectively train a significant adult to do everything for him, simply by being entirely passive. Teaching assistants especially, report this as a particularly delicate matter to deal with.

Speech and Language Problems

Speech defects are considerably above the norm in frequency. Mutism and primitive speech are quite common in the severe classification but not necessarily in others. Typically, the language use level of mentally handicapped students tends to be below the commonly accepted age norms.

Social Adjustment

Many of the students experience difficulty in social interaction for a variety of reasons. Because they do not find it easy to read a social setting, it is not uncommon for them to participate in it inappropriately, perhaps by being too loud, or too ebullient for example. Some students in an integrated setting may at first function in what is called "parallel existence". That is, because they do not know how to naturally ingratiate themselves with their peers, they simply go along in their own world, without really becoming a part of the general social environment. This will occur most frequently, when mentally handicapped students and so-called normal students interact with one another for the first time, especially if there has been no preparation. (It is very encouraging however, to observe a class of very young children. The uncritical, mutual acceptance one invariably observes, forces the conclusion that interaction like this is natural if integration begins early as a matter of course.)

Some students develop behaviours that the rest of the world may look upon as bizarre, and they often tend to indulge in these behaviours repetitively (known as *perseveration*) especially in times of stress or discomfort. As a consequence, a large part of educational planning is sometimes devoted to the control of these behaviours. Proponents of total integration argue — with considerable empirical evidence to support them — that inappropriate behaviours are eliminated more easily and quickly in the mainstream.

Academic Achievement

It requires little insight to conclude that students with a mental handicap do not achieve academically at the norm for their age level in most cases. Their achievement deficits seem to be most pronounced in reading comprehension and in arithmetic reasoning and problem-solving. A steadily growing body of research evidence suggests that the students pass through the same phases of cognitive development as everyone else, particularly the childhood phases, but they pass through more slowly and often attain lower levels of achievement. The implication here therefore, is that certain students may indeed learn much of a standard school curriculum, but will do it a great deal more slowly, and likely with less efficiency. This makes *time* and *regular practice* crucial items in the educational planning process.

The Importance of Self-Help Skills

For obvious reasons, the most immediate of which is physical health, an important part of educating the students is devoted to such items as hygiene, eating and dressing, use of the toilet, physical appearance, etc. While this aspect will be part of an educational plan only to the extent necessary, and that necessity of course, will vary according to the degree of handicap, it is nevertheless crucial to a student's sense of well-being and sense of self. Teachers of exceptional students generally, and those with a mental handicap most specifically,

"We just had a consultant spend a whole week teaching us all about 'Support Circles'. She calls them an "invitation to students to come into the life of another". The idea is that students in a class are encouraged to become a friend of a classmate who is mentally handicapped.

I have to admit I'm very ambivalent about it. Of course we encourage our kids to ignore differences and welcome everyone, but you can't force that kind of thing. It has to be spontaneous and genuine. Yes, I'm going to try Support Circles, but it feels awfully close to manipulation. I worry about the morality of it."

—*P.G.D., grade seven teacher*

find much truth in the old adages that connect "feeling good" to "looking good".

Self-Esteem

Research confirms that self-esteem among mentally handicapped students tends to be low. A combination of discouraging social experience and of repeated failure often leads to an expectation of poor performance. When this is overlaid with what seems to be a ready willingness to give over control to someone else, either peers or an authority figure, it is easy to understand why the students often avoid or ignore challenging tasks. The 'if-at-first-you-don't-succeed: quit' syndrome is often a tempting and comfortable one. Teachers must avoid the trap of becoming a controller — the easy route — and instead, by judicious encouragement and behaviour modification, demonstrate to the student that she can do the assigned task and should feel proud because of it.

Assessment of a Mental Handicap

The two major instruments used for assessing students who are thought to be mentally handicapped are the I.Q. test and the adaptive behaviour scale. The former instrument is discussed elsewhere in this text and its strengths and weaknesses in any case, are fairly well known. The latter item is less well known.

Adaptive behaviour scales (See Rating Scales, Inventories and Checklists, Chapter 13) usually present a battery of questions to be answered by the parent, or teacher, or other responsible adult. The questions cover the student's general performance — as judged by the adult — in areas like family/community/peer relations, self-care skills, independent living skills, cognitive and academic skills, etc. Generally, the validity and reliability coefficients of adaptive behaviour scales are not as high as those for I.Q. tests, but professionals in the field do not consider I.Q. tests as helpful as scales in ranking performance against an objective standard for general, successful functioning.

A widely used instrument in Canada, is the AAMD Adaptive Behaviour Scale (1974) by Nihira, Foster, Shellhaas and Leland. (Washington, D.C.: AAMD).

Educational Placement

Most jurisdictions in Canada offer variations of three basic placement types: the totally integrated class, the self-contained class or congregated class in the regular school, and the special school devoted to students with exceptionalities. (The latter situation is now less common.) Typically, the restrictiveness of the placement is directly related to the individual student's degree of handicap, with an increasing number of students identified as *educable retarded*, or *moderate* now spending the vast majority of their schooling in the mainstream.

Although Canada's direction in recent years has been to decrease institutional placement, many provinces maintain a number of residential institutions, most of which receive clientele whose handicap is judged severe or profound.

Strategies for the Classroom

(1) For teachers of students with mental handicaps, there is a prerequisite to education plans, instructional strategies, curriculum — all the trappings that gather nominally under "education". The prerequisite, quite simply, is a positive attitude: recognition and acceptance that these are students like any other, with strengths and needs and likes and dislikes and ideosyncratic behaviours *and a capacity to learn.* What distinguishes them, perhaps more than any other trait, is that they tend to learn more slowly. For teachers, the implications of their learning speed (perhaps learning *rate* is better) are significant.

Teachers, by nature, have faith that their students will learn (or else there would be no point to the profession!). When they have students with mental handicaps in a class, teachers need just a bit more of that faith: that quality reflected in the patience, the effort, the flexibility, and the sense of humour that together with enlightened instruction make classrooms successful. Without these intangibles — in liberal quantities — no amount of

tactic or technique can be effective. The teacher, as always, is the key.

(2) It is common administrative practice to arrange for teaching assistants in classrooms where one or more students with mental handicaps are enrolled. A principal reason for the popularity of the practice is that time and again, teaching assistants have proven their value. However, doubling the number of adults in a room does not double the achievements automatically. Whether an assistant is assigned to a whole class or specifically to a student (this latter option has come in for serious criticism as a form of de facto segregation) it is crucial that both teacher and assistant work together in an atmosphere of mutual respect and appropriately shared responsibility.

(3) In a similar vein, teachers recognize that when students with special needs are in their classes, they are expected to cooperate extensively with other professionals, other significant persons, and certainly with parents. In the case of students with mental handicaps, this support circle often widens considerably. Very active involvement by groups such as the Association For Community Living for example, often leads to the development of a team of key players in a student's life, who share information, ideas and concerns about that student and then take some wider responsibility for promoting his integration in the life of the community. Since school is a major part of a student's community, it is only natural that such a team will often involve and overlap the teacher's role. Thus in addition to their responsibility for individual instruction, teachers often find themselves part of a larger circle of action that includes other students, parents, and interested members of the community.

Sometimes the teams are organized under relatively formal structures (one such is MAPS*); at other times the situation is informal, often the result of the will and dynamism of a key player in the student's life. Either way, teachers of a student with a mental handicap should expect involvement that often goes way beyond the walls of the classroom.

*known variously as Multi-action Planning System and McGill Action Planning System. MAPS asks specific key questions about a student's life and develops a coordinated plan (e.g., 'What are our dreams for...?' 'How can they be fulfilled?'). See Forest and Lusthaus (1990).

For Discussion: The Case of Siobhan and Vern

There are two students with mental handicaps in the grade two class: Vern and Siobhan, both eight years, six months old. There are 26 children in the class, along with the teacher, a full time teaching assistant, and an itinerant resource teacher available up to ten hours per week. All instruction takes place in the classroom.

At three months, Vern was severely injured in a fall. It is uncertain whether his very poor gross and fine motor control stems from injuries to his body or to his brain, but the fact is that all his movements are slow and rather clumsy. His hearing seems to be normal but his speech is intelligible only to those who are used to it. Vern is cooperative but operates on a very narrow emotional plane. He never involves himself spontaneously in any activities, and often does not seem to be aware of activity around him. His classmates seem to accept his presence, but — with no malicious intent — generally ignore him. Vern is just "there". For dressing, toileting etc., he does not need much assistance but he does need to be directed. Vern does not yet recognize his initials (V.K.) and so far can only distinguish the color red.

Siobhan has no speech or physical difficulties but has the respiratory weaknesses that often accompany Down syndrome. She can count to 30-40 — more if encouraged — but there is no certainty she fully understands the relationship of, say, the word 'three' and the concept. Siobhan can recite the alphabet,

print her first name, and tell a coherent story. She does not write. At daily journal time she scribbles circles for a moment and then goes to an activity centre. (Vern, unless specifically directed, just sits.) Siobhan's classmates treat her in an entirely normal way as part of the class, accepting or rejecting her from time to time as they would anyone else.

The teacher is committed to cooperative learning and has planned these four units for the next month:

i) a math unit emphasizing linear measurement. An activity centre is set up for this unit.

ii) a drama unit in which students will prepare and present brief plays about safety.

iii) introduction of "power word time" (which will carry on for the rest of the year). The objective here is learning to use dictionaries. It will be a daily activity.

iv) publication of a "book". Each group will collectively prepare and publish a book on an aspect of the school (for parents' night).

The class has been divided into groups of four/five for these units. The teacher also plans to continue devoting a portion of the day to sustained silent reading. Her concern is how to involve Vern and Siobhan in all of the above in a way that they will benefit, without at the same time imposing on or detracting from the learning of the other children.

(4) Careful attention to *structure* both in direct individual instruction and in the general learning environment is another important factor for teachers to consider. Experience in both integrated and modified environments suggests that the students are much more comfortable when classroom routines and expectations are regularized. In this case, familiarity breeds, not contempt but comfort, and in the security engendered by this comfort, a teacher can usually assure more effective learning.

Establishing a structured environment may mean that the teacher arranges for and continually repeats certain sequences until they

are fully assimilated by the students. It may mean temporarily reducing the number of choices a student is expected to make. Very often a great deal of effort is expended by the teacher on what, in the grand scheme of things, may seem relatively trivial: colour-coded notebooks, for example, with red for one purpose, green for another, etc. Yet these are precisely the kind of arrangements that protect the students from confusing and overlapping demands and allow them to bring their available cognitive strength to bear on a learning task. Without a carefully established structure in which to learn, students with a mental handicap tend to expend a prohibitive amount of energy trying to establish it on their own. Some permit the perceived disorganization of an unstructured environment to carry them away into helplessness or counterproductive behaviour.

The challenge for the teacher is finding the right balance of structure and flexibility so that organization does not become more important than learning. An additional challenge is finding this balance in an integrated classroom, where there are many students whose need for a structured and carefully sequenced instruction may not be the same. Teachers in this type of classroom can argue with considerable authority that such a placement for a student with a mental handicap, with all its benefits, also means having to forgo a degree of the learning support that arises from a carefully arranged structure.

(5) Interestingly, just as advocates have tried to find a more palatable term for 'mental retardation', educators have tried to upgrade the vocabulary for a time-honoured *and effective* practice for all students and especially for those with mental handicaps: namely, 'drill' and 'repetition'. Whatever the currency of suggested replacements, the simple fact is that all students seem to need the opportunity to go over material a certain number of times until it is taken in, and students with a mental handicap are no different. (See NIM next page.)

(6) Momentum, or commitment within the individual is another concern. Students with a mental handicap regularly and successfully invite others to do their work for them, and equally regularly, back away from challenge and opportunity. Encouragement by significant adults is very important therefore. In fact, a teacher who establishes a sense of commitment in a student has usually led him or her through one of the most important steps of development.

(7) Particularly for students whose mental handicap is fairly extensive, the task analysis method has been found to be very successful. It is based on sequencing and operant conditioning, and because the procedure involves breaking down complex tasks into simpler components, it offers the student an opportunity not just for learning but for a sense of accumulating success. An example of task analysis follows.

Using the Task Analysis Method

Task analysis is a method of breaking down a general concept or skill into its component parts. The component parts are then arranged in a logical teaching sequence.

Teaching begins at *baseline:* the level where the student is functioning prior to instruction (or, one step below, where success is assured). Each step is taught in a variety of ways until 'overlearning' has taken place. Overlearning means practising the concept beyond the point of original mastery because the teacher cannot assume the student has mastered the concept on the basis of a single correct response. Instead the teacher should present the concept on numerous occasions, over a time period, expecting the student to respond correctly most of the time before being satisfied the concept has been mastered. Some teachers set criteria for mastery, e.g., four correct responses out of five consecutive trials.

The Task Analysis method makes it easier for students to experience a sense of achievement at each step along the way.

Illustration:

1st step: state *behavioural* objective; e.g. :
1. tell time to 1/4 hour
2. order an item from catalogue
3. correctly address envelope
4. measure length of room

2nd step: list all steps, operations and prerequisite skills necessary to do step 1.

3rd step: order these in hierarchy or logical teaching sequence.

4th step: find out where in this sequence the student is functioning (baseline). By simply testing the performance of each step, the teacher can quickly find out what steps in the sequence have been mastered.

An Example of Task Analysis: Steps 1-3

Objective: Student can count a handful of coins correctly (pennies and nickels only)

Task Analysis:
1. verbally identifies penny and nickel
2. states nickel = 5 pennies

3. counts rows of pennies — straight line

4. counts pennies scattered on desk

5. counts one nickel and several pennies — placed in straight line

6. counts, when arranged in a straight line, one nickel and several pennies when nickel is not first

7. same — scattered fashion

8. counts by 5's

9. counts rows of nickels (straight line)

10. counts nickels (scattered)

11. counts rows of several nickels and pennies when all nickels are placed first

12. counts (same as 11) but all nickels are not first

13. counts nickels and pennies scattered (the stated behaviour objective).

"Neurological Impress Method" (NIM)

The name — even the idea — is a touch controversial. To some critics the method implies brainwashing; to others it describes a technique that, neurologically, is impossible according to the current state of knowledge. Be that as it may, although the popular name for the technique may be unfortunate, many teachers have found their own applications of NIM to be very useful for students who have great difficulty assimilating information.

Essentially, the NIM method, although it is interpreted and applied in a variety of ways, means *carefully structured repetition of an instruction*. The basic ingredients, whatever NIM variation is used, are usually: (i) repetition (ii) very careful structure so that the repetitions are identical (iii) appeal to as many sensory modalities as possible.

An example of one NIM approach used to teach letters of the alphabet (or numbers, or perhaps even whole words) is a technique that appeals to several sensory modalities at the same time. In this interpretation of NIM, the instructor teaches, say, the letter 'a' by putting it before the learner, then while standing slightly behind her and to her side, speaks the letter 'a' into her ear, while simultaneously guiding her finger over it. The letter being traced may be of rough texture (e.g., velcro or sandpaper) so that in addition to hearing and seeing and tracing 'a', the learner feels it. Usually the learner is encouraged to speak 'a' with the instructor too. In some cases the instructor will also trace 'a' on the learner's back, adding a further tactile/kinesthetic impression. This is repeated and repeated for brief intervals, several times over a day until the student can recognize, and possibly write 'a' independently. Then the next letter is tackled.

Supporters of NIM insist on its worth as a teaching technique. Although the method had some academic credibility when first espoused by Grace Fernald (1943) a later popularizing of the idea of brain reorganization by Glen Doman, a physical therapist, and Carl Delacato, an educational psychologist (which came to be called the Doman-Delacato Technique) has been so fiercely criticized (Robbins, 1965, and many others) that the use of instructional styles associated with the notion tended to decrease. Teachers who continue to use variations of NIM however, argue that they are using it merely to instruct, with no claim whatever regarding neurological remediation. Calling it NIM is just a convenience.

Interestingly, the empirical evidence in support of the NIM style described above, is fairly consistent in showing that it takes quite some time for the student to acquire the first letter ('a') less for the second letter, even less for the third and fourth. Most learners acquire the remaining letters quite quickly (as though a neural impression or circuit has been established!) Given that variations of NIM are used almost exclusively in situations where nothing else seems to work, there is reason to give the method some thoughtful consideration.

9

Students Who Are Deaf or Hard of Hearing

Prevailing Misconceptions About Deafness

1. Deafness diminishes intellectual ability.

The basis of this misconception lies in the fact that in school, deaf students sometimes lag academically because of their difficulties in communicating with people who hear and can use spoken language easily. Intellectual ability is distributed among the deaf in the same way as it is for the hearing.

2. Deafness leads automatically to muteness or to inability to speak.

People who are born deaf or become deaf prelingually, usually have difficulty developing the ability to speak with clarity, but the connection between deafness and the inability to speak is not absolute. Many deaf people, in any case, prefer to sign.

3. Profoundly deaf people live in a world of total silence.

Even people with profound deafness can respond to some sounds, particularly the vibrations.

4. A hearing aid restores normal hearing.

Hearing aids amplify sounds and do not necessarily restore normal hearing. Although hearing aids have become very sophisticated, there are other even more high-tech (and sometimes controversial) devices now available.

5. Teaching sign to the deaf will retard their development of spoken language.

The teaching of sign language does not, of itself, retard the development of spoken language. However, if a deaf person chooses to learn or to use sign exclusively, the development of facility in spoken language may be affected.

6. Deaf people compensate by learning to read lips.

Many deaf persons use *speech reading* in which the receiver notes facial expression, hand gestures, and other body language in addition to simple lip movement. However this skill does not come more easily to deaf people than to anyone else. Reading of lips alone is often not helpful because of similarities in the words of spoken language, and because of the inconsistencies in the lip movements of speakers.

Types of Hearing Loss

Most hearing losses are conductive or sensorineural. In the case of *conductive* hearing loss, sound is reduced or blocked before it reaches the inner ear. This may occur as the result of infection, or trauma, or wax build-up or other cause. Sometimes the blockage can be cleared, or the sound amplified to reduce the effects of conductive hearing loss.

In *sensorineural* hearing loss, the problem is in the reception of sound in the inner ear or in the transmission of electrical impulses along the auditory nerve. Sound may reach the inner ear but because of problems in the inner ear structures, it may not be transmitted meaningfully even with amplification. There are many possible causes for sensorineural hearing loss, including such apparently simple diseases as mumps or measles, along with more complex viral infections like meningitis, and a range of congenital disorders and types of trauma. Attempts to correct sensorineural loss tend to be more radical and the results less predictable.

Some specialists in the field distinguish a third type of hearing difficulty which they call *central auditory dysfunction*. It is described as an inability to correctly interpret (i.e., in the brain) sound that comes from the auditory nerve, even though sensitivity to sound may be otherwise normal. Central auditory dysfunction is still pretty much a mystery and is not yet universally accepted as a valid explanation of hearing difficulty.

Hearing loss is also described in terms of *bilateral* (both ears) or *unilateral* (one ear). Typically, the loss is classified by the amount of hearing capacity in the subject's better ear.

Classifications of Hearing Loss

An individual's hearing loss can be described in terms of sound frequency or hertz (Hz), or in terms of intensity or decibels (dB), or both. (A simple metaphor for this can be found in the controls on a radio. The volume control increases or decreases the decibel rating of sound that issues from the speaker, while the frequency or pitch is modified by how carefully the tuner is set to the signal, and also by the tenor/bass setting.) Most human speech falls between 250 and 4000 Hz, and in most cases,

comfortable human conversation has a dB rating of around 35-50. (See Figure 9-A.)

Source of Sound	dB Rating	Freq.(Hz)
Middle C (piano)	varies	500
whisper	10-20	3500
rustling leaves	30	2000
normal conversation	35-50	250-4000
crying baby	60	750
helicopter	100	4000
rock music	115	4000

Figure 9-A

Most hearing assessments in Canada are conducted by *audiologists* who specialize in the evaluation and treatment of hearing loss, or by *audiometrists* who specialize in the measurement function. While assessments produce an impressive amount of technical diagnostic information, the most helpful information for teachers is classification of a student with hearing loss according to level of function. A very popular classification of this type (Goodman: see ASHA Vol. III p. 262-3) is presented in part in Figure 9-B. This classification describes hearing loss in functional clusters, and thereby implies certain kinds of educational response.

It is important to note that the characteristics described in Figure 9-B do not describe a deaf person in any absolute way. Deaf and hard of hearing persons are as completely individual as anyone else, and therefore attend or tune out like anyone else. Another difficulty with classification is that, despite a certain presumed level of function in a deaf or hard of hearing person, that function will invariably be affected by the style and expressive quality of the person sending the communication.

Some Issues in the Field

■ Although there are a variety of matters that concern both educators and specialists regarding the deaf and hard of hearing, the single, most overwhelming and consuming issue is the matter of communication method or style. On the surface, the issue appears to be a simple one of oralism versus manualism: that is, whether a deaf person should learn to develop and fully use whatever residual hearing he has available in order to communicate as normally

Loss Range	Classification*	Implications
0-26 dB	Insignificant.	No serious ones.
27-40 dB	Mild hearing loss; hard-of-hearing.	May have difficulty with faint or distant sounds, with conversations, and may have loss in groups, or settings with much ambient noise.
41-55 dB	Moderate.	Frequent difficulty with normal speech, especially in conversations, groups, and class discussions.
56-70 dB	Moderate/severe.	
71-90 dB	Severe.	Great difficulty with even loud or amplified speech. The latter may seem faint and distorted. Subject usually requires amplification and intensive speech and language training.
91 dB+	Profound hearing loss; deaf	May be aware of loud sounds and vibrations, but generally connot deal with even amplified speech without extensive training.

(*Note that some jurisdictions choose to modify classifications such as this one for their own purposes.)

Figure 9-B

as possible with people who hear, or, whether the emphasis and energy should be devoted to learning how to sign, in order to communicate with other signers (who, by and large, will be other deaf persons, family, and teachers).

Underlying the issue is what advocates of manualism especially, call the *deaf culture*. Supporters of manualism argue that being deaf means being part of a culture that is distinguished by among other things, its own language. They argue that because experience shows most deaf persons do not become comfortable participants in the *hearing culture*, to deny them their own language therefore denies them their own culture and forces them into one where they are at risk, or at the very least are not full participants. Simple observation forces the conclusion that significant numbers of deaf people support this view. The phrase *deaf community* is frequently used (especially by the deaf) to describe deaf persons as a cohesive group who share their own entertainments, activities — and language. This tendency toward self-exclusion does not prevail at all to the same degree among other groups with a readily apparent exceptionality.

Supporters of oralism counter that the world is dominated by, and made up mostly of, hearing persons, and that deaf persons who do not avail themselves of the opportunity to be part of the dominant culture are denying reality and relegating themselves to what is in effect not a culture, but a sub-culture with all that this implies. Some advocates on this side of the issue suggest that it may be advantageous for deaf persons to develop skill in both styles, either simultaneously or separately, in order that they can make a choice. The issue is often a particularly agonizing one for parents, for in the case of very young children, they must make make the decision on their behalf since it is usually advantageous to begin either method as early in life as possible.

Teachers too are inevitably involved in the issue, both practically and ethically. The teaching of reading is one area that can be affected if a student is using ASL (American Sign Language) as her predominant means of communication. For example a phrase that in print is written, "Yesterday I went to the store.", is typically signed in ASL as "Yesterday me store go." Because sensitivity to syntax is such a powerful component in learning to read, it follows that some deaf children using ASL may have an extra hurdle when learning to read English text.

Another matter for teachers is sensitivity to the intensity of this debate among the deaf. While a teacher's primary role, naturally, is to instruct, that role can be potentially more complex if the student (or her parents) have objectives which relate strongly to one side or other of the communication and culture issue.

■ Further complicating the matter of educating deaf and hard of hearing persons are debates within the oralism and manualism philosophies themselves. Even after a decision has been taken to emphasize one approach or the other, there are disagreements over what is the best technique to choose. For supporters of signing, American Sign Language has become the overwhelming choice, but that choice, among deaf persons, is not unanimous. There continues to be a significant number who argue for such manual methods as Signing Exact English (SEE).

■ In recent years, sophisticated surgical implantation technology has generated more possibilities — and difficult decisions —for dealing with significant hearing loss. One of the more vigorously debated technologies is the *cochlear implant*. In this procedure*, a receiver is implanted either within or outside the cochlea (part of the inner ear) and an external component transmits signals to this receiver. The present state of cochlear implant technology does not restore normal hearing, but there is evidence to suggest that it can dramatically improve a subject's ability to speech read (Clickener, 1991). Controversy about the procedure and the technology arises over the suitability of candidates, the type of implant to use, and the impact on the subject.

Somewhat less controversial is an at-the-ear, skullbone-anchored hearing aid system, which stimulates the inner ear by transmitting signals to the skull. This implantation technology was initially limited to subjects with conductive hearing loss, and has enjoyed a significant level of success. Research is being extended to subjects with sensorineural loss as well.

*The technology is highly complex, and a full description of it is beyond the purposes of this text. More detailed information is available from the Canadian Hearing Society.

Typical School Placements

☐ Special Residential schools. Canada has nine large residential schools, all of which offer day programs as well.
☐ Special day schools, to which students commute from their homes.
☐ Self-contained special classes within regular elementary or secondary schools.
☐ Part-time integration programs. Students may attend some regular classes in a regular school. A signing interpreter, or an FM amplification system or other support might be used. This type of program may have a resource room component, especially if a trained teacher of the deaf is available to work directly with the student and to consult with the regular class teachers.
☐ Itinerant teacher programs. Specialist teachers offer assistance in classrooms. In this program, the student is in regular class full time.

It is worth noting that at this writing, enrolment of deaf children in special residential schools is decreasing to the extent that these schools are widening their mandate to include other exceptionalities because spaces have become available. More deaf and hard of hearing students, it seems, are going to and staying in their neighbourhood schools.

Communication Approaches and Supports

Oral Approaches

A deaf or hard of hearing child who learns via an oral approach typically learns to take advantage of auditory, visual and tactile input. Much attention is given to auditory training, speechreading, amplification and talking. Usually, oral programs emphasize the development of residual hearing and the development of intelligible speech. Research suggests that significant successes in this type of program tend to occur in fully integrated school programs, and in subjects with above-average IQ test scores, whose parents are fully involved and supportive, and who have above-average socioeconomic status (Geers & Moog, 1989; Paul & Quigley, 1990).

Speechreading

This is a process wherein a person receives a message principally by observing a speaker's face, paying special attention to the lips, and expressions and gestures in the face, body and hands. Speechreading is enhanced if the receiver is aware of and familiar with the context of the speech, but complications make this method only one avenue among others for deaf persons to receive information. Very few rely on it exclusively.

Auditory Training

This process teaches a child to use what residual hearing she has. Also called the *auditory method* and *auditory learning,* it operates on the principle of teaching the child to learn how to listen rather than just learning how to hear. Advocates argue that only a very few children are unable to benefit from this training especially if it is begun as early as possible. Essentially, the method involves first the development of awareness of sound, then the ability to make gross discriminations among sounds in the environment, and finally the ability to discriminate among speech sounds. Supporters argue for the earliest possible use of amplification, as well as simultaneous training in speech production.

Amplification

There are dozens of types of hearing aids available today, and most of them are quite powerful and versatile. In many ways, aids are like a public address system, amplifying sound. Their usefulness to deaf and hard of hearing persons depends on a number of factors such as how early one was used, power, quality, etc.

A more recent and popular development uses amplification and modulation technology via FM radio bands. In the classroom, the teacher (and/or other students) wears a transmitter and the deaf student a receiver. For the deaf student, the amount of classroom ambient noise is usually less obtrusive, with the reception coming principally from whoever is wearing the transmitter. The system is cordless.

Technical developments have made telephone communication easier for the deaf. Most of Bell Canada's payphones are compatible with hearing aids for example, and with TDDs (Telecommunications Devices for the Deaf). For

---

On Being a Deaf Kid: The Words of Bernie L.

"It was just no fun being a kid. You missed so much. I'm a 'profound' you see. When I was a kid nobody believed I could get anything anyway so I had no aids. These things help now. Wish I had them earlier. I wouldn't have missed so much.

Oh, the other kids were nice enough. Not all the time though. They called me 'buzz bomb' — you know those German V-2 rockets in World War II? No one could hear them until they whined at the last minute. Guess I was like that. I don't really know. I knew I was making some kind of sounds but I didn't really understand them. So because I couldn't communicate the other kids just left me alone. Ignored me.

When I was there they would include me. I tobogganed and skated and that. Hide and seek too. Sometimes that was bad. If this one boy, A___ was around he would always talk them into running away when I was hiding. I took it as a joke though.

What hurt me when I was a kid was they would never come to get me. Never ask me to be part. If I happened to be there it was OK. But they never came to get me. Nobody ever said 'Can Bernie come out?' "

---

jurisdictions with the 911 emergency system, the deaf have access through TDD.

Manual Approaches

American Sign Language (ASL)

ASL is a true language in itself, quite different from spoken language, and most emphatically not a translation of English into manually communicated words. ASL has its own vocabulary, its own grammar, its own word order, and its own history. American Sign Language is founded on combinations of symbolic gestures produced by the shape, the location, and the movement of the hands. Whereas methods like *Total Communication* (See next page) very often employ iconic signs, in which the shape of the sign encodes English as much as possible, the signs of ASL are unique. Many of the ASL signs symbolize concepts rather than individual words. ASL has no signs for the grammatical markers, such as *ed* and *ing*, that express verb tense and condition. Rather, users depend on facial expression and body language to replace voice intonation and enhance meaning. ASL tends to be learned by deaf children in special settings like schools, rather than being passed on by parents in the way that language is learned by most hearing people.

Cued Speech

While not very popularly used, cued speech is fiercely supported by its advocates. Cued speech uses eight configurations and four hand positions to supplement the visible manifestations of speech. According to its originator, Orin Cornett, cued speech can be learned in 12 to 15 hours.

Fingerspelling

This method spells out the letters of the English alphabet by using various finger positions on one hand. As a technique it is often used as one part of the *Total Communication* method and *Rochester Method*. The alphabet in Figure 9-C is the one presented by the National Association for the Deaf in the U.S. Members of the Canadian Hearing Society have varied in their endorsement of fingerspelling.

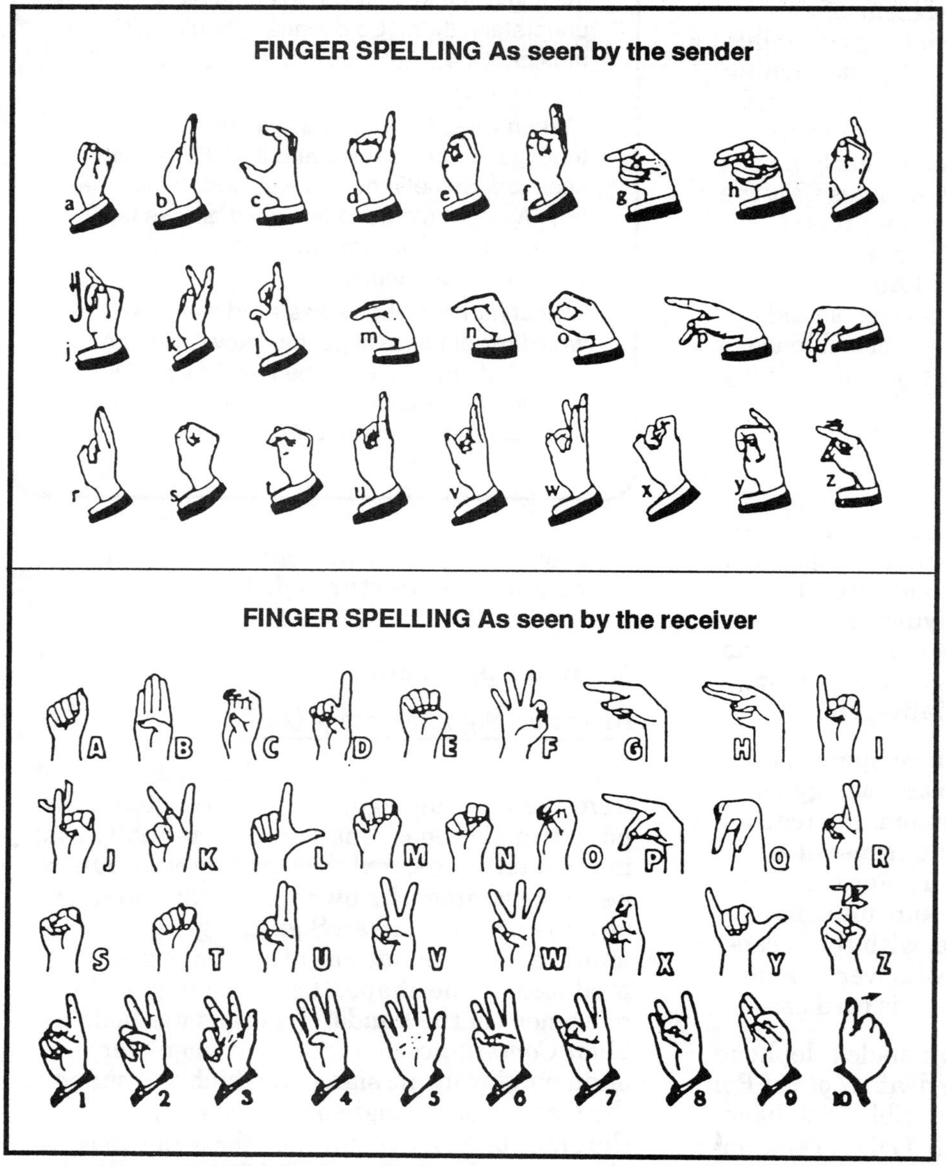

Combination Approaches

Although a deaf or hard of hearing person's communication approach is likely to emphasize one rather than several methods, she will invariably avail herself of other sources for information (like facial expressions, body language, etc.) in the same way as a hearing person. However, within the canon of communication styles advocated for the deaf there are approaches that operate from this multi-source position both practically and philosophically. Two of these approaches are the *Rochester method* and *Total Communication*.

The Rochester method uses finger-spelling in conjunction with speech, speech-reading, and amplification.

Total Communication may be defined as the use of speech, speech reading, finger spelling and amplification, along

Figure 9-C (Reprinted with permission of The Canadian Hearing Society.)

with the simultaneous use of a school-based manual system. In a school-based total communication system, signs are usually taught in the same order as language. This teaches the child to communicate manually using English syntax. Also, unlike ASL, the signs tend to attempt to reflect English syntax.

Educational Implications of Hearing Loss

❖ All other factors like quality of instruction being equal, deaf and hard of hearing students usually do not have an easy time in school, academically, mostly because of what is in effect, a language barrier. Studies over several decades (see Allen, 1986, for example) suggest that academic achievement is affected by five elements more than any other. These are the severity of the hearing loss, the chronological age at onset, intelligence, socioeconomic status of the family, and hearing status of the parents. (A deaf student of deaf parents is considered to have a better chance for academic success than if the parents are hearing.)

The same studies invariably point to achievement test scores for the deaf being significantly lower than the scores of hearing controls, even on specially adapted test instruments. However, it behooves educators to consider whether this lower performance is simply the result of a bad fit between the real abilities of deaf students and the way achievement is measured. Even though deaf students may lag in reading and other language skills, teachers must be on guard against interpreting a difficulty with language as an inherent lack of ability. Still, whatever the teacher's attitude toward her deaf students, the issue of language development and effective use will be a principal, likely *the* principal, educational consideration.

❖ The difficulties deaf students have in communicating often leads to exaggerated compensatory behaviours or to frustration that is expressed in ways which cause them to be unfairly labelled as disturbed, or odd, or even mentally handicapped. In the past it was not unusual to find deaf students of normal intellectual and emotional mein, placed in segregated classes because of what was perceived to be retardation or disturbed behaviour. There has even developed over time, a so-called 'psychology of the deaf', in which the characteristics of deaf people are sometimes described in very unflattering language. One result of this perception of the deaf, no matter what its accuracy or its origins, is reinforcement of the isolation that deaf students frequently describe as the worst part of living in a hearing world. Being aware of and responding to this factor is very important for teachers of integrated classrooms.

For Discussion: The Case of Maggie

Sometimes when Maggie fails to get through to someone, she throws her books, or pens (she has thrown her shoes on occasion) at the uncomprehending offender. Interestingly, this behaviour rarely if ever occurs when someone fails to get through to her. The explanation may lie partly in the fact that Maggie's deafness seems to impede her expressive skills much more than her receptive ones. She wears a pair of hearing aids which help somewhat but not a great deal, but she speech reads exceptionally well, and Maggie, fortunately, is very bright. The combination seems to have helped Maggie a great deal in receiving.

Where this student encounters continuing difficulty is in her sending: her speaking. She has problems modulating her voice, shaping tones and of course, problems in proper pronunciation and enunciation. The result is a flat, nasal sound usually with very little variance in pitch. And she is very hard to understand. Few of her classmates have the courage to tease her anymore, but they also have difficulty understanding her, and tend to stay away from her as a consequence.

Maggie is well ahead of the class in math. She does brilliant projects in science. Her notes, her desk, her person are each a model of neatness. She reads (silently) with the class comfortably. Oral reading, in which she insists in taking part is not pleasant for her, the class, or her teacher. She is excused from French and music (for speech therapy).

The premier issues with Maggie seem to be social and communicational.

❖ Whether a deaf student has an interpreter, or has amplification devices, or uses total communication — whatever the approach — communicating, for him, is very hard work, both as a consequence of the concentration needed to receive information and of the effort needed to send it. Deaf students get very tired and teachers must recognize this.

❖ Meaningful cooperation with the hearing world can be difficult to achieve. Deaf persons often describe their experiences with others in societal control (e.g., police, and other officialdom) as unsatisfactory. An important responsibility of educators because of their potential for extensive contact with deaf and hard of hearing persons is to sensitize the hearing public to their needs.

Strategies for the Classroom

The following suggestions are collected from deaf and hard of hearing students who were asked to offer advice to teachers and educational assistants in regular classes.

(1) Seat her toward the front of the room and to one side with the better ear toward the teacher and class. Otherwise seat in the second seat from the front, second row from the window, or similar setting, but always with light on the teacher's face.

(2) Permit the student to move her seat if the teaching centre moves to another part of the room.

(3) A deaf student needs to see the speaker's face. Seat him two to three metres away from the place where you do most of your talking. Keep your hands away from your face.

(4) From time to time attempt to keep your mouth near the level of the student's eyes. For example, instead of always standing, sit at your desk at certain times.

(5) Be sure to have the student's visual and aural attention before giving assignments or announcements.

(6) Make a practice of asking *both* hearing and hard of hearing students to repeat directions for the benefit of the whole class. Ask the student to repeat instructions to ensure he understands.

(7) Do not turn your back while talking. Do not talk while writing on the chalkboard; a moving target is impossible to speech read. Do not walk around the room while talking about important things.

(8) Don't use loud tones or exaggerated mouth movements. Use the same tone of voice and the same inflection you use for everyone else. Avoid gestures. Excessive gestures draw attention away from the face and lips. They're embarrassing too.

(9) Many words sound the same — blue, blew; tax, tacks. This is confusing enough. But many words that do not sound the same look the same on the lips — e.g., *bat, pat, mat* look alike as do *bad, pad, mad*. Words that look alike on the lips are called homophones. Even an expert at speech reading misunderstands directions or questions. It is essential, therefore, that when dictating spelling words for example, you use them in sentences to give the student a clue.

(10) It may be helpful to explain to other students that many words look alike. Let the class try to speech read a few sentences. This procedure will help others in the class to understand. Understanding helps eliminate teasing and unfair judgements.

(11) During a discussion, ask questions to ensure that the person with hearing loss understands. If she does not understand, restate the material in a different way. Perhaps she was not familiar with the key words that you used, or some of them may have looked like other words.

N.B. (12) Names of people and places, especially new ones, are very difficult to understand. It is well to place new words or terms on the chalk board and discuss new material from this vocabulary.

(13) Assign a 'buddy' to help explain things. A buddy can be a great fallback, but watch out for too much dependence.

(14) Try rephrasing rather than repeating. But be sure a rephrase does not add confusion.

(15) If the person with a hearing loss is completely lost, say quietly "I'm talking about . . ." This often gives her a fresh start. But be discreet!

(16) If the student seems to have trouble with certain words repeatedly, use these words often in as many ways as possible.

(17) Find out if he has a good ear and speak to that side.

(18) If your class has group discussions or cooperative learning activities, a round table is better for a deaf student than a rectangular one.

(19) If you have a good relationship with your deaf student, you can tell him when his speaking is too loud or when it's getting on other students' nerves.

(20) Encourage participation in extra-curricular activities. Deaf students are like any others. They take their lead from their teachers.

(21) If a visit is being planned, or a visitor is coming, prepare for it. Write new and unusual words on the chalk board; help the deaf student become familiar with the names of persons or objects she will be seeing. Explain any special rules ahead of time when you can be sure that she understands them. The brief discussion will help her associate lip movements with new words and promote her understanding of their meaning. By telling the student in advance what unit of activity will be studied, she has an opportunity to find material on the subject and will be able to follow along much better because she will be more familiar with the vocabulary. Always, in history, or science, and geography lessons where there will be new vocabulary or new concepts, try to give the student a brief written statement e.g., "Today's topic is the Introduction of The War of 1812. Key words are Niagara Frontier, Sir Isaac Brock, York, James Madison", etc.

(22) Deaf students tire more easily than others. You can help by planning the day's work so the periods when they must pay attention are interspersed with other activities.

(23) Encourage the student to keep trying. Please be patient. Repeat instructions as often as necessary.

(24) If possible, try to help the student learn to use a dictionary pronunciation key.

(25) Note that many students hear better on some days than others.

(26) Talk with the deaf students every day. Talk often, rather than for a long time. Ask questions about movies seen, T.V. programs, hobbies, travel, work, etc.

(27) A hearing aid makes speech louder. It does not make speech clearer. It also amplifies all the other noise. See if some of the other noise can be reduced.

(28) If it has not already been investigated, look into the possibility of using an FM system. This system can be more effective in a classroom than a hearing aid.

> *(Charlie B. became deaf at age 43 owing to an accident.)*
> "This being deaf — for me, anyway — it's like — well, almost like living at one end of a tunnel. I mean — blind people can hear the world around them. 360 degrees. But when you're deaf, all you get is the slice you can see. If you can hear, you're at the centre of the world, right in the middle of what's going on. But if you're deaf, you're always out at the edge. It's not easy being out there all the time."

10

Students Who Are Blind or Partially Sighted

Prevailing Misconceptions About Blindness and Partial Sight

1. Blind people have no sight at all.

Only a small percentage of legally blind people have absolutely no vision. The majority have a useful amount of functional vision.

2. Legally blind people use braille as their primary method of reading.

The majority use print — often large type — as a primary source of reading. An increasing trend among blind people who cannot see print is to use audio technology — recordings and other conversions of print — rather than braille.

3. An extra sense enables blind people to detect obstacles.

Blind people do not possess an extra sense. They often develop an "obstacle sense" provided they have the ability to hear.

4. The blind automatically develop better acuity in their other senses.

Through concentration and attention, blind persons often learn to make very fine discriminations in the sensations they obtain. This is not automatic, but rather represents a better use of received sensations.

5. If partially sighted students use their eyes too much, their sight will deteriorate.

Only in rare conditions is this true; visual discrimination ability can actually improve through training and use. Strong lenses, holding books close to the eyes, and using the eyes does not harm vision.

6. Blind children automatically become good listeners.

Good listening is primarily a learned skill. Although many blind people develop good listening skills, it is the result of effort because they depend on these skills for so much of their information.

7. Seeing-eye dogs take blind people where they want to go.

The proper term is **guide dog**. It does not "take" the blind person anywhere; the person must first know where he or she is going. The dog is primarily a safeguard against dangerous areas or obstacles.

Definitions of Blindness

Legal blindness in Canada is defined as a distance acuity of 20/200 or less in the better eye. That means the person must stand at twenty feet or less to see an object which would normally be seen at two hundred feet. Persons whose visual field is reduced to an angle of twenty degrees or less at its widest diameter are also legally blind. A partially sighted person is one whose distance acuity is 20/70 or less in the better eye. It is important to recognize that someone with visual acuity of 20/200 can probably read, or at least *see*, print. Total blindness, i.e., inability to see anything at all, is actually uncommon.

Classifications are usually presented as follows:

Near normal vision. These individuals are able to function without special training, but will use corrective lenses.

Moderate functional impairment. People in this group require specialized aids and lighting.

Reduction in central vision. A moderate field loss. People with this disability may qualify for special services as legally blind.

Poor functional vision and possible poor central vision with marked field loss. For this condition, standard correction is of little or no benefit. Usually strong reading aids and other technologies are needed instead.

Blind. Total field loss as well as total detail loss. May, in some cases, distinguish between lightness and dark.

Some Typical Causes of Blindness

Retinal detachment: The retina can become separated through injury or disease, making it incapable of receiving images.

Retinoblastoma: an intraocular tumor that is often malignant. Usually the eyes are removed and the child is fitted with prostheses.

Retrolental fibroplasia: a condition occurring in babies who are exposed to a greater than normal concentration of oxygen post-natally.

Rubella: a syndrome occurring as a result of maternal rubella infection during the first months of pregnancy.

Sympathetic ophthalmia: When there is a penetrating wound to one eye, the other eye may reflect the same characteristics as the injured eye.

Some Typical Causes of Partial Sight

Albinism: The eyes are light sensitive. Minimum illumination is needed, and tinted glasses are usually prescribed.

Astigmatism: This defect causes an error in refraction. Images are blurred and there is generally poor visual discrimination. Glasses are prescribed, usually with positive results. Good illumination usually helps too.

Cataracts: Any lens opacity is a cataract. Such an opacity causes blank areas in what is seen. Depending upon the nature of the opacity, adjustments in lighting are usually necessary.

Colour blindness: A child is unable to distinguish colours. More boys than girls are affected.

Glaucoma: a problem caused by increased intraocular pressure. Glaucoma patients require constant medical attention and sometimes suffer headaches. Quite often peripheral vision is poor. Good illumination is recommended.

Hyperopia: The hyperopic eye is far-sighted. A student with this condition usually functions well in gross motor activity but finds reading and other near work difficult and tiring until correction is provided.

Macular degeneration: The centre of the field of vision blurs causing most detail to be lost. Some peripheral vision usually remains but with limited strength.

Monocular vision: Through disease, accident, or defect, a person is left with only one seeing eye.

Myopia: The myopic eye is near-sighted. Distance vision is blurred so that gross activities can be difficult. A student with this condition is more comfortable with reading and other close work.

Nystagmus: The involuntary movement of the eyeball caused by this problem makes focusing and fixation difficult.

Optic atrophy: The optic nerve sustains permanent loss of its ability to carry clear images to the brain. A person may have restricted fields of vision. Visual behaviour may be inconsistent.

Peripheral vision: This is the ability to see only those activities and objects outside of the direct line of vision. Because of defective central vision the student may have to tilt the head or raise or lower the eyes in order to read.

Retinitis pigmentosa: Pigment deposits in the retina cause loss of peripheral fields resulting in tunnel vision. Major difficulties occur in dim light. Good illumination is needed.

Strabismus: An imbalance of the eye muscles causes failure of the two eyes to focus on the same object. The eyes can cross or eyes deviate upward or downward. Early treatment is vital, or a "lazy eye" (amblyopia) can result.

Tunnel vision: The field of vision is so reduced that a child sees only what is directly in front. It creates the same visual image that others see when looking through a tube or a straw. This severely affects a person's mobility and the collection of information from the environment.

education, and time, are devoted to this matter especially when they are young. At the same time, because they are normal human beings in every other respect, blind people naturally wish to live the lives that the rest of the world does. A great deal of the initial social exchange between visually disabled people and the sighted people in their lives is devoted to finding a mutually comfortable, appropriate and effective means of associating.

■ The failure of individuals and families to have regular eyesight examinations continues to be a nagging concern of health care professionals and educators. Infants as young as three months can now be tested with considerable accuracy. Optometrists urge that all children be examined by three years of age and again at school entrance. This is because many vision problems are more correctable if a response is made early. It is also important to begin teaching visual *efficiency* early, if visual *acuity* is poor or weakening. Testing is especially important if there is a familial pattern of such problems as strabismus, cataracts, etc. Despite the logical and impassioned arguments of both educators and health professionals, the response of families and even educational jurisdictions to the need for early and regular eye examinations is, surprisingly, less intense than one might expect, given the ease and limited expense with which these examinations can be conducted.

> **On Being Blind: Words by Ginny de V.____**
>
> "... what took me till adulthood to realize, was how much sighted people talk to each other with their bodies — I mean — I still don't actually see it, but I'm more sensitive to it now that I know. You see I always talk a lot — can't you tell? — and most of the time I just keep on going until someone stops me — well, wouldn't you?
>
> Anyway I didn't understand that sighted people have all these ways of saying 'shut up' without actually saying it — you know? Like — they turn away, or they stand up suddenly. Stuff like that. I never interpreted that as 'shut up' even when I knew it was happening, until someone told me about it. I'm glad I was told though. It helps to know. That's one of the things about being blind. Everybody treats you with kid gloves. We don't need that. We're people too. We've got to be told to shut up too just like everybody else. I mean ..."

Some Issues in the Field

■ Perhaps the most significant issue is successful adjustment to the world at large by blind and partially sighted people. This adjustment calls for mobility and a sensitivity to the environment that is natural in sighted persons but not so in those whose vision is limited. Much of a blind person's energy, life force,

■ Treating learning disability as a vision problem was not uncommon in the early to mid-1970's and still has some residual currency today, even though evidence of the connection is hard to find. A student presumed to have learning disabilities should always have his vision checked, but only to determine whether his academic difficulties are being caused by poor vision, not to find a visual/learning disability connection.

Teachers' Checklist of Possible Vision Problems

Although the ultimate diagnosis of a student's visual problem — or even its existence — would naturally be determined by an optometrist or ophthalmologist, teachers can play an important role in early detection. While this is a more common occurrence in the very early grades, teachers of older students should not exclude themselves since eye disease and poor vision can begin at any stage in life and grow serious rapidly. Any of the characteristics in the Teachers' Checklist, especially if observed over time, might indicate real or potential visual impairment.

1. Appearance of eyes
One eye turns in or out at any time?
Reddened eyes or lids?
Encrusted eyelids?
Frequent styes on lids?
Eyes tear excessively?

2. Complaints by student
Headaches in forehead or temples?
Burning or itching of eyes after reading or deskwork?
Nausea or dizziness?
Print blurs or moves after reading a short time?

3. Behavioural signs of visual problems
Head turns while reading across the page?
Loses place often during reading?
Needs finger or marker to keep place?

Rereads or skips lines unknowingly?
Too frequently omits or substitutes words?
Complains of seeing double (diplopia)
Misaligns number columns regularly?
Squints, closes or covers one eye?
Tilts head extremely while working at desk?
Consistently shows gross postural deviations?
Orients a worksheet unusually?
Must feel things to understand?
Disorderly placement of words or drawings on page?
Blinks excessively at desk tasks?
Blinks to clear chalkboard after near task?
Holds book too closely?
Avoids all possible near-centred tasks?
Closes or covers one eye when reading?
Squints to see chalkboard?
Rubs eyes a great deal?

Some Educational Implications of Special Visual Needs

❖ Empirical evidence suggests that in the classroom, especially among younger students, cognitive abilities in the blind and partially sighted tend to develop more slowly than the norm. There is a good deal of support for the view, however, that this apparent lag is owing more to differentiated early learning experiences rather than to any inherent intellectual difference. Blind children simply have not had the opportunity to experience some of the things that sighted children have.

❖ It is difficult for students with serious vision problems to develop a spatial map of their environment. However, it is possible to develop the concept of space with other senses, such as noting the time it takes to walk various distances, or feeling the dimensions between objects. Because the amount of information that can be taken in at one time is limited, the process is understandably slower. This fact makes the time to acquire learning an important factor — as it is with almost all students with exceptionalities.

❖ For students who cannot see, or who see poorly, it is often difficult to understand abstract concepts without the aid of concrete materials. Such students then, will benefit from three-dimensional models, exaggerated bas-relief maps and globes, manipulative games and materials.

❖ Blind and partially sighted students are often overprotected by the adults in their lives and treated over-delicately by fellow students.

Although this is not an unnatural response, it is important that independence be a prominent and continuing objective in the education of these students. Fostering this independence calls for frequent and delicate judgments by the teacher.

❖ Blind students must be taught social and communicative skills that many sighted persons acquire naturally (at least some of the time). Most cultures, for example, attach great importance to whether or not a speaker looks at her listener, and many advocates for the blind urge that this habit be taught. However, some so-called natural skills are much more difficult to teach. For example, sighted people make constant use — albeit subconsciously much of the time — of a system of communication that has come to be called 'body language': important markers that indicate responses like reinforcement, enthusiasm, reluctance, disagreement, uneasiness, etc. Body language thus enables an alert speaker to detect the need to modify a particular communication. Sometimes even more important, it is body language that indicates whether or not a communication is finished — or should be! For obvious reasons, the very notion of body language, and the means of dealing with it is something that blind and partially sighted students cannot be expected to acquire naturally.

❖ The less a person is able to know the world through sight, the more important it becomes that he be a good listener. Although it was assumed in the past that good listening skills automatically develop as a consequence of sight deprivation, it is now known that such skills must be taught.

❖ Teachers of the very young must be particularly conscious of the fact that many children are not aware of a visual problem if they have one. Or if they are aware, they often do not understand its extent or its implications. This is important for the teacher, not just in discovering the presence of the problem, but in helping the child to deal with it.

❖ For teachers, a point of importance is recognizing that academic success is more closely related to social, cultural, and familial factors than to degree of visual impairment.

Education and Communication Technology

Braille

Louis Braille's adaptation of a cipher system developed by one of Napoleon's staff for communication in darkness, has been in use by the blind for over 150 years. Braille is a tactile communication method. Cells of from one to six raised dots on paper represent the letters of the alphabet (and numbers). Although it is a direct transliteration of English (or other language) braille resorts to contractions regularly to save time and space. (For example, in English the letter 'r' by itself means 'rather'.) Although it has been established that braille is easier to read than raised letters of the alphabet, it is still a much slower process than reading print is for the average sighted reader.

Students can begin learning braille in the first grade, and have a number of technologies available to them, beginning with braille books. A brailler is a six key device not unlike a typewriter. (Integrated classrooms where a brailler is used must become accustomed to its noise.) There is also the *Optacon** which converts print into braille electronically.

Computer-Assisted Technology

Computer technology continues to develop at a rate that almost outpaces the capacity of special education to use it effectively. Some examples of recent technology — to which modifications are continually being added — are the *Versabraille II+** a laptop computer that combines brailler and word processor technology, the *Kurzweil Reading Machine** which converts print to audio output, the *Dragon-Dictate** a speech-activated word processor, and the *Braille Blazer** which prints braille at 10-15 characters per second.

Optical Aids

Teachers and their blind and partially sighted students are assisted by still other devices which, although they may appear simple in comparison to computer technology, are remarkable examples of technical common sense.

* Brand names are used in these descriptions. Further information about these and other technologies is available from provincial and territorial ministries of health.

These include items like embossed rulers and tape measures, braille watches, three dimensional maps, hand-held and stand mounted magnifiers, special lighting, etc.

For Discussion:
The Case of Stanley

Stan is now seventeen. He has been legally blind since the age of three, owing to macular degeneration which was first noticed just after his second birthday and developed rapidly. (When there is macular degeneration, the centre of a person's field of vision blurs and most if not all detail is lost. Very often peripheral vision will remain but the person has difficulty seeing anything at a distance, and problems distinguishing details, even colours.) Stan has a serious case.

He is of average intelligence, and other than the obvious modifications in his education and day-to-day living, Stan has no particularly outstanding physical features or character traits.

Except one. Stan has absolutely refused to accept — even acknowledge — his visual handicap. He refuses assistance of any kind, not just visual aids, but any form of special accommodation or remediation as well. In school for example, he will refuse an advantageous seat (one with better lighting, or one that offers more to his peripheral vision) and will deliberately choose a disadvantageous location. He is failing most academic subjects in his grade eleven year, but has been reluctant to accept any kind of tutorial help. He works hard, but without the extra help the school and his peers can provide, he will undoubtedly miss most of his credits this year.

A confrontation is imminent in Stan's physical education course. Gymnastics, with a concentration on box horse activity, parallel bars, rings, etc. is on the program next month. The physical education teacher insists on special treatment for Stan, who has already refused to accept it.

Educational Placement

Increasingly, and with marked success, blind and partially sighted students are being educated in the regular classroom. Special assistance may be delivered by an itinerant specialist teacher who provides advice on strategy, materials, and possibly on curricular modification. Such modification may be intense instruction on how to listen, how to make "mental mobility maps", etc. The assistance may also take the form of one of the educational aids listed above. Or it may be a combination of aid from several sources. As with all other areas of special education, teaching assistants in the classroom have proven to be invaluable for blind and partially sighted students.

For some students, a resource room is their primary placement. This arrangement may offer a more certain guarantee of the specialized instruction they may need, but still permits a high degree of integration with the rest of the school.

A more specialized placement, used particularly for students whose vision problems are quite seriously disabling is an entirely self-contained classroom, or even a residential school devoted to blind students (and students who are blind and have other special needs as well). In these environments, where there are usually very low pupil-teacher ratios, students receive regular school curriculum adapted to their needs, along with very specialized instruction related to their blindness.

Strategies for the Classroom

(1) It is usually very beneficial for a teacher of a regular class with a blind or partially sighted student to establish the practice of holding regular, informal, and private discussions with that student to work out special means of communication,* or to clarify misunderstandings, to develop routines, and otherwise plan for the — usually simple — special accommodations to the student's needs. It is an ideal time for both student and teacher to learn and discover.

*A quite loquacious blind student in one of my classes did not sense that her extensive contributions to class discussions often wore out her classmates' receptivity. We worked out a simple and very subtle pencil tap so that she would know when to quit. —K.W.

(2) It may be necessary for a teacher to set up the classroom with the expectation that physical arrangements will not be altered, at least for a significant period of time. While this may contradict the style a teacher likes to follow, it may be a necessity for simple reasons of safety.

(3) At the same time there is the student's normal need to be physically mobile, to explore, to expand her capacity, as well as the need to perceive the self as both part of and separate from the environment. A great deal of professional skill is demanded of teachers in marrying this need with the obvious requirements of safety and efficient function described above. The key phrase is *responsible independence*. Students need supervision of course, but the ultimate goal of it must be, as with all special education, to become unnecessary.

(4) Another vital phrase is *common sense*. A student with partial sight for example, should always be permitted to sit near the chalkboard, to borrow notes, to have another student take carbon-paper notes. (Yet the exceptionality need not be emphasized. If other students are blindfolded in an activity, the blind student should be too.) An overhead transparency can be photocopied for someone who cannot see the screen. Partially sighted students almost always respond to better lighting. Additional time may be necessary for tests or a variety of other activities. Doors should always be fully open or fully closed. Name the students being addressed; if an instruction is given to another child, a blind child may automatically follow it with perhaps disastrous results. By the same token, be explicit in giving instructions, particularly those involving movement from one place to another. A blind student cannot be expected to compensate for obstacles. If told to "come here", he may well come in a straight line regardless of hazards, because of his trust in the teacher.

(5) Teachers, assistants, and sighted fellow students often have to make allowances for communication style. Blind and partially blind students usually do not reinforce others with eye contact or facial expression — a phenomenon that takes some getting used to. In the same vein, the students often place great interpretive value on the expression and tone of their teacher's voice. This can be very important in some situations. Also, when a blind person responds to a communication with total silence, it may be because he is taking in and interpreting available cues. This too, requires adjustment from the teacher.

(6) "Blindisms" are characteristic mannerisms such as rocking, head shaking, hand shaking and eye poking. Most advocates suggest that teachers adroitly discourage these behaviours for they may isolate the student as irremediably different in a way that goes beyond merely being blind.

(7) Many blind people have grown to associate physical contact with being guided. Gestures such as patting and hugging may have negative connotations for some students, or may be misinterpreted. (Another reason for having regular, informal meetings.) When a blind person is being guided, let her be the one who maintains and controls the physical contact. Don't grab her arm and steer; let her hold your arm.

(8) A *tactful* classroom buddy or advocate is always helpful, but this should never be an unnaturally long-term arrangement.

(9) Perhaps the single most important role a teacher plays is being the classroom leader in developing a positive attitude (a crucial role in any case). Sighted students will take their cue from their teacher in determining how to react to and inter-relate with a blind student in their midst. An accepting atmosphere for this student, with realistic expectations, will build his self-esteem, his sense of success, and his willingness to deal with the world. It will also contribute in a major way to the maturing of all students in the class.

11

Students Who Are Gifted

Prevailing Misconceptions About Giftedness

1. Gifted students always outdistance their peers academically.

It does not always happen that a gifted student's achievement reflects his or her ability. Perhaps for this reason as much as any other, giftedness is included in the special education corpus. Another factor is that some students' gifts are expressed in non-academic ways (which some educators distinguish as 'talent'; whether or not they imply a hierarchy by this distinction is moot).

2. Gifted students should be able to accommodate their own needs.

Our educational system is often uncongenial to the gifted. They require effort and support just like any other exceptional students.

3. Gifted students are bored with school, disruptive, and antagonistic.

Usually they enjoy school, are well adjusted, and get on easily with peers and teachers. But like any other student they will react to neglect or inequity or other issues they see as important.

4. It is common for emotional instability to accompany giftedness.

On the contrary, gifted students are usually in good mental health and tend to have fewer emotional problems than the norm. Increased experience with gifted students over the past few decades suggests they may be exceptionally sensitive to matters like injustice, world issues, etc.

5. An I.Q. test score is the best way to identify giftedness.

Very high I.Q. test scores are common among the gifted, but this is only one means of identification. These instruments are far too narrow to be a sole criterion for they are unable to measure or even highlight characteristics like artistic ability or creativity for example.

6. Gifted students work harder than others.

Strong task commitment has come to be one of the accepted markers of giftedness, especially among educators, but this factor is sometimes paradoxical, for a student's task commitment may not become evident until he or she is identified and working in an environment that stimulates the commitment.

7. Gifted students are physically inept, self-absorbed and narrow-minded

For the most part, they look and act like any other students, although teachers generally report them as above average in health, moral responsibility and social adeptness.

Characteristics of Gifted Students

Any attempt to describe the characteristics of gifted students reveals just how interwoven are matters like ability and desire in the human psyche, and how crucial are the matters of opportunity, environment and circumstance.

Although educators and parents agree more or less on the substance of the characteristics listed here, there is considerably less consensus on their relative priority as features of a gifted student, or on the number that should be present in an individual to make him gifted, or over whether these are necessarily stable, life-long characteristics. Every classroom teacher, for example, will notice in many of her students, from time to time, any or all of the characteristics listed below. But then she will be compelled to reflect on whether or not the characteristics she has observed are situation-related and temporary; or whether they have always been present and genuine in the student, just waiting for exposure by the circumstance.

There are other concerns too, like distinguishing high verbal ability (a commonly accepted characteristic) from mere artfulness and facility; and distinguishing genuine, inherent abilities from those that are stimulated as a consequence of the student's life at home. (Not to mention the issue of whether such a distinction should even *be* an issue!) Nevertheless, the simple fact is that some students appear to have abilities that stand out from the general run of things, and in the best of all worlds these students should be identified and allowed to develop in the very special directions to which those abilities point.

People who advocate for the gifted, argue quite rightly that circular debates invariably spiral downward, and that at some point it is necessary to act. Fortunately, some resolution of the uncertainty has been achieved by using a *cluster* system of characteristics to identify and describe gifted students.

What follows here first, is a list* of generally agreed upon characteristics, and below that a description of the notion of clusters.

- wide range of abilities both academic and otherwise
- well developed attention span, and a deep curiosity
- ability to grasp, retain, synthesize, and act upon information
- ability to work independently, and to fulfill responsibility
- capacity to adjust easily to new situations and demands
- able to offer innovative responses
- superior vocabulary and reading ability
- considerable energy and above-average health
- well-developed capacity for abstracting and conceptualizing
- more interested in questions than answers
- highly developed sense of consequence and forward planning
- able to perceive unusual diverse relationships
- persistent in meeting goals
- advanced sense of moral and ethical judgment
- trusts and will defer to intuition
- thought processes accelerated

Describing the Gifted by 'Clusters'

The practice of identifying and describing gifted students by clusters or groups of characteristics has had a major and beneficial effect on educational and administrative practice. Quite simply, in recognition of the relative instability of characteristics used to describe gifted students, educators and parents have generally turned to a style of identification that sees the characteristics in clusters that are fluid and overlapping, and that must be applied flexibly, in light of the dynamic interchange between a human being and his environment. This view holds that where genuine giftedness is present, a number of related characteristics form a sort of composite, with the characteristics applying some but not all of the time.

*A list of this nature can be subdivided and extended ad infinitum (and many writers in the field do so!). Readers seeking a list with finer distinctions than this one might wish to turn to Clarke (1988) among others.

One of the most accepted presentations of this style of identification by cluster was first offered by Renzulli (1978).

The Renzulli Description

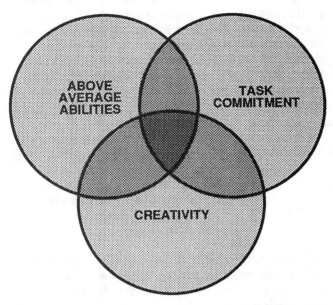

Renzulli's *Enrichment Triad Model* presents giftedness as an interaction among three basic clusters:

    i) above-average general abilities;

    ii) high level of task commitment;

    iii) high levels of creativity.

    Students who are gifted, according to Renzulli, are those capable of developing this composite set of traits and applying them to any potentially valuable area of human performance. What is significant in this approach, in addition to the substance of the three clusters, is the fact that there is recognition of an interplay among them, thus incorporating a dynamic reality. There are times, quite naturally, when the degree of task commitment glows and fades in an individual. Everyone is more (or less) creative at some moments than at others. And abilities may well be relative to the nature of a task. Renzulli's presentation accommodates all of this, which probably explains why it gained very rapid acceptance among educators and continues to be widely used in Canada, usually with local variations.

Unfortunately, it has not led gifted education entirely out of the woods. Renzulli himself, in subsequent articles, has argued that general ability is less important than specific performance in an operational definition of giftedness. (Which means of course, that everyone can be gifted at some time: another major consideration for educational authorities!)

The Sternberg Description

Another point of view that is at once intellectually exciting, and certain to keep the field of giftedness unsettled, is Sternberg's (1981) *Triarchic Theory of Intellectual Giftedness* which posits that the phenomenon must be viewed in terms of the internal world of the individual, the external world of the individual, and the interface of these two worlds as it unfolds through experience.

An individual's practical, functional intelligence, and hence, her degree of giftedness, involves the ability to select appropriate environments: environments that are right for her talents. It then involves the individual's ability to adapt to those environments, and to shape them in ways that will enhance the talents and put them to effective use. Such an individual then, not only knows *what* and *how* better than most, she also knows better *where* and *when* to use the what and how! One reason for the positive reception of Sternberg's position among teachers is its appeal to the notion that creativity, adaptiveness and old-fashioned common sense and shrewdness must play a major role in gifted behaviour.

The Gardner Description

In *Frames of Mind* Howard Gardner (1983) proposes a theory of multiple intelligences: linguistic, musical, logical-mathematical, spatial, bodily-kinesthetic, interpersonal and intrapersonal, suggesting that each of these is independent in function, and that if one intelligence is more powerfully developed than another, it will take over for a weaker or less developed one.

Gardner's very persuasive writings, supported by effective research, emphasize the multifold aspect of human intelligence (illuminating yet again the inadequacy of I.Q. testing with its implied notion of intelligence as a single, internal construct). His work has been instrumental in expanding the view that there is considerable growth and plasticity in human growth, that this plasticity may be modulated by genetic constraints, and that humans are predisposed to certain intellectual operations and styles of operation, all of which can be addressed by education.

The Importance of a Balanced View

The practical appeal of such views as Sternberg's and of Renzulli's, Gardner's, and those of other thinkers in the field, continues the ferment that both plagues and enriches the attempts of educators and parents to define giftedness and properly identify its educational candidates. Because these views lead away from the notion of giftedness as a single construct (the I.Q. notion) toward a view of giftedness as an expression of several contributing factors, students can be more fairly identified. Above all, the idea of giftedness as a construct standing on a number of foundations, gives more credence and importance to creativity, to commitment, and to the expression of ability in ways other than the narrow confines allowed by academic achievement alone.

"Imagination is more important than knowledge."
—Albert Einstein

Some Issues In The Field

■ It is a concern to educators and parents that despite a universal widening of the definition of giftedness, in many boards the I.Q. test score still plays a disproportionately dominant role in identifying students as eligible for special programs.

■ Programming and placement, i.e., how to deal with students once they have presumably been identified as gifted, is in constant debate. At one time, the heat in the programming-for-the-gifted debate arose primarily over whether or not these students should be congregated in separate schools. Proponents of this approach argue that a totally separated (but not totally isolated) environment can offer a much more enriched experience where the students are challenged by interchange with others like themselves, by special teachers, by an atmosphere of intellectual ferment, and by the momentum of exclusivity where elevated goals will obtain. The argument goes further to posit that a congregated environment will offer an intensity of role modelling less likely to be available in the mainstream. There are reasons to accept the validity of this position. Empirical

evidence particularly, has long demonstrated the stimulating power of high expectations in a specialized, highly-charged, intellectual environment.

On the other hand, there are also strong arguments in favor of integration. A principal tenet holds that although segregated environments may be successful, they are so specialized as to be unrealistic, and therefore counter-productive. By extension, experience in a rarified environment may mean the gifted student will be ill-prepared to perform effectively in the real world.

Ultimately, like most arguments over mainstreaming, whether to congregate gifted students in special schools, or integrate them, is probably unresolvable on a universal basis, not least because of the politics involved.

■ Where decisions have been taken to maintain gifted students in an integrated environment, issues over programming inevitably arise; issues such as:

enrichment: providing special activities in regular classes for selected students. Proponents say that this keeps the gifted student rooted in reality, and that given Renzulli's notion that everyone exhibits giftedness from time to time, there is less risk that potential giftedness will be ignored. Detractors state that enrichment is simply an inadequate response, and that it does not qualify as gifted education.

ability grouping: In an integrated environment, the gifted are selected out for differentiated instruction in more or less homogeneous groups within a regular class, or in congregations outside the class on a regular, part-time basis. Supporters of this placement and programming style usually advance the congregation argument described above, while detractors say the procedure fosters elitism.

acceleration: Although more uniformly supportive evidence can be found in favour of this technique than any other, it is the least used programming method, usually because of the fear of negative social and emotional consequences for the accelerated student.

Most school districts, especially the larger ones, tackle the issues above, by offering a variety of programming styles for students identified as gifted on the quite reasonable premise that a variety of programs is necessary to be effective in educating a variety of superior abilities.

■ The interpretation of, and programming for *talent,* unusual ability in, say, music, or athletics, or drama, or the visual arts (And why not carpentry?) is a continuing debate in the area of the gifted. Because these abilities are not necessarily accompanied by superior academic achievement, the issue is first: whether to classify them as examples of giftedness; second, and likely far more important: how — even whether — to offer programs aimed at developing these talents. An increasing practice in larger jurisdictions now is to develop 'art schools' for the talents that come under that rubric. (However, it is an interesting comment on our culture that exceptional ability in areas like carpentry or design or other *trades* have very little special accommodation.)

■ Almost every program for the gifted endures the accusation of meritocracy and elitism at one time or another, no matter how egalitarian its admission prerequisites may appear to be. For this very important, if somewhat insidious reason, special education for gifted students is often in jeopardy. It is not unusual therefore, for the mere existence of specialized programming for the gifted to be dependent on the vigour and determination of parent advocacy groups, acting in support of determined educators who feel this kind of special education is not just a practical but a moral obligation.

■ Many boards of education are very reluctant to formally identify students in the primary grades as gifted, and equally reluctant to authorize congregated classes or formal, differentiated programs for them. This attitude has taken hold first of all, because the developmental elasticity at ages 4-5 to 8-9 can make confident identification difficult. Secondly, primary education has usually been held to be very adaptive and flexible, and more individualized, so that in theory at least, the gifted can be easily accommodated in the mainstream. Further, in primary education there is an importance attached to social skills that in some schools takes precedence even over the development of academic and cognitive skills. The attitude is not the product of any insidious intent, or even neglect on the part of boards of education. Rather, it is likely the outcome of a vigorous thrust in the province to mainstream all students to the maximum possible extent, especially in primary grades. However research such as that by Karnes, M.B., et al., (1985) and a strong position taken by the Association for Bright Children, have given impetus toward establishing primary level programs.

For Discussion: The Case of Jasmine

On all of Jasmine's report cards since about Grade 5, teacher comments have regularly included the "She-could-do-better-with-more-effort" variety. The teachers have all seen the I.Q. test scores which imply Jasmine's superiority, and expect a lot of her. Jasmine however, does only the very bare minimum. She never takes advantage of extra activities, and sometimes does not get even the required ones finished. The young lady herself, (she is 16) feels she is "doing OK", says she is "not all that smart", and has a battery of excuses and reasons for not performing any harder. She insists that she is being pushed unreasonably.

Jasmine's parents are no less frustrated than her teachers. They are upper middle class professionals who either do not comprehend, or refuse to understand her attitude. The result is that they tend to put more pressure on her to which she responds with even greater resistance. Jasmine's friends like her, and she is somewhat of a social leader in her class. However they tend to avoid her if possible in cooperative activities during school hours because of her reputation as a counterproductive force.

Only one teacher on the present staff has been able to inspire Jasmine. This teacher is described by her principal as "off-the-wall" and a "rebel". Her elective course in Great Human Ideas has had a very positive effect on Jasmine, to the extent that Jasmine's essay on social responsibility was published — after being aggressively sought after — by the community's daily newspaper. Jasmine's parents have taken this as an indication that the school is not stimulating her natural gifts, and have requested a meeting to discuss her program.

■ More males are identified for gifted programs than females, and both educators and parents have had difficulty finding concrete and agreeable explanations for this. There is no conclusive research that points to biological difference as an explanation. Yet, explanations that point to traditions of male dominance in our culture have equally sparse research support.

■ The field of the gifted is regularly accused of burying itself in complexity, with inordinately interwoven and complicated models for identification, equally intricate models for program, and constant, involved requisites of review. There is considerable empirical evidence to support this. Some jurisdictions in Canada, for example, while recognized for their commitment to educating the gifted, have such amazingly intricate and time-consuming patterns of identification — and the programs to match — that it is conceivable that some students may not be receiving appropriate programs for the simple reason that they (or their parents) lack the will or the means or the stamina to crawl through the web of bureaucracy.

How Students are Nominated for Gifted Programs

1. Despite the acknowledged weaknesses of the I.Q. test, it continues to be a main screening device. The WISC-III (see Appendix B) is the most popular test used, although a few jurisdictions use the Stanford Binet Intelligence Scale (Rev. IV, 1985) despite criticism of its alleged cultural bias. More recently the Cognitive Abilities Test (1983) has been used in addition to and occasionally instead of the WISC. For younger children, the Kaufman Assessment Battery for Children (1984) has gained some popularity.

What is administratively significant about I.Q. tests, (and cognitive tests) is that they produce a quantified statement, a *number*, irrespective of whatever else they offer, and in most jurisdictions this number becomes an entry level border for admission to programs. The established figure varies from one jurisdiction to another (Figures of 140 and 130 Full Scale score on the WISC are typical). The work of such people as Sternberg and Gardner notwithstanding, the use of numbers it seems, and faith in tradition, has not yet been seriously shaken.

2. Tests of creativity are sometimes used to identify gifted especially in jurisdictions where creative behaviours are given credence as a major cluster. However, because the validity of these tests is so much in question, their use is being replaced generally, by teacher and peer nominations.

3. Achievement tests are used as initial screening mechanisms for giftedness much in the same way as in the assessment of retarded performance. Theoretically, the student who scores significantly above his or her age level (usually 2 or more grades) is a potential candidate for gifted programming.

4. Teacher nomination is a principal method of screening for the very early grades, but studies suggest that teachers are sometimes not particularly able in making the identification (Perks, 1984). Accuracy improves when teachers use a clearly defined scale to identify the students especially if the scale correlates the academic behaviour of the students with what is expected of them academically in the succeeding years (which inevitably raises the concern that students who "play the game" are most likely to have an advantage).

On Teaching the Gifted: The Words of Natalie B.

I was uneasy when the principal told me I had the gifted class that fall. Oh, I've taken the proper courses. But really, the course was the problem. It frightened me. So many teachers taking it had GBA Syndrome: Gifted By Association. It's a real problem in this field.

But after a year and a half with this class, I feel better. I've always been very curious about everything. That really helps because it rubs off on the kids. And I've always liked getting into a subject deeply. And creativity — well — it's in all of us. We just have to turn it loose.

What I think you really need to teach the gifted is ... is ... empathy. You have to get right inside their heads. Or try to. It even helps to be a bit naive, I think. That way you discover with them. It helps them pursue a subject for themselves and for its own sake, instead of for the all-knowing adult that's running the show.

Yes. I love teaching the gifted now ...

---

5. Parent nomination is shown by research to be generally more accurate than teacher nomination (Ciha et al., 1974) although this aspect is not without its own difficulty. Parents from lower socio-economic groups seem more likely to report giftedness than parents from higher socio-economic areas. As well, parents often lack opportunity for comparison in being able to predict their child's future success in school. Nevertheless, parents have the best knowledge of a child's early development, and this knowledge can be crucial.

6. Peer nomination is becoming more frequently used, despite the self-evident drawbacks and the lack of research clarifying its value.

7. Self nomination has developed as a recent practice as well. In this case, the student nominates himself or herself in the initiating stage of the identification process. Very often a self-nomination accompanies a nomination by teacher or parent, and more often than not is presented because the student has been asked to do so by one or both of the latter.

Organizational Models

Most boards adopt some form of organizational model to fulfill programming requirements for the gifted. Thus, where gifted education is formally offered, it is usually quite specifically organized on a broad jurisdictional basis (unlike programs for the learning disabled for example, or the mentally handicapped, which are more usually shaped by immediate, local demands and resources). What follows here are some of the models currently in use — with local modifications.

The Enrichment Triad

This model (Renzulli, 1977) believed to be the most widely used in Canada, has three levels of activity.

Type I is *General Exploratory Activities*. These are designed to expose pupils to exciting topics, ideas, and fields of knowledge not ordinarily covered by the regular curriculum. They include such items as visiting speakers, field trips, demonstrations, interest-development centres.

Type II involves *Group Training Activities*. These consist of methods, materials, and instructional techniques designed to develop thinking processes, research and reference skills, and personal and social skills.

Type III activities are *Individual or Small-Group Investigations*. In these, students investigate real problems and topics using appropriate methods of inquiry. The success of Type III activities very much depends upon the interest and task commitment of the individual.

An important modification of the Enrichment Triad is the *Revolving Door Identification Model* (Renzulli, et al., 1981)) which is designed to deal with problems in identification, motivation and curriculum. In this model, the resource room teacher is a consultant and the classroom teacher is directly involved in the students' special projects. Students are not permanently in or out of the program, but can apply for special consideration to work on projects of their own choosing. The resource teacher helps the student to focus or frame the area of interest into a researchable problem; suggests where he can find appropriate methodologies for pursuing the problem like a professional enquirer; helps him to obtain appropriate resources, provides assistance and encouragement, and helps find appropriate outlets and audiences for the creative work.

The Autonomous Learner Model

This is a program (Betts, 1986) developed principally for the secondary school, and is developed for a three year timeline. It adapts to the departmentalized structure of high schools, and anticipates that students will be withdrawn for single periods at specified times of the week. The student progresses through five stages:

i) orientation;

ii) individual development: students learn the attitudes and concepts necessary for life-long learning;

iii) enrichment activities: students explore outside the curriculum and become aware of resources they can use;

iv) seminars: students present the results of their personal pursuits and findings to larger groups for evaluation;

v) in-depth study: students are given opportunity to pursue an area of interest on a longer term basis.

The Purdue Three-Stage Enrichment Model

This is a half-day or full day withdrawal program (Feldhausen & Koffoff 1986) used mostly in elementary schools. There are three basic components:

i) divergent and convergent thinking abilities, in which the program concentrates on problem solving, decision making, forward planning, etc.;

ii) creative problem solving abilities, which offer strategies and techniques in creative problem solving of real problems;

iii) development of independent learning abilities, which requires the student to engage in the development of a product through learning and investigation and then share it with an audience.

This Purdue type of program is quite popular (under names like "Challenge", "Upward Bound", etc.) because it offers enrichment and opportunity without taxing the already scanty resources that typify so many elementary schools. Needless to say the quality of these programs varies dramatically according to the teacher in charge.

Other Strategies

Other responses to the need for educating the gifted use more time-honoured approaches. These range from congregated schools for the gifted to a variety of in-school programs.

For example:

• Enrichment in the classroom: A differentiated program of study offers children experiences beyond the regular curriculum. This model is delivered by the regular classroom teacher, with or without assistance from a consultant or resource teacher.

• Consultant teacher program: Differentiated instruction is provided within the regular classroom by the classroom teacher with the assistance of an educational consultant or specialist.

• Community mentor program: Students interact on an individual basis with selected members of the community to study topics of special interest to them.

• Independent study program: Differentiated instruction consists of independent study projects supervised by a qualified adult.

• Learning enrichment service: Generally, this is a networking system that combines many of the above ideas in an organized way.

Although the content and methods in the styles above do not differ widely from those of the more formal models (assuming they are well-run) they are not as well-received, principally because, their defenders say, these alternatives lack the aura that attaches to a program with an impressive title and a more apparently formal design. Critics on the other hand, say that less formalized structures are much more susceptible to casual, ad hoc programming, and are at greater risk of arbitrary cancellation.

Strategies for the Classroom

"Achieving potential" is admittedly a buzzword in all of special education, but its use requires no apology for it identifies what special education is all about. The phrase has extraordinary personal and societal significance in the case of the gifted. A program for gifted students must be based on the idea of achieving potential, and from that premise alone proceed to accommodate their unique needs. Part of that program — in some cases perhaps all of it — will be met in the role played by the classroom teacher. Each individual teacher of the gifted brings to a program, or a class, or a student, his own unique nature, as well as his own unique talents and interests and skills and background, all of which in the right circumstances, go a long way toward fulfilling the notion of achieving potential. In other words, as with any teaching-learning situation the teacher is the key.

There are however, certain absolutes to which teachers should subscribe, irrespective of their own preferences, styles, and areas of interest. These are planning goals which include the following:

• Establish an environment which shows clearly that intelligent thought, analysis, and creativity are valued.

• Encourage students to discover and develop their special abilities. Provide the time, space, materials and opportunities for them to do this at the sacrifice, if necessary, of the laid-on curriculum. (In this sense the teacher is much more of a facilitator than an instructor.)

• Arrange learning experiences that go beyond the normal acquisition-of-knowledge level. Gifted students need to go higher, deeper, and wider in their pursuit of a subject, pushing past the usual limits. Very often the teacher acts as a consultant, using her maturity and experience to help the student find a productive critical path, or a method of investigation.

• Provide opportunities for students to interact with adults, other students, and with various experts so that they will be challenged, not just to know about *things*, but about *people*, and so that they will learn to see their own place and their responsibility in the human connection.

• Create an atmosphere where risk-taking, speculation, and conjecture can be undertaken safely. The teacher recognizes that trial and error are part of learning and that the only real failures in a classroom are those which erode self-esteem. If the teacher herself takes risks, and fails, the student invariably will learn from this too.

The Characteristics of the Teacher

More than in any other area of special education, the literature on the gifted goes on at great length on the ideal teacher. Most texts spin out lists of desireable characteristics that, viewed cynically, could only force the conclusion that truly effective teachers of the gifted are a composite of genius, encyclopaedic information-storage, intuitive splendour, and sainthood. Realistically, truly effective teachers are effective no matter what their responsibilities.

And one would hope that all teachers are effective. Yet common sense dictates that the gifted and talented will naturally respond better to teachers with broad interests, extensive information and abundant creative energy. Not that students who are — say — learning disabled or behaviour disordered would not benefit from such teachers as well. The difference may lie in the horizons implied by achieving potential. The needs of a student with a learning disability or a behaviour disorder, for example, are usually more immediate and more focussed. But for the gifted, achieving potential provokes images of more distant horizons. The "miles to go before I sleep" of Robert Frost's famous poem, *Stopping By Woods On a Snowy Evening*, simply seem more numerous, and more significant in the case of the gifted, and therefore generate more concern about the teachers who will show the way.

For Discussion: The Case of Verna, Hon, and Devon

A district-wide achievement test for grade four students pinpointed three students in one class of a neighbourhood school. Verna, Hon and Devon obtained a grade equivalent score over 7.0 in every subtest. Following board policy, the principal arranged that they be given an I.Q. test, on which Verna's full score was at the 99th percentile; Hon's at the 97th and Devon's at the 98th.

Verna is an exceptionally cooperative, pleasant and able student, and a class leader. She is gentle, sensitive, personable and an especially effective peer tutor. Her academic achievement record is a string of A+s. Hon's record reads the same way. He too is cooperative and very able, but considerably more intense than most children in grade four. He works very hard and imposes considerable stress on himself. In a recent class discussion on hobbies, he explained that his hobby was school work. Devon on the other hand, is remarkably unstressed and very easygoing. Although he is as able as the other two, he does not work as hard. Still, the teacher feels that his results are easily a match for those of Verna and Hon. Devon's passion is hockey. His mother asserts that uninterrupted, Devon would play 24 hours a day! He plays for the community 'rep' team and is being wooed by three other teams.

This school has a congregated class for gifted grades four, five, six students, which enjoys an excellent reputation throughout the board. The grade four teacher has been told that she may nominate <u>one</u>, and only one — there are no possible modifications — of Verna, Hon, and Devon for possible admission to this class. (One criterion for admission is that applicants' I.Q. test scores be at the 92nd percentile or above.)

Verna's family is part of a small, very religious and very traditional farming community. Her parents are quite supportive of her, enjoy her achievements, and support her possibly joining the special class. They have, however, made it clear that when she is at school-leaving age, her formal education will come to an end. Hon's family vigorously support his joining the class. They are themselves very high achievers and community activists. Devon's mother is widowed and Devon is her only child. She is enormously pleased with every one of her son's achievements and enthusiastically supports the idea of the special class.

Each of the three children, individually and privately, has told the teacher they would really like to join the special class.

The teacher must decide.

12

Students With Physical Disabilities

Neurologically-Based Conditions • Chronic Health Needs • Multiple Disabilities

Prevailing Misconceptions About Physical and Other Health Needs

1. Students with special needs arising from conditions like spina bifida or Tourette syndrome or asthma are usually candidates for special education.

There is no reason to assume that physical disabilities or neurologically-based conditions or special health needs necessarily make a student educationally exceptional. Where conditions like spina bifida or asthma or Tourettes are primary or sole conditions, the distribution of intelligence, and distribution of other abilities like hearing or vision are similar to that in the rest of the population. It is possible, in some situations, that the medication used for treatment may have side effects that could make an adjusted program beneficial for a student, and it may be best to deliver such a program through special education services.

Another matter is that students with chronic needs often miss a great deal of school because of hospitalization or illness cared for at home, and may need a remedial program which special education is best equipped to deliver.

2. The physical condition of students with cerebral palsy cannot be remediated or improved.

Although it is considered irreversible, therapy, prosthetic devices, and sometimes surgical procedures, can make a positive change in the lives of people who have cerebral palsy.

3. When disabling conditions are neurologically based, there is always a consequent diminishing of intellectual capacity.

There is a higher incidence of mental handicap among people with cerebral palsy, but the connection is not absolute. Other conditions such as spina bifida, muscular dystrophy, or convulsive disorders, generally have no connection with levels of intelligence.

4. Conditions like epilepsy and Tourette syndrome indicate a predisposition toward mental illness.

People with these conditions are no more or no less disposed to mental illness than people who do not have them.

5. People with spina bifida are invariably incontinent.

Lack of bowel and bladder control is a genuine problem which accompanies the severer cases of spina bifida, but milder cases generally do not have this effect.

6. Arthritis is a disease of the elderly.

It is found in all ages.

7. Advances in medicine are reducing the incidence of physical disabilities and chronic conditions.

The number of children with these conditions is increasing because medical advances, particularly in post-natal care, have increased the birth and early years survival rate.

Describing the Needs

The primary distinguishing characteristics of students with a physical disability or other neurological or health need, are the proper concern of the health professions. Still, because these students are also *students,* it follows that teachers and teaching assistants will be involved, and must necessarily therefore, have some information about each situation. From an educational perspective, some specific, bio-medical knowledge about students can be useful for developing an appropriate program. Certainly this knowledge can be very helpful in understanding a student's emotional needs and learning patterns. However, it is important that teachers approach medical information principally from an educational and cooperative perspective, and not from a diagnostic or treatment point of view. In just about every single case (with the notable, frequent exception of neurologically-based conditions) a student with a special physical or health need of this type will come to the teacher already defined and classified by health personnel. The teacher's role is to respond educationally.

The descriptions that follow are quite brief and offer only preliminary information. Teachers who find themselves responsible for the instruction of a student diagnosed with one of these conditions, are usually wise to learn more about the particular condition, *and* the peculiarities of the individual student's case, since epilepsy, for example, or Tourette syndrome or brain injury will manifest itself in a variety of ways across a population, and with dramatically varying degrees of difference.

Cerebral Palsy

This is a condition caused by damage to the brain before, during, or after birth. It is chiefly characterized by motor disorder. It is not progressive but is not considered curable although physical therapy can be helpful in improving comfort and mobility.

Approximately fifty per cent of people with cerebral palsy have *spasticity,* slow, laborious, poorly coordinated voluntary movement. About twenty-five per cent have *athetoid* cerebral palsy, characterized by regular, involuntary, writhing movements. *Ataxic* cerebral palsy, characterized by poor coordination, balance and posture, affects approximately fifteen per cent. People with ataxia may be ambulatory; most others generally require a wheelchair. (There are further types of classification such as *hemiplegia* (involvement of right or left side of the body); *diplegia* (legs are involved to a greater extent than the arms) etc., which teachers may wish to investigate as they encounter particular cases.)

Other matters associated with cerebral palsy are mental handicaps (not an absolute connection but the incidence is significantly higher than in the general population) speech and language problems, sensory loss, especially visual and auditory difficulties, and epileptic seizures. An ongoing debate over cerebral palsy arises from the fact that average I.Q. test scores for children with this condition are lower than the general average. However, appropriateness of I.Q. tests, their administration and interpretation are often suspect in these situations.

Spina Bifida

Spina bifida occurs in the spinal column when one or more vertebrae do not close during pre-natal development. The resulting condition varies from few consequences to serious consequences. The most severe type is spina bifida with *mylemeningocele* which usually results in irreversible (so far) disability, the most obvious being lower body paralysis. Less severe conditions such as *spina bifida occulta* and *meningocele* do not necessarily involve lower body paralysis although people with these conditions may require crutches or leg braces to help them walk. Spina bifida is often accompanied by *hydrocephalus,* an enlargement of the head caused by pressure from cerebrospinal fluid which if not diagnosed and treated in time, can cause brain injury. Usually, the medical response to hydrocephalus is the installation of a shunt (a short tube) in the spinal column to help this fluid drain. Hydrocephalus and the presence of a shunt, indeed spina bifida itself, usually do not preclude a student's normal progress through school. However, educational experience with children who have hydrocephalus is beginning to reveal that the condition may also produce a higher than average chance of learning disability, owing to possible anomalies in the structure of the brain. The connection, at this stage, is more suspected (through empiricism) than proven, but teachers would be wise to be sensitive to the possibility.

Brain Injury

Often the result of an accident or other trauma, a brain injury is almost invariably an unique condition. While the area of the brain that has suffered the injury may be responsible for a constellation of human characteristics, there is no certainty that these characteristics will be affected, or that the effects will be short or long term. Educators dealing with a student diagnosed as brain injured, perhaps more than with any other exceptional student, must truly begin their assessments and programs with no assumptions or preconceived notions.

Epilepsy

Epilepsy is not a disease, but rather a symptom of a brain disorder that leads to seizures. There are several types of seizure; the two most commonly occurring are tonic-clonic and *absence seizure* (formerly called 'grand-mal' and 'petit-mal').

In the first type, the tonic-clonic, an individual loses consciousness, most often convulses, and falls. Breathing may stop temporarily. The individual may lose bowel and bladder control, or may bite the tongue. After one to five minutes or so, the individual regains consciousness, but may experience confusion and headache and often goes into deep sleep.

An absence seizure may occur several times a day, usually when the person is sedentary. It is very brief and may not even be noticed. It is characterized by what is often called a "clouding of the consciousness", during which the individual's eyes may stare at apparently nothing, or the hands will move aimlessly. The return to normal is usually abrupt.

Students with idiopathic epilepsy (of unknown origin) seem to function entirely normally between seizures. Those with symptomatic epilepsy (from brain damage) often have to cope with the consequences of the primary condition, of which epilepsy is one factor. Children especially, who have epilepsy that is expressed in tonic-clonic seizures seem to be extremely sensitive to the fact that they have the condition and teachers often find themselves more challenged by the emotional consequences than by the physical consequences of the seizures. Also, these students are sometimes very heavily medicated and the potential side effects can have an impact on their learning.

It is not unknown for teachers to be the first to suspect absence seizures, since one-on-one learning situations are good opportunities for observation, especially if the teacher is attempting to assess why a particular student's style is marked by significant ups and downs of understanding.

Finally, how a teacher deals with the post-seizure factors can have a most important impact. Reassurance and

"You get tough being a parent of a disabled kid. You develop a thick skin but sometimes you lose your cool. Like the time I took Tobin for his checkup and there was this new doctor. He was kind of confused. He had a couple of patient records in his hand when he came into the examining room, and he obviously didn't know who we were. But then he looked at Tobin and said: 'Oh — you're the athetoid.'
That's when I lost it. I punched him. He deserved it. Tobin is my son! He's my boy. And he laughs and cries and eats and sleeps and tries like hell to live like other kids. Sure he's got athetoid cerebral palsy. He doesn't talk and he spends half his life force grinding around in that damn wheelchair. But he's not an athetoid! Tobin is a human being ..."
—Verna D.

emotional support for the student who had the seizure, is crucial; equally vital is how the teacher educates the other students about epilepsy. (The Epilepsy Association has excellent material to assist in this.)

Tourette Syndrome

Once considered extremely rare, and likely because of that, very little known or understood, Tourette Syndrome (TS) is now believed to be far more common, and to have far more impact on the classroom. TS is a neurological disorder characterized by repetitive physical movements like facial tics and/or vocal sounds. According to Hughes (1990) it is an inherited condition that usually manifests itself in childhood. It is a lifelong disorder, although the symptoms have been known to disappear for long periods or even disappear altogether, with and without medication.

The implications for teachers and students are significant, partly because of the way the condition manifests itself and partly because TS may well be far more common than originally thought. Until 1972, only 50 cases of TS had been medically documented (Levi, 1991) and most teachers and even medical personnel were unaware of it. Very hard work by the Tourette Syndrome Foundation and some enlightened presentations on commercial television dramas have led to far more awareness about TS. However, prevalence data now vary widely. The prevailing opinion has been that TS affects one in every 2000 individuals (about the same prevalence as blindness) but a study cited by Comings (1990) suggests that as many as one out of every four students in special education in the United States may have some form of TS-related exceptionality.

The most common characteristics of TS are involuntary, multiple motor tics, involuntary uttering of noises, words and phrases, and what is often called "large personality" (i.e., behaviour seen as compulsive, loud and forceful; students with this symptom of TS may engage in ritualistic hopping or tapping — not unlike people with autism — and feel compelled to redo whole pieces of work several times because of even the tiniest error). Parker (1985) says that common learning difficulties associated with TS are difficulty in getting started (or finished), problems with comprehending verbal instructions and with space-time directionality. Given these descriptions, it is not hard to understand how TS can be confused with learning disability, mental handicap, schizophrenia and other conditions.

Medication to control TS symptoms is improving all the time, although it may have side effects that have an impact on a student's behaviour and academic performance.

The role of the teacher, as usual, is very important in the case of a student with TS. Understanding, empathy, common sense support and remediation strategies are obvious needs. Perhaps the most vital matter in assuring the student's security and sense of well-being is the way in which the teacher manages the effect of the TS on the student's peers and classmates. The Tourette Syndrome Foundation has some very helpful literature for teachers and it is a given that this should be read by any teacher who has a student with TS in his or her classroom.

Autism

Anyone dealing with severe autism in a child for the first time can be very intimidated by the experience. Because the condition is fairly rare (rate of 4-5 per 10,000), and only recently delineated as a disorder (by Kanner in 1943), and because its characteristics seem so resistant to educational — not to mention medical — intervention, autism holds place as one of the very most difficult areas of exceptionality. The health field, particularly psychiatry, has had great difficulty with autism, not just with treatment but even understanding it. Much of its early literature is devoted to distinguishing autism from childhood schizophrenia. Another body of literature suggests that 70-90% of children with severe autism are also mentally handicapped. Yet, more recent discoveries, through what is called 'assisted communication' suggest that the presumed connection between autism and mental handicap may not be accurate. In Ontario, the Ministry of Education classifies autism under the general category: *Communication*. The U.S., in 1981, removed autism from the category: *Seriously Emotionally Disturbed* and put it under *Other Health Impaired*. It is not hard to understand therefore, when medical and other experts have such difficulty, why educators are uneasy in the face of decisions about children with autism.

There is no test to confirm severe autism, but there is agreement on a constellation of observable behaviours.

1) avoidance of human interaction; little or no eye contact; little or no apparent wish for affection;

2) bizarre gestures and vocalizations; obsession with objects (often spinning objects) and compulsive need for an unaltered environment;

3) perseveration; extreme reaction to situations or sounds (or absolutely no reaction);

4) muteness or non-use of language for communication; sometimes echolalic;

5) frequent incidence of *pica;* ingestion of non-food material, like sand, plasticene, feces, small objects, etc.

The children may have a period of normal development from infancy, with evidence of autism beginning to show at 1½ to 2½ years. Although the symptoms may diminish in intensity by adolescence, the impoverishment in human relationship usually continues, along with a lack of social competence and limited or improper use of language.

Help From Support and Advocacy Groups

Teachers often find support and advocacy groups very helpful when planning program and strategy for an exceptional student. Members of organizations like The Epilepsy Association, The Learning Disabilities Association, The Association for Bright Children, The Tourette Syndrome Foundation, The Canadian Hearing Society, The Canadian National Institute for the Blind (there are many more) are invariably well-informed and current, and usually quite aggressive in seeking out information, supporting innovative practice, or dealing with slow-moving bureaucrats, and reluctant, sometimes poorly informed health professionals. All of these are issues a teacher invariably faces, and most of the time, regular contact and help from the appropriate advocacy group can be quite helpful in addressing them. Most associations, for example, have education programs in kit form or videotape which are available to teachers who wish to enlighten their classes — or their colleagues — about a particular exceptionality. Also, it is not unknown for an advocacy group to be the principal catalyst in bringing service to bear for a student for whom nothing hitherto had been available. Advocacy groups are also a remarkably effective first line of emotional support and information to a family which has just learned that a child has been diagnosed.

Multiple Disabilities

Students identified as multiple-disabled or multihandicapped have more than one exceptionality. There is limited evidence to show that certain single handicaps are more predisposed to be accompanied by others. In fact, a particularly vicious myth that continues to prevail is that all multihandicapped students are severely mentally handicapped. Another frequently posed myth is that all of these students have no oral language.

However there does seem to be a higher prevalence associated with certain exceptionalities. Kirk and Gallagher (1979) for example suggest that approximately 44% of children with cerebral palsy have uncorrectable visual impairments. Meadow (1980) found that a third of children with hearing impairment have additional disorders. Projections, mostly from American data, suggest an estimated 1 in 2500 children in Canada have a multiple handicap (Winzer, 1987).

This particular area of special education occupies a considerable amount of professional attention. In situations, for example, where it has been decided that a multihandicapped

---

For Discussion: The Case of Tahira

It is hard not to notice Tahira because of the large, powered wheelchair in which she spends most of her time. She is a thirteen year old, very beautiful girl with a type of spina bifida that will likely make her a wheelchair user for life. There are no secondary exceptionalities, but she does require a structured hygiene and toiletting program. Tahira also has only about 50% use of her left arm. (She is naturally right-handed.) In her native Calcutta at the age of four, she fell out of a wheelchair and broke the arm, which subsequently was not set properly.

In academic matters Tahira is a class leader. She is very able, an excellent writer, a "math-whiz", and possessed of what seems to be a prodigious memory. The IPRC which placed her in a regular class when she was in grade four (upon arrival in Canada) identified her as physically handicapped and recommended regular class placements with the support service of a health aide. The IPRC also recommended a yearly review because there was indication Tahira may be gifted. So far however, her identification or placement have not changed.

What troubles her grade seven teacher — and her classmates — is Tahira's sadness. She appears to be constantly and increasingly morose, and cries several times a day — not dramatically or noisily, but quietly: a steady flow of hushed, doleful tears. Tahira's schoolwork is beginning to deteriorate. She tends now, not to finish things, or if she does finish, to do work that is well below the level of what she has proven she can do.

---

student will not be mainstreamed in a regular class, finding an appropriate special class can be difficult. A jurisdiction may have a total of 4 or 5 students with deafness/blindness and a special class for them, but it may have only one student diagnosed deaf/blind, physically disabled and mentally handicapped. And it may have a total of three students who are identified as autistic (one of whom also has visual impairment). The tendency, in situations where these children are not mainstreamed, is to identify them as multihandicapped and place them in a single self-contained class. The rationale for this would likely be that such congregation will allow individualized programming and easy access to support services, will take cognizance of those areas where programs may overlap, and be economically feasible. More recently, it has become more common for students with multiple, severe disabilities to be integrated into a regular class with appropriate support, very often, a teaching assistant or health aide (or even both).

Whatever the identification and placement of a student with several exceptionalities, three features are common in a program:

i) it is highly individualized;

ii) there is a significant amount of support available from specialized educational and health services;

iii) there is a well-above-average degree of communication and cooperation (at least attempted) with the student's home so that education and habilitation can be coordinated over more than a school day.

Chronic Health Needs

There are other physical problems and conditions that may be present in students of either regular or special education classes. Teachers will encounter students with cystic fibrosis, scoliosis, congenital malformations, muscular dystrophy, diabetes, cancer, asthma and other chronic conditions, not to mention situations like poliomyelitis or encephalitis from which a student may recover but with some disability as a result.

It is not the place of a text like this to present a catalogue of handicapping conditions.

The descriptions above are included as examples of the kinds of possibly more frequent situations that may be present in a classroom, and as examples of the kind of general information about these conditions that a teacher may require. It is important to repeat here, that the teacher's main responsibility is to educate, with all this implies, not to treat; and to cooperate in the health care aspects that are part of the needs of these students. Attending school, simply being in school, is a crucial element in the normalization and growth of a student with a non-sensory physical exceptionality.

Some Issues in the Field

■ A particular concern to teachers is how to react in an emergency situation. It is this concern that sometimes leads them to resist placement of these students in their classes. Usually the resistance can be overcome simply with information and education about the particular exceptionality.

However, a constant — and justified — complaint of teachers is that they are not kept adequately informed about students with health needs. Changes in medication, environmental triggers (e.g., of an epileptic incident), crucial times of day: all these factors can be very important to the accommodation of a student with special health needs, and teachers quite rightly argue that poor communication from health personnel, inefficient bureaucracy in a school or larger system, not to mention stringent privacy regulations, makes their jobs more difficult and even puts the student at risk. (All of which substantiates the wisdom of regular, direct communication with parents who, for obvious reasons, will likely be both helpful and informative.)

■ An extension of the information issue is the currency of technical information about a condition or a disability. For example, students with severe autism have been generally regarded as mentally handicapped (Konstantareas, 1987); yet discovery of an incredibly simple technique called *assisted communication* is generating a re-evaluation of this notion. In assisted communication, a resource person helps someone with autism to use a keyboard to communicate. The "messages" that have surfaced as a result of this technique reveal a hidden well of intelligence and ability in *some* autistic individuals who previously had been considered unable to communicate — even catatonic — and mentally handicapped as well. Teachers often feel they are not offered the kind of professional upgrading that leads to awareness of new techniques like assisted communication.

■ Families often experience psychological havoc when they have a child with physical disabilities, or neurological condition, or chronic health need. Such a child inevitably demands a disproportionate amount of the family's resources in love, energy, money and time. Needless to say, families react in different ways, and their feelings usually have a profound effect on the way the child reacts in turn to the world at large. In whatever way the family — and the child — react, the teacher, teaching assistant and a wide number of personnel in a school are inevitably drawn into this reaction, so that relative to their other students, schools almost invariably find themselves expending equally disproportionate amounts of love, energy, money, and time. How a school deals with this fact, morally and practically, can become a matter of serious debate.

Educational Implications

❖ Canadians live in a culture obsessed with beautiful bodies. Health and strength are not enough; we must be well-formed and attractive. It is not surprising therefore that to the

> A frequent difficulty for teachers and teaching assistants is finding information on rare conditions and disorders. Very often, the best source is an advocacy or support group. Within the past decade, for example, support groups have been founded for Rett syndrome, tuberous sclerosis, and Williams syndrome. Children with the latter condition, sometimes called elfin-face syndrome, along with certain physical manifestations, show extraordinary intrapersonal differences in ability. Tuberous sclerosis is marked by lesions in the brain and other organs, often the skin, and is very frequently accompanied by serious developmental delay. Rett syndrome has so far been found only in girls. Children with the condition, after normal development, begin to lose purposeful hand skills around age 3-5, followed by a diminution of general physical ability and reduced cognitive functioning. Teachers can usually obtain an address for the support groups with the assistance of a provincial department of education, or through the community support department of larger hospitals.

physically exceptional especially, there is not only a battle to overcome the limitations imposed by their own bodies, there is also a battle to be accepted by others without stigma. The same phenomenon applies to behaviour. To people with Tourette syndrome, for example, the band of acceptable or so-called normal behaviour in our culture appears very narrow, so that when their condition expresses itself, they feel very much singled out. Therefore a teacher with one or more of these students in his class often finds himself dealing as much with behaviours — the disabled students', his own, that of other students, the culture at large — as he does with curriculum and instruction. Exceptional students will have negative feelings about themselves if it is obvious that others around them do. Conversely, they will become independent and self-sufficient in response to the expectations of others. Self-acceptance and self-awareness will develop in kind with the open and honest appraisal that significant people in their lives give to them.

The classroom teacher has an enormously important role to play in this. For example, teachers will often react with caution to someone in their midst who has a surgically implanted shunt, or who has a leg brace, or who may suddenly convulse or experience an asthma attack. Such caution of course is reasonable, but it is important that the caution be just that, and not fear. Fear and ignorance are potentially as great a threat to exceptional students as the primary handicaps themselves.

❖ The treatment of conditions like epilepsy or Tourette syndrome often involves the use of medication which has sedating side effects. Teachers sometimes find they are adjusting, not to an exceptionality, but to the treatment of that exceptionality. In fact it is not uncommon for a student to be identified and placed in special education principally because of the effects of the medication which is being used to control a primary condition.

For Discussion: The Case of Olaf

It was not until the beginning of November, when his family relocated from Florida, that Olaf joined the grade four class, and right from that first day his teacher was convinced there was something wrong, or at least different, about the boy. The other students noticed too.

For one thing, Olaf always entered the classroom ritualistically. He would stop just inside the door and with his left index finger, tap each of the three adjacent light switches and then the thermostat cover. He then walked along the left wall, across the back, and down the window wall, tapping each separate window sill before going to his seat. There was no behaviour like this when he left the room, but after a week the teacher couldn't help noticing that Olaf always stepped into the hall with his left foot, and would adjust his pace at the doorway to make sure this happened.

The teacher is committed to a cooperative learning style, and has a high level of tolerance for what he calls "learning noise".

As a consequence, no one was immediately aware that Olaf makes clucking noises with his tongue quite frequently and in a variety of situations. For periods of time (i.e., over several days) Olaf goes through bouts of unusual body movements too, particularly snapping his head forward and back. He also drums his fingers a great deal. The movements disappear though, for equal periods of time.

What has brought the matter to a head is this: the teacher is in his first year; he is held in very high regard by everyone, especially his students. They have begun to complain about being distracted by Olaf. The boy has not helped matters by seeming to have become quite aggressive and noisily assertive of late. When the teacher spoke to the principal about the matter, she did not seem to take it very seriously, attributing the behaviours to that of a typical ten year old in a new and somewhat stressful situation. The teacher does not agree but does not know what to do next.

❖ The normal adjustments that every teacher makes to accommodate her students' personal needs are often intensified in these cases. The students often miss a great deal of instructional time, being absent through illness or away for therapy, etc. The teacher may have to make allowances in scheduling and in monitoring so that matters of the students' personal hygiene can be addressed. As well, students with particularly serious disabilities often have attendant behavioural, even psychiatric problems that can call upon the full extent of a teacher's patience and stamina.

❖ Since a disabling condition like cerebral palsy can affect a student's progress through the natural stages of development, teachers can safely anticipate that some students with severe conditions may not be working at the same academic level as their peers, and must therefore make adjustments in program.

Strategies for the Classroom

(1) Where there are no secondary exceptionalities to deal with, such as learning disability or mental handicap for example, the teacher of a student with non-sensory physical limitations, or neurological impairments or chronic conditions, will likely treat the student in the same way as he or she treats everyone else, making allowance only for special needs in day-to-day functioning. These might include help in the administration of medication, help in the effective use of a prosthesis (artificial replacement for a body part) or some other adaptive device necessary for daily living.

(2) A classroom teacher may be asked to play a role in developing a child's use of an enabling device. A good example is the Blissymbolics Communication System, used by some non-verbal people (very often those with cerebral palsy). This is a worldwide graphic system of communication through pictographs and idiographs (e.g., ⌂ = house; •/ = before, or in front of).*

*Canada is a leader in the development and use of Blissymbolics. Teachers wishing further information may write the Blissymbolics Communication Institute, 350 Rumsey Road, Toronto, Ontario, M4G 1R8

(3) Continuing developments in computer technology accelerate far ahead of the capacity of texts like this one to describe them, and of course, teachers need to stay abreast as best as they can to utilize this progress on behalf of their students. The Apple Corporation, in particular, is held in high regard by educators for its work in the field.

(4) Because many children with physical handicaps are absent from school frequently, the degree to which a teacher cooperates in out-of-school assistance can be a very important factor in academic success. Many jurisdictions appoint what are called 'itinerant' teachers, or teachers of the home and hospital-bound, whose teaching load usually involves on-site instruction at home, in hospital, or in other institutions.

(5) It is rare but not unheard of, for the classroom teacher to be the catalyst in the discovery of a condition such as absence seizures for example, which in a large and chaotic family may not be noticed if they are mild and infrequent, but in the more structured demands of school become evident. Such relatively unknown conditions like Tourette syndrome sometimes go undiagnosed even through adolescence.

(6) Effective communication among teachers, parents, and health care professionals is absolutely essential but is ignored with discouraging frequency. It is often incumbent upon the teacher to initiate this, usually by direct and regular contact with the parents.

(7) Students in both regular and self-contained classes — most especially younger children — will invariably take their cue from teachers when seeking out how to react to and behave toward people with disabilities. Accordingly, teachers need to take a very positive leadership and modelling role.

Teachers also need to show other students tactfully, how to be helpful without taking over, how to react with empathy not pity, and how to treat their colleagues' exceptionalities with common sense.

13

Assessment in Special Education

The Contribution of Assessment

An educational assessment is a gathering and then interpretation of relevant information about a student, obtained from a variety of sources: observations of the teacher, teaching assistant, and parent, formal tests of the student, behaviour and ability profiles of the student, to name just a few. What is discovered in an assessment, at least theoretically, is some insight into a student's abilities, intelligence, strengths, needs, behaviour, and so on. These discoveries help educators and parents to make more informed decisions about identification of students, especially those who are exceptional or suspected of being exceptional. Matters of placement, of performance and specific need, and certainly the structure and content of a student's program, can all be focused and refined by the results of an assessment.

No single element in the special education process offers more potential value for understanding an exceptional student's situation. Yet, no single element in special education consistently proves more disappointing, especially to practitioners — teachers, teaching assistants, parents, and others with direct, daily responsibility — for the simple reason that the nature of a human being is enormously resistant to precise and absolute explanation.

No matter how much teachers may desire specialized information about their students, and parents about their children, and no matter how acculturated we may be to the belief that such truth can be revealed, the simple fact is that the very best an educational assessment can produce is a kind of "loose probability".

But however loose, it is nevertheless an important probability. Education itself is not an exact science, and effective teaching is often much closer to art than it is to the mechanistic principles of mere instruction. What an assessment does for an exceptional student is provide information which is gathered and organized in a way that at the very least, confirms in a presumably unbiased way, the view of the people working with that student; and at the very best, reveals factors that no one had known or possibly even suspected. Granted there are reasons to harbour doubts about some of the procedures and components in an assessment, and quite possibly, reasons to be wary of results, but to ignore the potential contribution of an effective assessment to an exceptional student's case, would be a disservice indeed. Assessment has an important role to play. What shapes the value of that role is the quality of the assessment procedures and the way the results are interpreted and applied.

When Are Assessments Done?

One point at which an assessment is usually carried out is prior to any formal discussion about a student. Generally, except in cases where there is recent and relevant data already available, assessments related to any formal procedure tend to be fairly thorough. Usually they will tap a number of sources of information and use a variety of strategies. Usually, a committee will then use the assessment as one of the bases for identification and possibly, placement. At any review point, assessment will again play a role. Whether it will be as extensive as the original will vary from case to case.

In other situations, less formal, smaller assessments fulfill similar purposes. For example, a teacher bringing a case to a School Team will usually offer an assessment based on observation, classroom performance and possibly, the use of a rating scale/checklist or even the results of a formal test instrument, provided such is available and that the teacher is competent to administer it and has permission to do so. (In a situation like this it would be rare for a teacher to conduct a formal, extensive test, like an I.Q. test, although if the results of one are available to the Team, they might be considered — usually at the discretion of the parents and principal.)

Another common procedure is screening. This is a fairly formal procedure in which groups of students are screened via an achievement test or test of cognitive abilities or other instrument. (Some districts develop their own system for screening to be used along with, or in place of a commercially published test.) The purpose is to discover, in a general way, whether there are any students at risk or potentially gifted. Those discovered are usually assessed then, in a more formal and extensive way to confirm (or disconfirm) their suspected risk or giftedness.*

Very specific assessments are sometimes conducted to evaluate a student's progress within a program. Often this is done by first establishing base line data and then obtaining comparative data after a period of time has passed.

*According to Lerner et al. (1981) about 85 percent of exceptional students are first identified by screening.

The same data are sometimes used to make a wider, more general analysis: viz., the quality of the student's program, the effect of the teaching strategies, the appropriateness of the placement, etc.

Ultimately, the timing and frequency of assessments are a factor of board and school policies, adjusted (in the best of all worlds) to the needs of a specific situation. The methods by which the assessment is carried out, and the actual components, are again a matter of board and school policies, but in practice these elements are very much controlled by the immediate personnel involved.

Who Conducts Assessments?

In larger jurisdictions especially, there is often a complete — and unfortunately, quite separate — unit responsible for assessment. Known by descriptors like 'psychological services' or 'psycho-educational services' or 'psych-support', etc., this unit generally does almost all the assessing for special education except for teachers' in-class evaluations. Much of it is conducted by psychometrists or graduates in psychology with psychometric training. Smaller jurisdictions, for obvious reasons, often use alternative arrangements. It is not unusual in smaller boards for classroom teachers to be given greater responsibility for doing assessments, although in practice, with boards of every size, the more complex an exceptional student's situation, the more likely an assessment will be conducted by someone for whom this is a primary professional role.

It is not unusual for a school to have fully qualified special education teachers do assessments. This has distinct advantages in that these teachers can take the next step — designing the program implied by the assessment — quite naturally and effectively.

Parents sometimes obtain an assessment privately, even though by law, they have access to any data the school has. They may offer these data to the school (or to a committee) or may choose to keep it to themselves. A committee will usually accept and consider a privately conducted assessment, even though, technically, it is not usually obliged to.

Privacy regulations regarding assessment information are constantly subject to review, debate and change. Generally, whether or not an assessment may even be done, is a matter of parental permission, school policy, and provincial and federal law. The same factors govern the results once an assessment is completed.

Components of an Assessment

Curiously, the pieces that together make up an assessment are often described collectively with an artillery term: assessment *battery*. What follows here is a description of components that may be used in a battery. Not all of them would be used in a particular case, although certain of them will almost always be included. (It is difficult, for example, to conceive of an assessment being useful and valid without the observations of the teacher and teaching assistant.) The decision regarding what components to use is typically governed in part by school and board policy. For example, many boards have complex and stringent requirements for identifying students as gifted, and specify that certain test instruments be used as part of the identification procedure. Some boards discourage or even forbid the use of certain components. However, once board and school policies are met — and on the matter of components these policies are flexible for the most part — how an assessment is actually conducted, and what is used, will typically be the choice of the professional personnel involved, and that choice will vary according to their knowledge, competence, and personal preference.

Formal Tests*

Intelligence Tests

Traditional intelligence testing continues to be very popular in Canada in spite of the grave concerns of many educators about the value of the procedure. Generally, I.Q. tests give a reasonably accurate assessment of what an individual has been taught (and what he remembers) and of what he has been exposed to thus far in his life. In this sense, an I.Q. test is a

*For descriptions of formal tests popularly used in Canada, see Appendix B.

Keys to an Effective Assessment

For reasons of economy, availability of personnel and appropriate instruments; because of of politics, and because of the chronic problem of special education: lack of time, not all educational assessments will meet every one of the criteria listed here, every time. Yet when these criteria are not met as a basic standard, the results of any assessment should be weighed accordingly.

❶ Has the assessment used a broad spectrum of sources (e.g., teacher, parent, other professionals if appropriate, test instruments if appropriate)?

❷ If test instruments have been used, are they known to be *valid* and *reliable*? Is the examiner adequately trained in the administration of the tests and interpretation of the results?

❸ Was the assessment individually tailored? (i.e., Did it take into account matters like the the subject's dominant culture, his language, age, school experience, physical abilities?)

❹ Was the assessment 'ecological' in the sense that it examined the whole student in relation to her total environment: (e.g., program, classroom situation, home situation)?

❺ Does the assessment imply or recommend responses: avenues of remediation or enrichment (as opposed to presenting only an enumeration of deficiencies)?

❻ Do key persons in the life of the subject (teacher, teaching assistant, parent) acknowledge that the assessment has sampled genuinely representative factors?

measure of current performance. What continues to be hotly debated is whether the tests measure intellectual potential, and can thereby be legitimately regarded as *predictors* of future school performance. Despite the weight of opinion against this use of I.Q. tests (Partenio & Taylor, 1985; Clarizio, 1982) they continue to be used for the purpose.

The most widely used I.Q. test by far in Canada has been the *Wechsler Intelligence Scale For Children - Revised,* (1974), now in Third Edition (1991) known as the *WISC-III.* More recently, assessors have turned somewhat to other I.Q. tests like the *Woodcock-Johnson Psycho-Educational Battery - Revised* (1990) and the *Kaufman Assessment Battery for Children* (1983) and even further, to alternative procedures that do not use intelligence tests at all.

Projective Tests

Gestalt psychology and psychoanalytic method propose that an individual will project her inner life, especially her feelings, when presented with an ambiguous stimulus like a picture of an inkblot. When asked to draw pictures of a situation or an object (e.g., her family, or a tree) or when asked to describe "what is going on here" while being shown a picture, an individual will, according to this theory, expose more of her deeper self than she would if asked directly. Projective tests have been fiercely criticized for lack of norms, insufficient standardization, entirely subjective interpretation, and even for revealing more about the examiner than the subject! Although their use is declining in Canadian schools, they still appear in some assessments. Some examples are the *Rorschach Inkblot Test* (1932) and the *Human Figure Drawing Test* (1968).

Tests of Academic Achievement

These are the most widely used formal test instruments of all — and possibly the most abused. There are achievement tests for large groups (e.g., the *Canadian Achievement Tests,* 1983) and there are individual tests as well (e.g., the *Peabody Individual Achievement Test,* 1970). Administrators of achievement tests can be anyone from a classroom teacher to a professional psychometrist. Publishers provide detailed administration manuals and in addition, recommend that examiners attend training seminars.

Very often in special education, achievement tests are used as screening tests. Other uses include general comparison, since the test results are calculated in terms of the results — called *norms* — developed across a wide, randomly selected population. In other words, the test-takers reveal where they stand *in terms of the test,* relative to a general population.

Diagnostic Tests

The term is misleading. These tests do not diagnose in any absolute sense but rather, present specific information about a student's performance in a specific area. The true purpose of these tests is to suggest areas for remediation. Subtests of the *Woodcock Reading Mastery Tests - Revised* (1987) for example, deal with specific areas like 'Word Identification', 'Word Attack', and 'Word Comprehension', presumably giving indication of the extent to which a student is competent in these areas. Critics of this and other similar tests question the value and even the validity of this kind of subskill breakdown in an area like reading, although they acknowledge it may have value in mathematics where the steps in the process of subtraction, for example, can be broken down and illuminated more clearly.

Tests of Cognitive Ability

The jury is very much still out on the issue of whether or not testing for cognitive ability is any different at all from testing for intelligence with the I. Q. instruments already in use. De-Ruiter & Wansart (1982) describe cognition as a process of extracting meaning beyond the figural information available in the environment in a way that allows the individual to apply it to new conditions. In less elevated academic terminology, cognition is simply *thinking* . Whether testing for thinking is any different from testing for I.Q. is moot. In Canada, supporters of the distinction generally opt for the *Canadian Cognitive Abilities Test* (1982).

Perceptual-Motor Tests

These claim to measure things like 'visual-perceptual skills', 'visual-motor skills', and 'auditory-perceptual ability' — so-called skills which should not be confused with straightforward information from the five senses. Perceptual-motor tests enjoyed extensive credibility in the 1970's until research began to question their validity, and even whether they should be used at all (Kavale & Mattson, 1983) because the tests purport to measure skills which, empirically, have never been shown to exist. In 1986, the Council for Learning Disabilities published a position statement that opposed the measurement and training of perceptual and perceptual-motor functions as part of learning disabilities services. The fact that perceptual-motor tests like the *Bender Visual Motor Gestalt Test* (1938) and the *Beery Developmental Test of Visual-Motor Integration- Revised* (1982) continue to be used in Canada is a tribute either to the staying power of the instruments or the (un)willingness of people to read and accept research findings!

Developmental and Readiness Tests

These are primarily administered by classroom teachers — especially teachers of early grades — to determine the level of ability of students. For exceptional students, their purpose is generally for screening. Very often these instruments are used in conjunction with checklists and skills inventories. Two of these, popular in Canada, are the *Boehm Test of Basic Concepts - Revised* (1986) and the *Brigance Inventories, (various)*.

Informal (Teacher Made) Tests

Owing to an erosion of faith in formal tests, there has been an increase in the use and

---

For Discussion: The Case of Lareyna

Lareyna's parents insist that their daughter is allergic to a variety of substances, especially moulds and fungi that, according to a magazine article they have read, occur regularly in a typical school classroom, lodged in the rug and on a number of other surfaces. The family doctor, who has a particular interest in allergies, has diagnosed Lareyna as having 'environmental hypersensitivity syndrome'. She has written the school as follows to explain the syndrome and the concept of 'total load':

> *"Briefly, 'total load' refers to all the elements in the environment that might cause reactions in individuals. The tolerance level, or level at which the load is 'total' for people with environmental hypersensitivity syndrome will usually vary, as it will with everyone, but almost always is well below normal. Physical reactions include watery eyes, red and runny nose, rashes, headaches, sick stomach and sometimes fainting. Frequently there are emotional reactions, including depression, anger, mood shifts, restlessness, attention deficit, etc."*

The doctor went on to offer the opinion that Lareyna's learning might be affected by the allergies too.

Lareyna is thirteen years old in the eighth grade. Until this year, she had been an average to above average student. This year her grades have dropped somewhat but not overwhelmingly. She has expressed some hitherto atypical defiance and rudeness in class, and her peers have reluctantly reported that they "can't get along with Lareyna" at recess or in cooperative ventures.

The teacher states that he has never once noticed any of the physical reactions in Lareyna. He is supported in this by the three other teachers who share responsiblity for her. All four agree, nevertheless, that Lareyna has changed this year, but tend to put it down to puberty and the presence of a new student in the class who has modified the behaviour of the entire group.

The parents have taken the position that 'environmental hypersensitivity syndrome' accounts for the change in their daughter and want the school to cleanse the environment by, to begin with, removing rugs and installing air exchangers. The school is understandably cautious. The principal wonders what might be accomplished if a full educational assessment of Lareyna is conducted before there are any further discussions.

---

acceptance of informal measures designed by classroom teachers to meet their own immediate purposes for particular, individual children. The disadvantage of these measures is that there are no norms for them and they do not usually have acceptance beyond the immediate situation. But then, that is not their purpose. Their advantage is that they can often be truly tailored to meet specific needs. For example, an informal test can be designed to reveal the presence or absence of a very specific skill, and thus may provide a picture of *why and when* a student fails to grasp a skill (like subtraction) instead of simply confirming that he has not grasped it (which the teacher already knows in any case).

Other informal measures may include a teacher's using parts of rating scales and checklists so that she can be more certain to have covered all the points. Informal inventories are used here as well. Still another practice (one of questionable legality, and efficacy as well) is to use parts of different formal tests to put together the desired information about a student.

Medical Information

This is included only when it is germane. Information may range from data about hearing, sight, and physical ability, to the general health and neurological conditions that may be relevant to a student's situation. These data, if available, will come from the appropriate health professionals; they are almost never prepared by a school board. Experience has demonstrated that without cooperation and impetus from parents, these data, along with accompanying, useful advice, are often hard to come by. Health professionals are understandably wary of privacy regulations, but at the same time, often show a curious reluctance to share more than sketchy information with schools.

Rating Scales, Inventories and Checklists

These instruments usually offer descriptive statements about areas like behaviour, attitude, self-esteem, self-care, etc., in lists. Each item in a list is followed by a frequency ranking (like 'almost all the time, frequently, sometimes, occasionally, rarely') or sometimes just by 'yes' or 'no'. Responses are entered by the student's teacher, or teaching assistant, or parent, or social worker, or child care worker (sometimes all of these for comparison and time/place/situation diagnosis). A reasonably popular example of this type is the *Child Behaviour Checklist* (1983).

Some rating scales are designed to be completed by the student. The *Coopersmith Self-Esteem Inventory* (1983) for example, presents statements to the student like 'I often wish I were someone else' followed by 'like me__' and 'unlike me__'.

Most often the results of these scales are used to determine a developmental profile from which educational, or social or self-care objectives are developed. Occasionally, the information may be used to indicate a developmental level, and sometimes decisions about placement, for example, will be influenced by the level indicated. The *AAMD Adaptive Behaviour Scale: School Edition (1981)* often called an adaptive behaviour 'test' is frequently used this way.

The rating scale type of instrument invites, quite obviously, considerable subjectivity, and interestingly, is both praised and criticized for this factor.

Interviews and Informal Commentary: Teachers and Parents

Any effective assessment procedure will seek out the opinions of the responsible adults who associate with and have responsibility for the student most directly. In Canada, most schools invite the classroom teacher, and sometimes the teaching assistant, to meet with a committee to present information. Very often this face-to-face discussion is preceded by written information that may vary from a simple referral form to anecdotal information to a fully developed case study. This latter, the case study, if properly completed can be a most effective adjunct — sometimes the very core — of an assessment. (See page 134 for more on the case study.)

Parents can usually offer vital information to an assessment or evaluation team. Their information is invariably current and intimate (if biased, sometimes); they also have the advantage of knowing the student's full history.

Reports and Analyses: Other Professionals

For reasons that do not require elaboration here, it is obvious that members of the behavioural science professions can offer very helpful insights into the situations of certain students. What educators must weigh however, when receiving information from these sources, is the proportionate amount of time any one of them has been able to spend with a student, and of that time, the amount in an actual classroom situation. Because of this factor, together with what seems to be somewhat of a weak track record for predicting behaviour on the part of these professionals,* educators often find it more helpful to use assessment information from these sources for general understanding of a syndrome rather than for specific program planning.

*Faust & Ziskin (1988) in a major review that traced expert psychiatric and psychologic testimony in the U.S. court system during the twentieth century, shocked both the legal and behavioural science professions by showing that the predictions of behaviour by these experts in testimony proved later to be wrong more than half the time! The fact that this excellent study has had almost no impact on practices in the judicial system or on behavioural science practices, suggests how firmly entrenched is our cultural urge to believe in supposed expertise.

Some Important Terms in Assessment*

Band of Confidence: a relatively new means of reporting test scores. Because of the Standard Error of Measurement factor (See below) a test score can never be considered absolutely correct. Thus some test manuals now offer a range *around* the given score about which there can be some confidence.

Criterion Referenced Test: a number of specific behaviours or performances are stated (e.g., Subject knows the alphabet? Can count from 1-20?). These are the criteria. The subject's ability in this particular area is then assessed. (See Norm Referenced Test.)

Grade Equivalent: a subject's raw score on a test is applied statistically to produce the school grade he would be in if he were in the sample group of students used to determine the norms for the test. (A subject's grade equivalent of 6.2 means that if he were in the group sampled to produce the norms, he would stand at the second month of sixth grade.)

Norm Referenced Test: a test which rates a subject's performance relative to the results obtained in a known comparison group (or *norm* group).

Norms: the results obtained by a supposedly representative sample of students as a particular test was being developed. Students who write the test after it is then published, have their results compared to these norms to produce scores like Percentile, Stanine, Grade Equivalent, etc.

Percentile Rank: a subject's percentile rank of 82 means that she scored higher than about 82 per cent of the norm group.

Reliability: the level of consistency and dependability of a test. (Will it produce similar results over variable conditions?)

Split-half Procedure: this involves administering the same subject(s) half of a test instrument (e.g., the odd-numbered questions) at a different time from the other half (e.g., the even-numbered questions).

Stanine: a reporting scheme for test results based on an equal interval scale of 1 to 9. (5 is average; 6 slightly above, etc.).

Standard Error of Measurement: the extent to which a subject's score is "out". These data are reported (or should be!) in the technical manual available with published, formal tests.

Validity: the degree to which a test measures what it purports to measure.

* See also glossary in Appendix B.

Alternative Assessment Procedures

Alternatives to traditional assessment procedures are continually being suggested to school systems. Four of these are described briefly here.

Ecological Assessment

This concept includes an amalgam of formal and informal methods, along with careful evaluation of the teaching-learning variables in the student's case. The idea is to examine the context in which the student learns, as well as the student himself. Thus, matters like the teacher's management style, the curriculum, teaching strategies, and instructional materials are examined; work samples produced by the student are evaluated, as well his success and error patterns inside and outside of school, etc. All this is in addition to the use of the usual formal test instruments. While ecological assessment is most attractive in principle, sheer management and economic factors make it very difficult to do.

Curriculum-Based Assessment

This concept involves the measurement of a student's performance in terms of the curricular outcomes the school has established. Many observers suggest that curriculum-based assessment, despite the extensive explication and argument that surround it, does not differ very much from the way evaluation in schools was conducted well before special education became a commonplace factor. In the case of an exceptional student, this kind of measurement is not a true alternative since all it really does is reveal (or confirm) that the exceptional student is not responding appropriately to the curriculum, and therefore needs to be assessed in other ways in order to discover what can be done about it.

Supporters argue however, that curriculum-based assessment emphasizes the identification of a student's personal, unique and complex characteristics as they relate directly to what he is supposed to be learning, and that this is superior to the type of assessment which is concerned principally with establishing the presence of some disability.

For Discussion: The Case of Mohinder

In five months, Mohinder will be seven years old. He is a polite, disarming, little boy just finishing grade one. His teacher describes the child as an "adequate to sometimes very good" student. The program in grade one is rather traditional. The teacher's style is not rigid, but not flexible either. The class tends to move as a unit with only limited independent study. There is a full phonics program, lots of 'creative' math, and although the room is equipped for several activity tables, there is usually only one set up at a time.

Of the four reading groups in the class, Mohinder is in Level 2. Yet the librarian reports him as a regular visitor who has independently read every Curious George and Clifford book she has. The teaching assistant (part-time) reports that recently, while playing a game with her, Mohinder anticipated her questions by reading the instructions upside-down. In the same week, during a math exercise using manipulatives, Mohinder, left to his own devices for only a short time, instead built a wonderfully

elaborate maze that won the admiration — and the total attention — of all the children in the class.

Mohinder frequently imagines the presence of 'friends', usually animals with whom he acts out elaborate dramas. Recently, he successfully got grade one to see several multi-coloured horses come from his pocket on command, after which they cheerfully interacted with all the children in a kind of circus. Unfortunately, the teacher could not see them, and Mohinder had to spend some time on the 'Reflection Chair'.

Mohinder's Mom says that he always speaks enthusiastically about school, and will deny being ill if there is a threat that he has to stay home. She had once suggested to the principal that it might be interesting to assess Mohinder, but he replied that assessing the boy at his tender age might not produce any useful data. Meanwhile, Mohinder has made another visit to the 'Reflection Chair', this time for drawing an extraordinarily long penis on Elmer the Safety Elephant with an indelible pen.

To be effective, curriculum-based assessment must be done frequently; it should be specific (i.e., directed exactly at what has been taught); the results should be considered as a reason for possibly adjusting the instruction in addition to just determining how the student is doing; and, testing should consider small, subskill gains in addition to the acquisition of more global matters. (See Salvia and Hughes, 1990, for more.)

Learning Style Assessment

An initially well-received proposal in the 1980's offered the idea that by examining how a student learns, and discovering under what conditions, or through what style of presentation she learns most naturally and effectively, it would be a relatively straightforward case of making appropriate adjustments when she does not learn. While the idea was successful in promoting attention to individualized programming, as an assessment method it has proven very complex for the rewards it might generate. Another problem is that in the development stages of their growth, students' styles are not necessarily stable and therefore accessible to reliable measurement.

Dynamic Assessment

Feuerstein (1979) and his colleagues propose an alternative that is most exciting, conceptually, for special education. Generally critical of traditional assessment procedure for its habit of assessing a student *statically,* i.e., at a single point in time, with all the attendant drawbacks, Feuerstein argues for dynamic assessment: in essence a test-teach-test model that stipulates the subject first be assessed to reveal needs; then it directs the examiner to interact constantly with the subject, teaching him the content and concepts that were first assessed in an attempt to address the needs; and third to re-assess to see if the subject has learned, and to identify what strategies were the most successful in the process. Feurstein's thesis is that it is more valuable to discover whether and what and how a student can be taught (his word is 'modified') and what strategies work best in the teaching, than it is to simply learn or have confirmed what he cannot do. Although dynamic assessment has a minority of firm converts in Canada, it has not gained the attention it perhaps deserves.

Some Issues in the Use of Formal Tests

■ More than in any other area of special education, the issues and concerns — the problems — of assessment are very much interwoven and interrelated. One issue spills over into another in a way that makes both more serious than they might be individually. A good case in point is the issue of test mystique and the issue of just how accurate is the picture of a student that a test produces?

The mystique factor is powerful. Educators, including those who should know better, seem to willingly ascribe to tests a kind of mystical capacity to open a window into a student's inner being, and the workings of her mind. The result is that these educators will often defer to test results or interpretations of test results — the supposed picture of a student — that contradict their own observations and conclusions, arrived at over months of intimate observations and analyses. Ironically, the professionals who administer and interpret the tests rarely push for this; in fact they are usually the ones who point out that a formal test instrument is just one of several looks at the subject. Yet so strong is the effect of a test result that almost everyone involved in a student's case will, however tacitly, acknowledge its superiority, with the effect that the importance of a test in the general assessment of a student can be shockingly disproportionate.

■ Other nagging problems are the aging of content, and the matter of cultural bias and tacit discrimination against lower SES groups. Producers of commercial tests claim to have addressed this matter in their revisions, but estimates of their success, as published in professional reviews, are conservative at best.

■ In tests administered to groups, the questions are typically phrased so that the answers can be machine-scored, with multiple-choice format being the most popular. Almost every question therefore, must be responded to with a single, confined answer. Such a structure invites a great many dull and simplistic questions, and devotes an excessive amount of space, time, and effort to minutiae. Needless to say, it also leaves little room, if any, for the reflective or creative student.

■ It is not uncommon, in tests of language and reading, to find lists of single words, out of context, to be read aloud. (See, for example, the *Wide Range Achievement Test-Revised,* 1983.) These subtests are called 'Reading', or 'Reading Recognition' with the results interpreted as a measure of general reading ability, rather than word recognition alone. The practice also assumes that testing an unnatural idea like word recognition is possible, and worth doing in the first place.

> The first time I saw Enny's file was a shocker. It was so thick! But what was really bothersome was what was in it. I mean — I know Enny is not easy. Autistic kids rarely are. But his file ... it was full of tests and reports and lists and all kinds of things, all of it describing what was wrong with him and what he does wrong. The thing is: we know all that already. Shouldn't there have been something about what can be done?"
>
> —*Bea. K. (mother of a 9 year old)*

■ In tests of achievement especially, each item tends to be scored with the same value (usually 1 or 0). Since the tasks typically increase in difficulty, Student A, who correctly answers only questions sixteen to twenty, earns the same score as Student B, who correctly answers only questions one to five. Granted, a careful item by item analysis would reveal that Students A and B attained a raw score of five by different routes. But in practice, consumers of test information rarely see, or have time to see, an item analysis.

■ Tests are usually rigorously timed, with all the difficulties that causes for slower thinkers (not to mention deep thinkers).

■ Over time, commercially produced formal tests have come to be called 'standardized' (distinguishing them from teacher tests which by implication therefore, are *un*standardized). Most test consumers have come to use 'standardized' as though these tests are based on a standard against which students are judged. This is not at all the case. Test results are indeed compared to a scale of values or 'norms', but these norms are not an absolute standard; they are the scores obtained from the population samples used by the test publishers to establish the basis for comparison. Publishers usually contend that the norms they have established represent the range of results (in a perfect bell curve) that could be expected in a normal or typical population. That claim notwithstanding, the comparison is still relative; it is not a standard. What *is* standardized in formal tests are the procedures of administration and scoring. A 'standardized' test is one which is administered and scored the same way every time, in order to reduce examiner interference.

■ Another well-established practice is to generalize test results. If Student C takes test XX in reading comprehension, and scores a grade equivalent of say, 4.2, those results are for that particular test. Yet it is regular practice by educators to make the assumption that the student's absolute reading level is 4.2.

■ Easily one of the most misunderstood and most ignored elements in formal tests is the standard error of measurement (SEM). Because no test is absolutely accurate, a subject's true score is never known. The score that a subject gets — his 'obtained' score — is actually only an estimate of his true score. What the SEM does then, is give a statistical reflection of how close to a true score the subject's obtained score actually is. If, for example, he scores 110 on a test with an SEM of 3.8, then approximately two-thirds of the time, statistically, his true score would fall between 96.2 and 113.8. The impact of the SEM can be very powerful (not least because it is so often ignored). If students are identified for a program on the basis of test scores, it is easy to see how the spread, the looseness, implied by the SEM can be significant.

■ Taken together, the problems with formal tests (not all of which by any means are the fault of the tests or the examiners) have led to a decrease in their use in Canada for assessing exceptional students. Although the testing tradition is still quite solidly established, alternative sources are more frequently being used, and tend to have greater credibility than they did. What still remains for special education, at least in some jurisdictions, is to narrow — hopefully eliminate — the gulf between the conducting of an assessment of an exceptional student and the developing of her program. See *The Gap Between Assessment and Program* page 22.

The Case Study

It is unfortunate that the formal case study is not used in education to the extent it might be. The probable reason is that case studies are thought to take too long to write or to read, and for some, they are difficult to write. Nevertheless a succinct, thorough case study can be one of the most effective tools in an assessment, most especially if the subject's situation has become complicated — as many do — and has attracted the involvement of a variety of personnel, some of whom may not know one another, or have never worked together. Because a case study provides an efficient executive summary, collating information from a number of sources into one document, it can become the principal base from which identification and placement decisions are made, and perhaps even more important, the base from which a student's program is written. There is probably no single element in an assessment procedure which more effectively brings together an exceptional student's history, current status, and needs.

Usually, an educational case study is prepared by the teacher nominally responsible for the student in question. An ideal study is as succinct as possible; it does not make judgmental or evaluative statements but reports fact. For a case study *in education* the following components are most often preferred:

I.   Demographic data
II.   Description of the Educational Issue
III. Family History
IV.   Physical and Health Status
V.   Social and Behaviour Matters
VI.   Supplementary Reports
VII. Assessment Data
VIII. Present Program
IX.   Recommendations

I. For reasons of privacy, the amount of demographic data is usually limited to bare essentials, including the obvious elements like name and address, age, birth date, school and placement, and parents' names.

II. The educational issue is the heart of the study and should give the reader the essence of the situation. Details that expand or explain are usually entered in different sections.

III. Appropriate, useful information about the family is often very helpful but for reasons of privacy, the writer of a case study should err on the side of less rather than more — unless the family situation is, in the writer's opinion, a major factor.

IV. Information about physical development is included only if germane. Where it is not an issue, the case study should state only that.

V. In some case studies, the section on behaviour and social matters will require some detail. The writer of a study, however, must be careful to avoid drama and to stick to relevant facts.

VI. Supplementary reports usually include medical data, reports from other schools or agencies, etc. In some case studies, it suffices to state only that these reports have been made, and then if possible, indicate where the originals may be available.

VII. Assessment data are usually the product of tests. It is important to include them, but often, because of privacy regulations, they may not be available to the writer of a case study. If possible, the writer should try to determine what tests were administered, under whose authority and when. At the very least, the writer should be able to state whether or not tests were administered.

VIII. Since an educational case study is written primarily for other educators, a description of program need not be elaborate. Usually an overview is sufficient.

IX. Recommendations are not usually made if the case study is going forward to a school team or to a committee. (On the other hand, if the study is not going forward, then this section becomes the whole purpose of the activity.)

Immediately following are two sample case studies.

CONFIDENTIAL

I. <u>Carter F-R.</u>   Date:_____12 Dec_____

Address: 123 Street   DOB: 12 Oct/19 xx   Age: 9.2

School: ABC Elem. , XXX, B.C.   Placement: Gr. 3-4

Lives with: Mother ✓ (Judith)   Father ✓ (Stanford)

Writer:_____Distribution:_____

II. Educational Issue: Carter appears to be extremely bright. Teacher nomination, peer nomination and I.Q. test results all match the school's 'gifted' indicators. His parents have declined to offer an opinion. Carter himself insists he is not very intelligent.

By the end of kindergarten, Carter could read fluently and do arithmetic at about the grade three level. He continues to excel in both areas. Carter has an impressive vocabulary and speaks in a very mature, very adult fashion, although he participates during class only when the topic is serious (e.g., world issues, etc.). He has never been seen playing, or smiling, or appearing to be enjoying himself. Several observers have commented that "he is a miniature 40-year old" and that "he's almost not a kid at all". Carter belongs to a chess club and has qualified for inter-provincial competition in an age group one above his own.

In his split grade 3-4 class, Carter leads somewhat of an isolated existence. It is difficult to tell whether this is his decision or not, although any invitations by peers to become involved are invariably declined. As a result, the boy has no friends in the class, and except for a fellow chess player in grade eight, none in the school.

A decision must be taken whether or not to transfer Carter to the self-contained gifted program at XYZ school. In discussions with his teacher, Carter has revealed that he does not see himself as very bright, that he feels deeply insecure, and that he feels no one likes or cares for him. This nine-year-old recently said to his teacher: "I am the saddest person I know."

III. Family History: Carter is the youngest child in an intact family of five. His father is president of a large import-export firm, and travels internationally about half the year. Mother is an opthalmologist with a well-established practice. His two siblings (age 22 and 24) are cum laude university graduates. One is studying for a doctorate; the other has started her own investment service. Carter's principal care-givers have been nannies, none of whom has stayed with the family for more than nine months.

IV. Physical and Health Status: No significant matters; Carter is very healthy.

V. Social and Behaviour Matters: Except for the social behaviour described in II., there are no exceptional matters in Carter's school behaviour. In class he is quiet but not withdrawn, and cooperative but not submissive.

VI. Supplementary Reports: A letter from XXX Academy, a private residential school where Carter was enrolled for two months in grade one, states that he was withdrawn by his parents "by mutual consent". There are no other reports on file.   ➡

VII. Assessment Data: In a board wide achievement test (C.A.T.) administered to the third grade during the week of 21 September, all of Carter's sub-test scores were above the 98th percentile. (See OSR.) Carter was given the WISC-III with the permission of his parents; his full scale score was in the Very Superior range; the verbal score was higher than performance by 2 points. Following the board administered test, Carter's parents had him assessed privately but have declined to share the results.

VIII. Present Program: Carter is in a split grade three-four class. (Officially, he is in grade three.) The program here is very organized and very much individualized, with emphasis on academic achievement. There is plenty of opportunity for enrichment and extra study. The other students in the class are, by and large, bright achievers.

IX. Recommendations: Carter will be presented to IPRC on 7 January. Recommendations to follow. (See OSR.)

Confidential

Divorah H.   Date: Nov. 30

Address: 456 Avenue   DOB: July 7, 19xx   age: 16.4

School: DEF S.S., xxx, Nfld.   Placement: Grade 10

Lives with: Mother — (Shoshona) (CAS group home: See N.L. for address, etc.)
                    Father — (Marty)

Writer_____ Distribution_____

II. Educational Issue: After almost one and a half years in secondary school, Divorah has earned only three credits. (The average, after one year, is eight.) Divorah appears to be entirely capable of academic success if she chooses to be. Unfortunately, her refusal to cooperate, and resistance toward help and guidance, along with missed school time have caused a significant academic lag, particularly where subjects have prerequisites. Because of this complication and because of Divorah's involvement with the CAS and juvenile authorities it is necessary to prepare a special design for the next stage in her school program.

   At the direction of the court, the school principal and the special education department are to develop a limited program of studies for her. She will take two credits at school during the next semester, and complete one via home study. At the end of the semester the court will re-examine Divorah's situation and make further recommendations. In the meantime, she will live in a CAS group home and continue as a ward.

III. Family History: Divorah has one sibling who is 18 and has left school. Her parents are separated; the mother reports that Divorah is the principal cause of the breakup. Mother owns and manages a laundromat. Father is presently unemployed.

➡️

Both parents are alcoholics; they have been "dry" for some time and attend AA. Although the CCAS has investigated allegations of abuse in the home, no proof was ever established. Divorah is an adopted child. She knew this long before her intransigent behaviour surfaced and there has never been any indication that the knowledge has affected her.

IV. *Physical and Health Status:* Because of very mild cerebral palsy, Divorah was late in learning to walk, and until about age eight, continued to have some problems with self-care and personal hygiene. She has a slight limp; her height is somewhat below average; and, although she is believed to be naturally left-handed, she uses her right as the preferred hand because in her words: "It works better". There are no other unusual health matters. Divorah has eyeglasses to correct an astigmatism but does not wear them.

V. *Social and Behavioural Matters:* Until Divorah reached puberty (approx. 13 years) there were no significant and ongoing inappropriate behaviours. After this time, her school record lists consistent misdemeanours, serious breaches of accepted norms of behavior, and regular truancy. The record shows, for example, that when Divorah was in grade eight, her parents were asked 42 times to come to school and remove her for the day. She has been suspended twice this year with the approval of the school board.

In grade nine, the vice-principal caught Divorah selling her Ritalin medication at school. She was given a second chance, but on the next day repeated the offence. Police were called but did not charge her until the third time it occurred. Shortly after, Divorah's mother, who was awarded custody after the separation (during grade eight) took her off the Ritalin. Divorah then ran away. While living on the street she was arrested for a felony; the charge is not disclosed under terms of the Young Offenders Act. In September of this year, Divorah was charged again and spent two months in a detention centre. She is now a ward of the Children's Aid Society and is living in a closely monitored group home.

VI. *Supplementary Reports:* Although there are extensive reports from the police, CAS, and other agencies, these are not available to the school. Medical reports issued during the early grades on the subject of Divorah's cerebral palsy have been removed from the OSR at the parent's request.

VII. *Assessment Data:* Peabody Individual Achievement Test, administered March 24, 19xx (Grade 5): Reading: 82nd percentile   Mathematics: 91st percentile
                    Spelling: 77th percentile   General Information: 51st percentile
There are no other test results available. It is known that CAS has administered several projective tests.

VIII: *Present Program:* Divorah has earned credits in English (Active Drama In The Classroom 111) Social Studies (Elements of Basic Geography 122) and Mathematics (Introductory Basics of Calculus 133). At the beginning of this semester, Divorah was enrolled in four courses (English, Mathematics, Family Studies, and Physical Education). She attended school only one day, was truant for ten days, and then after the arrest was placed in the detention centre. Divorah will not return to DEF Secondary School until the beginning of the next semester on January 18.

IX. *Recommendations:* The special education department in consultation with the School Support Team will make recommendations.

14

Practical Elements of Successful Integration

Prevailing Misconceptions About Integration

1. According to research, integration produces clearly superior outcomes for exceptional students.

Although this claim is regularly put forward, it is not borne out quite so clearly in a careful examination of the literature.*

2. For both exceptional and so-called regular students, the social benefits of an integrated situation are invariably greater than in other situations.

Empirical evidence and research together suggest that social benefits do indeed arise out of integrated situations, but not necessarily because of integration itself. Many other factors are involved. There is considerable evidence however, along with common sense, to suggest that integrated situations offer more realistic and natural opportunities for social development than might be available in some segregated situations.

*For ease of reading, this chapter does not include citations of the research. Readers are referred to the bibliography on page 169.

3. Support for integration among parents and exceptional students themselves is universal and unanimous.

Some parents and students, most notably people whose concerns relate to deafness, learning disabilities and giftedness, argue vigorously for alternative options like specialized settings. Further, it has been shown that the support of parents who favour integration tends to vary in response to the degree to which their particular wishes are fulfilled.

4. Classroom teachers are generally resistant to integration.

Survey research indicates that the vast majority of teachers favour integration and that they become progressively more positive as their experience with it increases. What sometimes appears to be an initial resistance among classroom personnel is more often a reaction against change about which they feel they have not been consulted. Also, evidence suggests that what makes teachers most wary, is lack of what they feel is appropriate and adequate information about students and their exceptionalities.

5. Teacher education fails to prepare teachers for integration.

While this may have been true of pre-service teacher education at one time, it is no longer the case generally. The quality of *in*-service education offered to teachers already in the field, however, continues to be very uneven.

6. Teaching in an integrated classroom requires radically different strategies and methods.

Especially in elementary school, and especially where a student centred approach is taken to instruction, teaching methods usually do not vary in any dramatically significant way. For secondary school situations, especially where the dominant approach is content oriented, or where the instructional approach is teacher-centred, there may be a need to investigate alternatives.

7. The achievement of so-called regular students declines in integrated situations because of the time teachers must devote to the exceptional students.

There is no extensive, clear research evidence to support this claim. Generally, the available research, in fact, refutes the claim, but much of that research can be fairly accused of demonstrating 'Hawthorne Effect'. Empirical evidence shows that declines in achievement are owing to factors that go way beyond the matter of integration.

8. A self-contained, specialized classroom setting does a better job of delivering the necessary and appropriate service.

Although this type of setting may be organized to deliver service effectively and efficiently, whether that is in fact what happens will have more to do with the program and the personnel than with the setting itself. The setting is not a guarantee.

9. Specialized, self-contained environments prepare exceptional students better for employment.

Comparative studies to support this claim are few, so far. What is available generally does not confirm it.

10. Integration is more costly. Or, integration is *less* costly.

Experience has shown that simply offering special education is more costly than either placing exceptional students in custodial environments, or denying them entry into neighbourhood schools. But once a jurisdiction is engaged in offering special education, how the available resources are deployed is an administrative matter. Thus integration can be more costly. It can be less costly too.

11. Inclusive schools demit their "failures" to a school offering self-contained placements.

The experience among inclusive jurisdictions tends to show that such occurrences are extremely rare, including those instances where parents have the option of withdrawing a student from a board and enrolling her in a different one.

12. To be truly successful, integration must be total and absolute.

Experience with integration is still too brief to make such claims. The western country with the longest history of total integration is Italy (since 1971). While Italy reports general success, its system was modified in the late seventies, at the request of parents who were supported by the Supreme Court, to allow for some segregation of exceptional students.

This type of modification appears to be happening in Canada as well. Some districts in the country, which hitherto have followed an inclusive policy in an absolute way, have altered their procedures for a few students who seem to need a more specialized environment, at least temporarily. The Ministry of Education in Ontario, for example, while quite strongly advocating a policy direction toward integration, acknowledges that practically, it may not be in the best interests of all students for the policy to be total and absolute.

For Discussion:
The Case of Erna

Erna's parents have appealed to the court, asking it to order the school board to provide a self-contained class for their daughter. Erna is severely learning disabled and, ironically, was the board's first ever student to be formally identified. That was when she was in grade three and had already repeated grade one and spent an extra year in a split grade two-three class. She then spent grade four and half of grade five in a self-contained class.

Erna is now in secondary school in grade nine. At 16, she is able to read only a very little, and does no math at all. Her battles with her parents, teachers and peers — the latter often physical — are legendary. Erna's counsellor says she is very depressed and quite possibly manic. Her parents believe Erna's suicide threats are serious.

School board policy where Erna lives calls for full integration of all exceptional students. There are no self-contained centres in the entire jurisdiction; all support service is delivered in regular classrooms. This system has been extremely successful since it was introduced three years ago and has wide and enthusiastic support from most faculty and parents. The media have described it several times as a model. Erna's parents however, contend that three years is long enough to demonstrate that this system does not work for their daughter and that her rights are being violated. The young lady herself has said she cannot work or concentrate in a regular classroom. The board contends that a self-contained setting has already proven to be an inappropriate placement for Erna; it would make no difference to her learning in any case, and would likely make her behaviour worse.

Where is Truth?
Problems with Research on Integration

Drawing firm conclusions from studies of human behaviour and achievement and social development requires a great leap of faith for the simple reason that variables in this type of research are so difficult, if not impossible, to control. Note, for example, the famous *"Pygmalion in the classroom"* experiment which has been replicated many times with differing — even opposite — results! (See also, the review by Faust & Ziskin, Page 130.) Studies of educational experience, especially the subject of integration, are particularly susceptible to this weakness. Unless a study is conducted under laboratory conditions — which logically, makes any generalization of the results suspect therefore — the researcher, not to mention the consumer, can only speculate about the reasons for an outcome. This profound weakness makes the generalization of research results on human subjects very difficult, so that educators encountering a study purporting to show the success or failure of integration, or the value or non-value of a strategy, can never be entirely confident that they are dealing with something applicable to their own situations.

The very attempt to control variables in studies of integration creates a paradox. The vast majority of these research projects are conducted on subjects with a similar exceptional characteristic (i.e., on a population of students identified as learning disabled, or physically disabled or gifted, etc.). While the results of such a study may well be illuminating within narrow parameters, what educators would prefer is for that same study to be conducted with a subject group representing a *variety* of exceptionalities, because that is closer to the reality of an integrated classroom. Yet such a design could well mean the variables are not being properly controlled, or at least, that they are not sufficiently controlled to permit confident, firm generalizations!

Research in education under real conditions faces practical barriers too. There are problems in getting access to subjects and situations. Thus the numbers (i.e., the number of students, or teachers, or schools, etc.) are often too small or the subject groups too unique for the results to be truly meaningful — which is one reason why so many research reports conclude by calling for even more research on the same topic.

(Another reason for the call, is that the researchers themselves are acknowledging limitations.) Ironically, despite the veritable flood of literature on integration over the past decade or so, there is still a desperate need for excellent, controlled studies that will permit general conclusions. Even the claim that a "weight of evidence" generally favours one conclusion or another about integration is difficult to accept if one reviews that evidence carefully.

Then there is misapplication of results and data by consumers of the research. It is not at all uncommon for an advocate of one point of view or another to quite blithely use research results on integrating, say, children who have multiple disabilities, to support an argument about integrating, say, children who are autistic.

Nor is credibility and rational discussion enhanced by the number of "gee whiz" reports in the literature, particularly in non-refereed journals and in newspaper columns, where cases of (usually) successful integration are glowingly described, creating by implication, the impression that there is no other way.

Unfortunately, experience — empirical evidence — on which educators quite rightly place a great deal of faith, often suffers from similar problems, most especially the unrepeatable uniqueness of each situation. And when the drawbacks in generalizing research and experience are compounded by the influence of personal opinion and philosophy, along with the ever-present trap of self-fulfilling prophecy, it is little wonder that when educators look for concrete support on matters regarding integration, they find a lot of confusion, contradiction, and fuzzy abstraction.

Where Research and Experience Agree

Fortunately, at least some credibility and practical value for educators can usually be extracted when research results on integration dovetails with practical experience: when both point to the same conclusions a significant number of times. Following here, are some points on which research and experience seem to find some common ground. Interestingly, these are all points that the literature on integration has advanced for some time in articles that do not report studies, but instead make arguments on the basis of common sense.

Integration in Secondary Schools: Not an Easy Matter

Integration in this setting encounters all the issues of every other setting plus some that are special. For one, a secondary school is governed by the pervasive notion of "standards" or "credit". Society, much more than for elementary schools, interprets certifications granted by the secondary panel as confirmation of certain levels of academic competence. For teachers in secondary school, accommodating this goal with the goals of special education looms as a very real challenge. The challenge is equally real for many exceptional students.

The traditional organization and curriculum orientation of secondary schools make it very difficult for teachers to implement the features that so frequently prove successful for exceptional students: intense individualization, in-class support and consultation, for example, and most of all, student-centred instruction. Case studies of successful integration at the secondary level generally illustrate organizational models that are quite radically different from the structure that these schools have known for a very long time. However, research consistently points to secondary school teachers' resistance to classroom methods that are not essentially teacher-centred, and to models that diverge from the traditional subject groupings.

The two most popular approaches to integration in the secondary school are the collaboration-with-the regular-teacher model, in which special education personnel work with exceptional students and their regular class teachers, and the home-base model, in which the exceptional students take at least one period a day in a credit course given by a special education teacher. While there is limited evidence to support a clear preference for either model, the latter seems to have somewhat of an edge. Even so, irrespective of whatever strategy is preferred, it has yet to be confirmed that total integration can succeed at the secondary school level without fundamental changes in both the structure and the very concept of the secondary school itself.

✦ Educators with experience in integration insist that the process must be treated on a *by-case basis*. The fact that one exceptional student integrates successfully into a regular classroom is no guarantee that another will, even if the previous conditions are duplicated precisely.

✦ Not just the professional ability of the classroom teacher, but the *professionalism* of the teacher: his willingness and active support, is pivotal to the success of integration. Active intervention and facilitation by the significant adults in a classroom have been shown to have a major, positive effect. This is especially the case if an exceptional student is integrated into a regular classroom after her primary class years, if it is a new experience for that regular class, and if the exceptional student has had very limited experience with regular classroom environments.

✦ What has always gone under the rubric of "good teaching" (admittedly, a phrase that is hard to define — except for those who benefit from it) applies to an integrated class in the same way as it does to any class. Most teachers find that the strategies and techniques and modifications and inspirations that have always produced effective instruction and management in their classrooms, i.e., the *art* of teaching, work equally well in an integrated situation. There are adjustments to be made when an exceptional student joins a class, but these tend to become instances of wholesale change in only two cases: one, when the integrated student's behaviour is more extreme than can be accommodated in the class *and* continues that way over an extended period; two, when the teacher's response to a newly enrolled student is more exaggerated than is warranted.

✦ The availability, and most certainly the quality of resource support can be vital factors. An effective teaching assistant, adequate supplies of materials, and a setting that can be modified to meet unique demands are important to successful integration — just as they are to any classroom situation. The role of administration is illuminated in this issue. Recent research along with extensive experience teaches that in addition to providing inspiration (on which administration seems to

have concentrated in the early days of integration) the leadership must also be facilitative and practical if integration is to succeed.

✦ The earlier that integration begins for students, the more likely it will prove best for all parties. Students who begin their schooling in integrated situations tend to regard them as natural reflections of the way the world works. By the same token, integration that is established arbitrarily, when students are older, often has a number of barriers to overcome.

✦ Students of all ages are generally far more accepting of differences among humans than many adults are prepared to believe, although the attitude of significant adults is still a very important formative factor.

✦ Once an exceptional student with very noticeable behaviours is integrated into a regular classroom, most of the time the behaviours soon tend to modify and become more like the norm for that classroom.

✦ There are turning points (a cynic might call them crisis points) in the chronology of integration cases. At around grade three, for example, there is usually a major instructional shift in regular classrooms as students move from "learning to read" into "reading to learn". This change may bring about a complete rethinking of the approach to some exceptional students. It may also have an effect on the student's self-esteem and sense of belonging. Other turning points often occur at early adolescence. At this point in students' emotional and physical development, any fragility in an integration situation might intensify. Another very important change occurs when students enter high school. Not only is there a completely new setting to adjust to, but the organization (e.g., rotary timetable) is wholly different, and often, much more difficult for some exceptional students to manage.

✦ The risk of unintentionally creating hidden or subtle segregation in an integrated classroom is very real. It seems to occur most frequently when resources are deployed directly and exclusively to the exceptional student(s) in the class and only minimally or not at all to the

> "There are no models."
> —Phil DeFrancesco (Hamilton-Wentworth, ON, Roman Catholic School Board, praised internationally for its success with full integration)

rest of the class. When this happens, an exceptional student may well be enrolled in a regular class, but will tend to lead an almost separate existence.

Certain settings seem more likely to provoke this outcome. One is the wall-less large room (often called "pod") in elementary schools, where several classes are grouped. Such a setting is extremely busy, and when teachers take advantage of the flexibility and fluid movement it invites, the temptation to turn over responsibility for an exceptional student to a teaching assistant, is very strong. Another setting is the secondary school which uses a floating team of resource support. It is not difficult to appreciate that a teacher presenting complicated, curriculum-specific material that is new to all students, may feel it is advantageous to make the resource team responsible for some exceptional students.

Practical Classroom Matters

If successful integration is best achieved on a by-case basis, for the simple reason that exceptional students are like all students — they are each unique and individual — then it follows logically that there can be no universal model for instruction, no how-to-instruct cookbook. For every class, a teacher must develop an instructional style that is appropriate to her nature, and to the needs of every student, not just the exceptional ones. Although the special needs of the latter can have a strong impact on that style, fortunately, the most effective way to respond to them is entirely within the context of simple 'good teaching'. What is appropriate style for instructing exceptional students, most of the time, is the same as what is appropriate for instructing all students. There may well be no models or cookbooks, but there are basic, universal principles.

The Principle of Structure

Structure in a classroom is that sense of organization, both explicit and implicit, created by the teacher so that the decks can be cleared for learning and development. In a sense, the more effective the structure, the more it is invisible. When a classroom is effectively organized, there is a feeling of confidence in the students that this is a place of purpose and value, a place that makes reasonable demands for good reason, and a place in which it is safe

For Discussion: The Case of Alessandro

Recently, a psychiatrist revised her initial diagnosis of Alessandro from "severely" to "moderately" autistic. 'Sandro is eleven and a half; he does not speak and uses only a few manual signs. Trials with a symbolics-type communication board and with 'assisted communication' were judged failures a year ago, although a teaching assistant (one of his staunchest advocates) in 'Sandro's self-contained class insists they should be tried again in light of his apparent development.

His behaviour has indeed changed. 'Sandro no longer has to be physically restrained from running head down at the wall — or at the nearest person — when he is frustrated. He no longer spins in dervish fashion until he drops; nor does he run away when the opportunity is available. But he still rocks his head from side to side for long periods; continues to be obsessed by spinning objects and, if excited, he will stuff things into his mouth and try to swallow them.

In September, 'Sandro will be enrolled into a regular grade six class. His teacher will have had one year's experience. Last year she spent three months as a substitute in 'Sandro's special class (in a different school). What will be her grade six class next year has had one experience with integration; a seriously mentally handicapped girl was enrolled for three months but the experience was very discouraging. Because of it, three children — including the girl herself — were withdrawn from the school by their parents.

'Sandro's soon-to-be grade six teacher must make two decisions: should 'Sandro's enrolment be delayed until mid-September? (The principal has offered this.) Should 'Sandro be included in the traditional four-day/night, grade six field trip to an outdoor education centre, in the last week of September? This is a yearly highlight for grade six. The teacher is not obliged to include 'Sandro. The teaching assistant will be going on the trip along with five parents, but 'Sandro's mother is unable to volunteer.

to make a mistake. When classroom procedures are so automatic they are generally unnoticed, there develops a kind of invisible momentum in which students become caught up, and are moved intrinsically to learn and to manage their own behaviour.

To have an effective structure, a teacher must of course adjust expectations and procedures to the age and grade level of her students. After that, it becomes a matter of establishing a reasonable, achievable set of organizational principles. To do so often takes a great deal of effort in establishing what may seem, in the grand scheme of things, inconsequential matters: e.g., classroom entering behaviours, note-taking and note-keeping, use of independent work time, of work centres, etc. Yet without a structure established for them, students — especially exceptional students — tend to flounder for lack of direction, or expend their available cognitive energies establishing their own notions of structure. Many simply permit the seeming disorganization to carry them away into impulsivity or learned helplessness. On the other hand, when a teacher narrows the organizational focus for his students, and makes it unnecessary for them to "get it all together" on their own, they are more able to apply their cognitive strengths to learning and self-management. Effective classroom organization is beneficial in any situation; in an integrated one it is essential.

The Principle of Encouragement

Encouragement is something all good teachers offer as a matter of course. It is encouragement, and all the other affective processes that are part of it, which helps to elevate teaching and learning above mechanics and techniques into dynamics. Encouragement infuses the way a teacher plans for her students, the way she organizes, the way she evaluates. With some exceptional students it may even be the only arrow in the teacher's quiver.

Moreover, encouragment is symbolic. It demonstrates a teacher's belief that, no matter what the apparent capacities of her students, she at least, believes they are capable of developing, of moving forward. Encouragement is an affirmation of the teacher's faith in a student's potential, and creates an impetus for students to believe in themselves and work toward achieving that potential. In an integrated class, encouragement from the teacher is contagious, and moves students to support one another. It can, in fact, be the glue that holds the whole class together, that makes it the kind of unit that is greater than the sum of its individual parts.

The Principle of Time

One of the serendipitous results of universal education for people with special needs was the discovery that, even though they may have a disability or handicap, there is no ceiling to their ability. Mentally handicapped and learning disabled people especially, are capable of much more than everyone used to believe. All that is necessary for many of them is more *time*.

The following equation expresses it best.

$$\text{quality of instruction} \times \left(\frac{\text{time spent}}{\text{time needed}}\right) = \text{degree of learning}$$

Putting numbers in the equation helps illuminate its meaning.

For example, if 'quality of instruction' is 5, and 'time spent' is 1, and 'time needed' is 5, then the 'degree of learning' will be 1.

$$5 \times (1/5) = 1$$

But what happens if the available time ('time spent') is increased: brought closer to the actual 'time needed'? In fact, what happens if the 'time spent' is the *same* as the 'time needed'?

$$5 \times (5/5) = 5$$

The degree of learning quintuples! Granted, these numbers are arbitrary, but they illustrate a point. If students are given sufficient time to acquire a concept or skill or technique, the degree of learning will — other factors being equal — increase. Given the reality that many exceptional students take longer to learn things, it follows that their education must take this into account. Of course, *time*, or rather, lack of it, is an irritant to which teachers of integrated classes point with regularity, and not without justification. Fortunately, most students identified exceptional, receive a modified program; they are, in a sense, freed (along with their teachers) in most cases from the coverage stipulations of the curriculum in order that this program can be followed. Usually therefore, a response to the time issue lies in this modification.

The Principle of Practice

A logical correlate of time is *practice*, for the need for repeated trials, constant reinforcement — call it 'drill' — is, in most cases, why available time is so important in the first place. Practice is also interwoven with structure, for one of the reasons that structure is so crucial is to create opportunity and establish a framework for regular practice. Also, notwithstanding the above, it has long been established both empirically and by research that practice is essential for learning. It is more than reasonable to assume then, that if exceptional students learn differently — the majority with greater difficulty — they will likely require more practice.

Very often, recognizing the need for practice requires an adjustment in attitude and approach for the teacher. Teachers have experienced success in school, and may well find repetition and drill tedious. For themselves and presumably for their students, going over and over the same ground has, naturally, limited appeal. Still, no procedure has yet been found that will equal the effect of repeating and repeating something until it is learned, until it has become part of the students' automatic repertoire.

> "The experience we've had now with full integration has been most instructive. For one thing, we've learned it's easier than we thought; for another, it's good for just about all the kids involved, and frankly, we should have done it years ago. But we're learning something that's troublesome as well. A few kids are not better off; in fact, they're much worse off. Common sense told us that would happen and the experience confirms it. However, somewhere along the road we lost our freedom of speech on the issue of integration. It's dead wrong for some kids, but you don't dare try to say that publicly."
>
> — *Bob L., principal in a Canadian jurisdiction with full integration.*

Other Practical Matters in Successful Integration

Understanding An Exceptionality

It is important for teachers and teaching assistants to understand the nature of a particular exceptionality when they encounter it for the first — or even second, third or fourth — time. Notwithstanding the accusation that a teacher therefore risks seeing the student only in terms of the exceptionality, it simply makes sense that the art of teaching a student who has, say, a learning disability, will likely be far more productive if the teacher understands the effects that a learning disability can have on a person.

This kind of understanding is crucial in determining goals and designing instruction for the student. It also goes a long way toward erasing the discomfort that affects many teachers when they first receive an exceptional student in their regular classrooms. A useful first step therefore, for teachers, is always to review information about an exceptionality. The chapter structure of *Special Education In Canadian Schools* is designed to accommodate this step.

Importance of Preparing the "Regular" Students

Just as the development of a teacher's own awareness about an exceptional student is important, so is awareness on the part of that student's peers. This is especially so if a class is receiving an exceptional student for the first time. It is doubly important if the student's needs will at first appear quite pronounced. There are some who take the position that a teacher should say nothing at all to a receiving class because drawing attention to special needs will only serve to exaggerate them. This position may have merit in situations where a class has been an integrated one from the beginning of its schooling; in fact, boards of education where full integration has been common practice for some time, say that advance preparation soon becomes utterly unnecessary. However, where experience with full integration has been more limited, there is sufficient empirical evidence to support a preference for preparing students ahead of time. Also, since survey research continues to expose a surprisingly high degree of ignorance in the public at large about special needs, it is reasonable to assume that the same ignorance may prevail among students as well. And what better time and place to begin enlightenment?

Naturally, preparing a class with this kind of information will require all of a teacher's tact and diplomacy, and should only be carried out with the permission — and the help, if possible

— of the exceptional student's parents, and ideally, if it can be done, with the help of the exceptional student too. If it is possible, teachers should avail themselves of the helpful material designed by support groups, precisely for this purpose.

The Matter of Collaboration

The introduction of special education into the wider world of education brought along an impressive array of new material, alternative strategies, administrative arrangements, and a broad range of expertise. When special education tended to be, in its early days, concentrated more or less in discrete units, somewhat separate from the mainstream, these specialties too, were frequently set apart. But the integration of exceptional students in the mainstream has accelerated the need to integrate these specialities at the same time. How teachers regard this special expertise, and how they use it, is significant to the success of integration. Sometimes the accommodation is not as smooth as it could be.

An essential professional behaviour in many teachers – that feeling of responsibility for and deep commitment to "my class" and "my students" — sometimes precludes the kind of collaboration, the sharing of responsibility, that is best for all concerned. While teachers will readily turn over responsibility for a particularly knotty problem to a so-called expert, they are often less disposed to work *with* that person toward a mutual objective. A similar phenomenon often occurs with new strategies. It is not unusual for teachers to adopt alternative strategies on the premise that a strategy by itself may provide the answer to a particular matter whereas in fact, any new strategy is only effective if it is integrated into the teacher's established, natural style.

What is necessary for integration to succeed, is that the teacher see herself as the central role player on a collaborative team. No classroom teacher can be expected to have all the answers, but when an answer comes from outside, it can be truly useful only if it is applied in the context that the teacher herself has established. For the sake of the exceptional student, who is after all, one of "my students" too, the teacher must continue to be the key.

A Space In The Daily Schedule

The research and experience which together show that teaching styles and strategies in an integrated class differ very little from those in any other class, have also suggested the importance of arranging a piece of time in the school day when teacher and students have an opportunity to catch their breath, so to speak. The pace, the demands, the work, the stresses, the shifts and changes that occur regularly during the course of a school day — all these take a toll on everyone. Among the realities all teachers and all students face is the fact that at the end of practically every school day, there is an accumulation of loose ends, of work begun but not completed, of possible misunderstandings and misapprehensions, of lessons that need practice and reinforcement, of matters that need attending to. When a class has exceptional students in it, this reality is often intensified, if only because of the extra demands of their special needs. This intensification, many teachers acknowledge, is really where the difference lies between teaching an integrated class and one that is not.

It makes sense, therefore, to structure the school day so that there is a piece of time in it when many of the loose ends can be tied, and the ruffled feathers smoothed; a time when much of the natural fragmentation of the day can be resolved so that the very next day starts on a more solid footing. Ideally then, teachers will organize the school day so that such a piece of time is available.

In elementary schools, experience suggests the end of the school day is the preferred time. In secondary schools, with the demands of the individualized rotary timetable, it is not so easy to make an arbitrary choice like this, but in the case of exceptional students, if at least one course is established as the students' "home-base course" or "strategies course", the time can be available here.

What happens in this time is that, for the exceptional students, and quite likely other students too, the extra things: the reinforcements and re-explanations and reminders — and enrichments, if those are the case — get done. Given that so much of the teaching-learning dynamic, whether students are exceptional or not, depends on the amount of time and practice and opportunity available, it is logical to make space for it in the daily schedule.

In the End, a Matter of Common Sense

For most exceptional students, integration into regular classes is an entirely workable placement, one that is beneficial to all parties. But a key word is *most*. Exceptional students, like any other students, cannot be lumped together in a way that denies their unique, individual characteristics. Because *most* exceptional students thrive in integrated regular settings, it does not mean therefore, that *all* do. Research points to this fact. Experience teaches it. And common sense underlines the reality of it.

Not that total integration of every exceptional student should be rejected as an impossible goal. Rather, it should be seen as a goal to be achieved through logical analysis of every exceptional student's situation. It means doing for every student, on a by-case basis, what makes the most sense.

What makes sense, first of all, is that for a few exceptional students — and the maturing of special education makes clear that it is only a few — their needs are so special that they require very special resources. To integrate these students without the immediate availability of the resources may well put them — and others — at risk, not just educationally and socially, but even physically. This reality triggers yet another. Although many educators and parents prefer to regard fiscal issues as a morally inferior encumbrance to be dealt with at arm's length, what makes sense is that without financial support, there would be no special education at all. It may well be, therefore, that the cost of providing highly specialized resources means that, sensibly, they often have to be provided in a specialized environment for the simple reason that to duplicate them universally, potentially drains away the very support that makes special education possible.

> "One thing I learned was that integration doesn't just happen by itself. You should have seen little Francis. Every day — I mean every day — he'd eat his lunch all by himself and then lean against the wall and watch the older kids. They never played with him, never even asked him. It broke my heart to see it."
>
> —Maha M. (student teacher)

What also makes sense is, that for some exceptional students, a more contained environment is not only in their best interests, but in the best interests of other students, of families, and of educators and support staff. While the majority of students, exceptional and otherwise, thrive in a regular classroom placement, there are some for whom a specialized placement is the only sensible choice. Indeed it is impossible to avoid the point that, for a very few students, choosing anything other than a special placement may restrict their potential and even deny their rights. However, this does not mean that such a placement is forever. One of the unfortunate elements in the polemic surrounding integration is the implicit doctrine that a special placement is permanent — even terminal! In a common sense view, this is simply not the case. In Canada, the recognition of parents' and students' wishes, and the professionalism of educators guarantees that cases are regularly re-evaluated, and when change is warranted, it happens.

Finally, common sense dictates the reality that integration will only succeed if there is effort from all parties. Students, exceptional and otherwise, have a vital role to play if only in acting naturally. From parents there must be cooperation, collaboration, and from time to time, an essential ingredient: compromise. Administration must facilitate; its role must range from the loftiness of inspiration and leadership to the nitty-gritty of making day-to-day things possible. And at the centre of it all is the classroom teacher. Ultimately, after all the available resources are pried loose and all the paperwork is filed, after all the consulting expertise is delivered, all the objectives established and the strategies decided, it is still the teacher who will make the final difference.

Appendix A

Special Education Legislation in Canada's Provinces and Territories

Alberta

The School Act in Alberta is currently under active review. This act states that a student who is determined to need special education is "entitled to have access to a special education program". Also, the Individual's Right To Protection Act in Alberta refers to the equal rights of all persons, regardless of physical characteristics. The province does not however, have specific mandatory legislation which directs schools to provide special education.

British Columbia

The legislation regarding special education in the province is permissive. The Public Schools Act and Regulations (presently under active review) are generally interpreted to mean that school boards have an option in providing special education or not providing it, although it is widely recognized that the boards offer special education at a rate and level greater than what the legislation requires. The Human Rights Code in the province promotes social and educational discrimination and promotes placement in the least restrictive environment. The Code, at this point, does not have the force of law but it is very persuasive in guiding educators in their decisions.

Manitoba

In 1984, the province mandated the provision of special education services by school boards. Preparation for this madating had been going on for several years prior to 1984.

New Brunswick

The province has mandatory legislation for special education, and to date, goes farther than any other Canadian province on the issue of class placement. In 1986 the province revised the Provincial Schools Act by eliminating the Auxiliary Classes Act and mandating the integration of exceptional students into regular classrooms. New Brunswick continues to participate in APSEA (see page 149).

Newfoundland

Newfoundland has mandatory legislation which was passed in 1979. School boards are required to provide special education or to purchase service elsewhere in the province or in Canada. Newfoundland particpates in APSEA.

Nova Scotia

The province has mandatory legislation which predates that in most of the country. While there continues to be disagreement as to just how mandatory it was, "Regulation 7(c)" by Order-In-Council issued in 1973, required boards of education to provide special education service. Subsequent revisions and additions to the legislation have established a zero-reject policy in the province. Nova Scotia participates in APSEA.

Ontario

Mandatory legislation was passed in 1980 in Ontario, to become fully effective in 1985. Regarded as the most stringent in Canada, it is at the very least, the most complex. (See Weber (1993) *Special Education In Ontario Schools.*) In 1991, the provincial government announced consultation on a potential legislative change which would require "almost all" exceptional students to be placed in "local community schools". Three years later the legislation had still not passed owing partly to fierce debate over who — educators or parents — determines "almost", and whether "community" means "neighbourhood".

Prince Edward Island

There is no mandatory legislation in PEI but the Department of Education follows a policy which holds that exceptional students should be treated non-categorically, and should be educated with their regular peers. Prince Edward Island participates in APSEA.

Quebec

The province of Quebec adopted a policy of equal opportunity for students with special needs in 1978. The following year saw a policy promoting integration. Quebec's Charter of Rights and Freedoms declares the right to universality in education, and in the Rights of the Handicapped Act (1978) prescribes specific programs that can be offered in special education.

Saskatchewan

The province passed mandatory legislation in 1978. Although integration is not specifically mandatory by legislation, the province makes clear in its policy manual that integration is a preferred choice of placement.

Territories

Both Yukon and Northwest Territories have mandatory legislation, follow a zero-reject policy, and officially avoid the use of categories.

The Atlantic Provinces Special Education Authority (APSEA)

Organizational Structure

The Authority is governed by a Board of Directors, three from each of the Atlantic Provinces, with a Deputy Minister of Education from each province in permanent membership. Two additional members from each province are appointed by the Lieutenant-Governor-in-Council for two year terms.

Programs and Services

APSEA supports a service delivery system which makes it possible for each child to receive an appropriate educational program designed to meet his or her individual needs.

The service delivery system includes a variety of educational settings and support for pupils who can be successfully integrated or partially integrated into the public school system. Integration, to a large extent, depends on the individual needs of each pupil, the level of family support, and the availability of support service within the child's home community.

Provision has been made by the Authority for individual provinces to purchase from APSEA those educational programs and services which will best meet the needs of persons who are visually impaired, hearing handicapped, learning disabled.

Provisions are also made for francophone pupils by purchase of appropriate service from some schools in Quebec.

There are two major categories of service offered by APSEA:

(a) on-campus — in resource centres;

(b) off-campus — through the resource centres to communities and schools in the individual provinces. (For a description of services see below)

Superintendent (and office of APSEA)
Atlantic Provinces Special Education Authority
P.O. Box 578, Halifax, N.S. B3J 2S9

Atlantic Provinces Special Education Authority
Resource Centre for the Visually Impaired
5940 South Street, Halifax, N.S. B3H 1S6

Atlantic Provinces Special Education Authority
Resource Centre for the Hearing Handicapped
P.O. Box 308, Amherst, N.S. B4H 3Z6

APSEA Resource Centre for the Hearing Impaired

The roots of this Centre are in the Halifax School For The Deaf where education of the deaf began in 1856. This school was closed in 1961 and moved to a new facility in Amherst, Nova Scotia. It was renamed the Interprovincial School for the Deaf and operated under the joint sponsorship of Nova Scotia and New Brunswick. In 1975 the Centre became one of the two resource centres within APSEA established by the Handicapped Persons Education Act.

Programs Offered

Preschool Programs

Programs are provided for hearing impaired children between the ages of 0 and 5 years. The program is family centred, with emphasis on a counsellor working with parents to provide support and expertise to create an appropriate language environment in the home.

Itinerant/Tutorial Support

These services are provided to hearing impaired students who are able to learn in a public school setting with the assistance of special equipment or special help. The services offered include assessment, itinerant/tutorial help to a maximum of five hours per week, classroom FM equipment, consultation, a visit by educational audiologists, and workshops for school personnel.

Day Classes

Day classes are established in various communities, enabling many hearing impaired students to remain at home and still receive an education. The classes are taught by trained teachers of the deaf, in some cases with the assistance of paraprofessionals.The students are integrated into the regular program as much as possible.

On-Campus

At the residential school in Amherst, students attend complete academic programs at the elementary, junior high and high school levels. Some are enrolled in programs for students with multiple handicaps. There is also a program for deaf-blind students, and a vocational program for technical-vocational education

Admissions

To be eligible for service, a pupil must be diagnosed by an audiologist as having a hearing loss which interferes with the development of language, resulting in educational delay. The pupil must be identified by the school district for referral in consultation with the parent or guardian. Referrals for preschoolers come from parents, clinics and public health nurses.

Residential School Placement

Placement in the residential school is considered when:

(a) a complete assessment has been conducted;

(b) the individual has not demonstrated progress in the local community after extensive collaborative effort between the school district and APSEA;

(c) a suitable educational provision, as determined by the Centre and the referring district or unit in accordance with its mandate, is not available to the individual in the district of residence.

Teacher Education

This is a July to June program preparing teachers to work in either French or English with hearing impaired students. It is offered in cooperation with the Université de Moncton and leads to a Master of Education Degree from that institution.

APSEA Resource Centre for the Visually Impaired

Although the roots of this Centre go back to the original Halifax School for the Blind, it has been part of the four province APSEA agreement since its establishment in 1975, and serves visually impaired children and youth aged 0 to 21.

Programs Offered

Preschool

This service is designed to provide home-based programs for visually impaired children before they begin school. The programs may include such elements as consulting visits or tutorial services or a preschool program or materials from the Centre's library, or a combination of these. There is an emphasis on multidisciplinary cooperation and on consultation with parents or guardians to determine realistic goals for the child.

Off-Campus

The variety of programs and services include:
  (a) an integrated school program provided by an itinerant teacher, for school-aged visually impaired pupils who can function successfully in a regular school setting.
  (b) a consultant service to help school officials provide appropriate programs.
  (c) a tutoring program
  (d) an orientation and mobility program
  (e) an extensive library service
  (f) an equipment and materials lending service (for items like low vision aids, braillers, etc.)
  (g) other consulting services.

On-Campus

Visually impaired students between the ages of five and twenty-one may be eligible for admission to Sir Frederick Fraser School. This residential school operates a junior department for students aged five to twelve. The intermediate department is for pupils ten to fourteen, and the senior for ages fourteen to twenty-one. There are also junior special and intermediate special programs for students who are developmentally delayed as well as visually impaired.

Residential School Placement

Placement in the Sir Frederick Fraser School is considered when:
  1) a school district or unit requests the service, and
  2) the student has been diagnosed as legally blind or partially sighted, and
  3) an assessment has been completed by the Centre in consultation with the district or other agencies, and
  4) the student has not shown the expected progress in the local community after extensive collaborative effort by the district and APSEA, and
  5) a suitable educational provision, as determined by the Centre and the referring district in accordance with its mandate, is not available in the district where the student resides.

The final decision to end a student's placement in a residential program is made by the Centre in consultation with the parents or guardian, and the school district.

APSEA Residential School Placement for School Age Learning Disabled Pupils

In recognition of the fact that that there are some situations in which severely learning disabled pupils cannot be provided for by the public system, APSEA, in 1980, authorized the first extension of its services to provide a program of residential schooling for such pupils. Generally, these students are enrolled at Bridgeway Academy in Dartmouth, N.S., or at Landmark School in Wolfville, N.S., both independent schools.

Eligibility For Placement

  1) The student must be identified by the school district or unit for referral to APSEA, and
  2) appears emotionally stable and is not handicapped in a sensory or physical way, and
  3) possesses at least average cognitive ability, but whose achievement is not commensurate with expectations in relation to ability. Further, the student has extreme difficulty in functioning within an age-appropriate curriculum/grade placement, and

4) has not shown the expected improvement after a trial period in a comprehensive remedial program at the local school or district or unit level, and

5) is twelve to sixteen years of age at time of entry, and

6) meets the entrance requirements of the residential school.

In the case of applicants who are being presented for admission to the APSEA residential program for severely learning disabled students, the referral is first made to the learning disabilities section of the Department of Education, for review.

Legislation in U.S.A. Public Law 94-142

This law (The Education For All Handicapped Children Act) was passed in 1975 and has subsequently been revised as the "Individuals with Disabilities Education Act".

Its major provisions include:

☐ a requirement that all children be screened to identify needs;

☐ a guarantee of free education;

☐ a stipulation that the student must be placed in the least restrictive environment that is appropriate;

☐ due process for parents and guardians; they have the right to consent regarding assessment, identification, and placement, as well as appeal rights;

☐ confidentiality;

☐ a requirement that parents (or surrogate) must be consulted prior to any decision;

☐ a specification that individual education plans (IEPs) must be developed for all exceptional students; (The IEPs must include entry levels, long and short term goals, strategies for instruction strategies and evaluation.)

☐ a requirement for appropriate teacher training.

The Council For Exceptional Children

The Council For Exceptional Children (CEC) is the largest international professional organization devoted to improving educational opportunities and practice for exceptional individuals. It was established in 1922. In 1968 a Canadian office opened to coordinate CEC activities here.

CEC members are teachers, parents, administrators, teacher educators and student teachers, and professionals from related services.

CEC has seventeen specialized divisions which provide additional focus on particular aspects of special education. Each has a leading publication in its field. The divisions are:

• Division for Physical and Health Disabilities (DPHD)
• Council of Administrators of Special Education (CASE)
• Council for Children With Behaviour Disorders (CCBD)
• Division on Mental Retardation and Developmental Disabilities (CEC-MRDD)
• Division for Children with Communication Disorders (DCCD)
• Division for Learning Disabilities (DLD)
• Division of Visual Handicaps (DVH)
• The Association for the Gifted (TAG)
• Teacher Education Division (TED)
• Division for Early Childhood (DEC)
• Council for Educational Diagnostic Services (CEDS)
• Technology and Media Division (TAM)
• Division of Career Development and Transition (DCDT)
• Division for Research (CEC-DR)
• CEC Pioneers Division (CEC-PD)
• Division for Culturally and Linguistically Diverse Exceptional Learners (DDEL)
• Division of International Special Education and Services (DISES)

CEC Policy on Inclusive Schools and Community Settings (Adopted by the Delegate Assenbly, 1993)

CEC believes all children, youth, and young adults with disabilities are entitled to a free and appropriate education and/or services that lead to an adult life characterized by satisfying relations with others, independent living, productive engagement in the community, and participation in society at large. To achieve such outcomes, there must exist for all children, youth, and young adults a rich variety of early intervention, educational, and vocational program options and experiences. Access to these programs and experiences should be based on individual educational need and desired outcomes. Furthermore, students and their families or guardians, as members of the planning team, may recommend the placement, curriculum option, and the exit document to be pursued.

CEC believes that a continuum of services must be available for all children, youth, and young adults. CEC also believes that the concept of inclusion is a meaningful goal to be pursued in our schools and communities. In addition, CEC believes children, youth, and young adults with disabilities should be served whenever possible in general education classrooms in inclusive neighbourhood schools and community settings. Such settings should be strengthened and supported by an infusion of specially trained personnel and other appropriate supportive practices according to the individual needs of the child.

Policy Implications

Schools

In inclusive schools, the building administrator and staff with assistance from the special education administration should be primarily responsible for the education of children, youth, and young adults with disabilities. The adminstrator(s) and other school personnel must have available to them appropriate support and technical asistance to enable them to fulfill their responsibilities. Leaders in state/provincial and local goverments must redefine rules and regulations as necessary, and grant school personnel greater authority to make decisions regarding curriculum, materials, instructional practice, and staffing patterns. In return for greater autonomy, the school administrator and staff should establish high standards for each child and youth and should be held accountable for his or her progress toward outcomes.

Communities

Inclusive schools must be located in inclusive communities; therefore CEC invites all educators, other professionals, and family members to work together to create early intervention, education, and vocational programs and experiences that are collegial, inclusive and responsive to the diversity of children, youth and young adults. Policy makers at the highest level of state/provincial and local governments, as well as school administration, also must support inclusion in the educational reforms they espouse. Further, the policy makers should fund programs in nutrition, early intervention, health care, parent education, and other social support programs that prepare all children, youth, and young adults to do well in school. There can be no meaningful school reform, nor inclusive schools, without funding of these key prerequisites. As important, there must be interagency agreements and collaboration with local governments and business to help prepare students to assume a constructive role in an inclusive community.

Professional Development

Finally, state/provincial departments of education, local educational districts, and colleges and universities, must provide high-quality preservice and continuing professional development experiences that prepare all general educators to work effectively with children, youth, and young adults representing a wide range of abilities and disabilities, experiences, cultural and linguistic backgrounds, attitudes and expectations. Moreover, special educators should be trained with an emphasis on their roles in inclusive schools and community settings. They also must learn the importance of establishing ambitious goals for their students and of using appropriate means of monitoring the progress of children, youth, and young adults.

Appendix B

Some Assessment Instruments Popular in Canada

The Wechsler Intelligence Scale For Children - Third Edition **(1991)** ("The WISC-Three") The Psychological Corporation.

Educators in Canada are very familiar with the Wechsler intelligence tests, likely because they have been by far the most popular instruments used to obtain an I.Q. Score. The original Wechsler Intelligence Scale For Children (WISC) was last significantly revised in 1974 (the WISC-R) and this version is still used in some boards. The most recent edition is the WISC-III (usually called the "WISC-Three"). Excluding the Coding sub test, 73% of the WISC-R is retained in original or slightly modified form in the WISC-III.

Although the manual for the test states that the instrument is intended for use with people aged 6 years O months through 16 years 11 months, it is not uncommon for the test to be used with students who are older or younger. (Adult and older students should theoretically be tested on the WAIS, the Wechsler Adult Intelligence Scale, and younger children on the WPPSI, the Wechsler Pre-Primer Scale of Intelligence.)

The WISC-R enjoyed significant credibility as a clinical and diagnostic tool and it is believed the WISC-III will have the same experience. Reliability and validity coefficients are high; it is particularly well standardized, and can produce some useful diagnostic information. The testing time is approximately 1½ hours, and the test is administered individually.

Test results give three overall scores: *Verbal Scale, Performance Scale*, and *Full Scale*. The Verbal Scale depends a great deal on vocabulary, verbal reasoning and general information, and is much more closely correlated with classroom activities and teaching than the Performance Scale which is much more closely related to visual and perceptual reasoning and to motor activity. *The Full Scale Score* is what is generally referred to as one's I.Q. (Although this is an improper way to express it. There is no sound evidence that anything such as an I.Q. exists, and professionals will always refer to this number by what it really is: an *I.Q. Test Score*.) It is usually irregular for classroom teachers to administer a WISC, but they may receive results. Ideally, the teachers will be given the sub test results as well as the Full Scale, Verbal, and Performance Scores, for these may have diagnostic information on which a plan of remediation can be based.

The Verbal Scale is made up of six sub-tests.

Subtest	What It Measures
Information	Long-range retention Memory of general information Intellectual drive
Similarities	Analysis of relationships Logical and abstract thinking Concept formation
Arithmetic	Ability to attend Retention of arithmetic concepts and processes
Vocabulary	Language development Level of education Level of abstract thinking Concept formation
Comprehension	Common Sense Organization of knowledge Social maturity Reasoning with abstractions
Digit Span*	Attention span Immediate auditory memory Auditory sequencing

*Usually regarded as an optional sub-test.

The Performance Scale is made up of seven sub-tests.

Subtest	What It Measures
Picture Completion	Alertness to environment Visual perception of relationships
Picture Arrangement	Visual sequencing Concept formation Synthesis of non-verbal material
Block Design	Ability to perceive, analyze, synthesize and reproduce abstract designs
Object Assembly	Perception of whole/part relationships Visual-motor integration
Coding†	Immediate visual-recall Visual-motor dexterity
Symbol Search†	Analysis of differences Attention to detail
Mazes†	Planning and foresight Pencil control

† Available at two levels of difficulty.

Generally, the Full Scale Scores are interpreted in this way:

Full Scale Test Score	Classification
130 and above	Very Superior
120-129	Superior
110-119	High Average
90-109	Average
80-89	Low Average
70-79	Borderline
69 and below	Mentally Deficient

The AAMD Adaptive Behavior Scale, School Edition ("The ABS") (1981): The American Association On Mental Deficiency.

This is an individually completed scale used principally to aid in classification, placement, and general programming decisions for mentally handicapped individuals. It has two parts, yields percentile ranks; age range is 3-69. The sub-sections deal with areas like social adjustment, community self-sufficiency, etc. The rater (test completer) can be the parent, teacher, social worker, etc.

Strengths and Weaknesses:

The ABS enjoys popularity with educators and health professionals who emphasize adaptive behaviour in assessing mental handicap. It is used most frequently to assess an individual's ability to thrive in a particular placement (independent, group home, etc.). Validity and reliability are criticized. Generally it is not used for severely handicapped persons.

The Behavior Evaluation Scale ("The BES") (1984): Pro-Ed.

The BES is a scale for evaluating behavior in students K-12. It is filled out by the teacher or other adult, and covers areas like learning problems, interpersonal difficulties, unhappiness/depression, etc. It takes about 15 minutes to complete, and produces a number that can be used to judge a student's behaviour comparatively.

Strengths and Weaknesses:

The instrument is useful for comparison purposes if it is completed by several of the significant adults in the subject's life. However, this or any evaluation scale should never be used as a sole determiner for identification or placement.

The Bender Visual Motor Gestalt Test ("The Bender") (1946; Koppitz Scoring System, 1963; rev. 1975; Pascal and Suttell System, 1951): The American Orthopsychiatric Association.

This is a standardized, individual or group test which assesses visual-motor integration and emotional adjustment through a series of nine abstract designs to be copied in pencil. The designs reflect certain principles of Gestalt psychology. The age range is 5-11 (Koppitz) or 15-50 (Pascal and Suttell); it takes 10-15 minutes to administer; and produces age level and percentile scores.

Strengths and Weaknesses:

For critics and sceptics, *The Bender* is one of the most difficult instruments to accept as valid, or even remotely useful. Despite the elaborate scoring systems, both the procedures and the interpretation of results can be very subjective. The test results, and even the tests themselves, are highly suspect as ten minutes spent by a subject copying designs can hardly be said to produce a valid measure of emotional adjustment. Moreover, since most ten year olds can copy the designs without difficulty, it is moot whether the tests are even a measure of fine-motor maturity. Criticism also involves the interpretation of copied designs as examples of emotional maladjustment, for in fact they may only be reflections of a personality style. Taken together, the weaknesses of *The Bender* are such that most professionals whose principal responsibility is in education, tend not to use this instrument.

Boehm Test of Basic Concepts ("The Boehm") (1967; Form A, 1969; Form B, 1971): The Psychological Corporation.

This test is a standardized, individual (or group, for screening) test of comprehension, quantity and time concepts designed to assess knowledge basic to early academic success. The grade range is K-2; it takes 30-40 minutes to administer; and produces a percentile score.

Strengths and Weaknesses:

Most young people find *The Boehm* interesting. Illustrations are clear. The test is well organized with an excellent manual, and is easy to administer. Unfortunately, no documentation is offered to support the concepts in this test as crucial to the early years of school.

Brigance Diagnostic Inventories ("The Brigance") (1981): Curriculum Associates.

This is an individual, non-standardized (but field-tested in Canada and the U.S.) instrument, designed to assess pre-academic, academic, and vocational skills so that teachers can more easily define objectives and plan individual programs. The grade range is preschool to 12; it takes 15-90 minutes to administer, and only in some subtests produces a grade or age level score. (There are several other similar instruments by Brigance.)

Strengths and Weaknesses:

There is an excellent, well-organized record-keeping system which will be of real assistance in planning student programs. This test can be administered easily by paraprofessionals under supervision. The somewhat informal procedures tend to encourage carelessness, but properly used, this test can be a useful planning aid.

The Canadian Achievement Tests ("The C.A.T.")(1983): McGraw-Hill-Ryerson.

This is a standardized, norm-referenced and criterion-referenced, group test, designed to assess achievement. The grade range is 1-12; it takes a flexible time period to administer (depending on the number and combination of sub-tests); and produces percentile, stanine, scaled, and grade equivalent scores.

Strengths and Weaknesses:

The major content areas of this test are reading, spelling, language, mathematics, reference skill. Given the many pieces to it, the test is reasonably easy to administer. It produces a detailed Student Diagnostic Profile (SDP) that can be very useful if all personnel are prepared to take the time to interpret it. Potentially a very valuable addition to the canon of available tests, it has been quite sharply criticized for being too unwieldy and threatening to both subjects and examiners.

Canadian Cognitive Abilities Test ("The C-Cat") (1982): Nelson Canada.

This is a standardized, norm-referenced group test designed to measure cognitive abilities in the verbal, quantitative, and non-verbal areas. The grade range is 3-12; it takes 1½-2 hours to administer; and produces standard, percentile, and stanine scores for age groups, and percentile and stanine scores for grade groups.

Strengths and Weaknesses:

The C-Cat has high validity and reliability estimates, and reviewers compliment it for careful norming and standardization. Supporters state that this test has better predictive value than I.Q. tests, although critics argue that cognitive ability by itself is not a simple or straightforward entity to assss.

The Canadian Test of Basic Skills ("The CTBS") (1988): Nelson Canada.

This is a Canadianization of the Iowa Test of Basic Skills and is very popular in Ontario. It is a standardized, norm-referenced, group-administered achievement test for K-12. *The CTBS* produces mounds of data. It can be hand scored, although a computerized scoring system is preferred. Scores range from percentile to scale to grade equivalent. Intra-class data as well as other, extensive comparative data can be made available.

Stengths and Weaknesses:

Although the *The CTBS* can be extremely time-consuming to administer, there are many educators who argue it is worth the effort. Validity and reliability data are generally good and the test generally is well-received by reviewers. The most severe criticisms are not directed at the test itself but at the general abuse to which achievement tests especially, are subject.

Detroit Tests of Learning Aptitude - 2 ("The Detroit") (1985): Pro-Ed.

This is a revision of a once popular standardized, individual test designed to measure general intelligence functions, such as verbal ability, reasoning, time and space relationships. The age range is 6-18; it takes 1-2 hours to administer; and it produces percentile scores, and a General Intelligence or Overall Aptitude Score.

Strengths and Weaknesses:

The revised Detroit is sharply criticized for lack of validity and reliability. Reviewers suggest that results should be interpreted cautiously, which is a more than mild dismissal.

Gates-MacGinitie Silent Reading Tests ("The Gates-MacGinitie"), Second ed., (1978): Riverside Publishing Co.

This is a standardized, norm-referenced, group test designed to measure silent reading skills. The grade range is 1-12; it takes 50-60 minutes to administer; and it produces grade level, standard, and percentile scores.

The Gates-MacGinitie is offered at eight levels, and gives two basic measures: vocabulary, comprehension. (The older, first edition also had a measure of speed and accuracy.) They are pen and paper tests completed by the subject(s) usually in groups.

Strengths and Weaknesses:

These tests are a useful screening device and are often used for test-retest procedures because alternate forms are available. However in their usefulness rests the inherent weakness: a silent reading score does not give any diagnostic information. The comprehension sub-tests are criticized as being not very well done. The questions often rely on factors not present in the passages to be read. They measure a very low level of comprehension. A most serious criticism is that the *Gates-MacGinitie* tests do not offer a teacher more than he or she already knows about a student, except a number with which to satisfy a bureaucracy.

Kaufman Assessment Battery for Children ("The K-ABC") (1983): American Guidance Service.

This is a standardized, individual, norm-referenced test of intelligence and achievement. The age range is 2½-12½ years; it takes 30-90 minutes to administer; and produces age level, standard, percentile, scaled, and grade level scores. Three dimensions — sequential processing (serial or temporal order problem-solving), simultaneous processing (a gestalt approach), and achievement — are assessed in 16 sub-tests, which in turn report four global scales: the three above plus a global estimate of intellectual functioning.

Strengths and Weaknesses:

It is a complex and involved instrument that requires expertise, time, and patience in the examiner. The authors urge examiners to take training courses.

An important feature of the test is its purpose of assessing disabled and minority students, and pre-schoolers, but as with the Woodcock-Johnson Psycho-Educational Battery (see page 160) *The K-ABC* does not yet have widespread acceptance. It draws heavily on neuropsychology and cerebral specialization theory, and whether or not a test based on these elements can be educationally useful is still uncertain.

Keymath Diagnostic Arithmetic Test ("Keymath") (1971): American Guidance Service.

This is a standardized, individual, criterion-referenced test designed to assess mathematics skills. The grade range is pre-school-6; it takes 30-45 minutes to administer; it produces grade level and percentile scores.

Strengths and Weaknesses:

Keymath is easy to administer, diverse, colourful, and widely applicable. It has some unique sub-tests (such as missing Elements) and is generally very motivating. On balance, *Keymath* is an excellent screening instrument, but is criticized for some elements of construction which leave gaps in the continuum of difficulty. Another criticism is that grade level scores tend to be inflated.

Leiter International Performance Scale ("The Leiter") (1948): C.H. Stoelting Co.

This is a non-verbal test producing mental age and I.Q. scores. Usually it is used for individuals with hearing and language difficulties, for severely disabled and for non-English speakers. The directions are pantomimed and gestured. Age range is 2-18. It measures areas like specific relationships, quantitative discrimination, immediate recall, etc.

Strengths and Weaknesses:

There are no time constraints and the scoring is very objective. Subjects usually enjoy the test process. However there is no leeway for partial scoring, which seems contradictory when there is no guarantee the subjects have fully understood the tasks, or are fully capable of responding. *The Leiter* is heavy and awkward to use and store. However it is a popular and potentially useful instrument for certain subjects. (There is an adaptation known as the Arthur (1950) Adaptation.)

McCarthy Scales of Children's Abilities ("The McCarthy Scales") (1972): The Psychological Corporation.

This is a standardized, individual, norm-referenced test of general intellectual ability which is frequently offered as an instrument to identify children with possible learning disabilities. The age range is 2½-8½ years; it takes an hour to administer; and produces mental age, standard, and percentile scores.

Strengths and Weaknesses:

The McCarthy Scales include several verbal tasks that are appropriate for children with suspected learning disabilities, and has good reliability support. Ironically, no exceptional children classified as exceptional were included in the norming sample, part of a criticism that suggests more validity studies are needed. This test also has a very small age range, which makes re-testing comparisons difficult as the child grows. It is not an easy test to interpret.

Peabody Individual Achievement Test ("The PIAT") (1970): American Guidance Service.

This is an individual, norm-referenced, standardized test, designed to give a wide measure of general achievement, with particular emphasis on reading, spelling, and arithmetic achievement. The grade range is K-12; it takes 30-40 minutes to administer; and produces age level, grade level, standard, and percentile scores.

Strengths and Weaknesses:

The PIAT uses a multiple choice answer format. It requires recognition of correct spelling (not written spelling) and tests sentence comprehension as well as mathematical problem-solving skills. It can provide a quick, overall, preliminary view, but should not be regarded as comprehensive or diagnostic. Nor should sub-test scores be regarded as truly and finally indicative of a student's ability in a particular area (like reading). Because validity studies on *The PIAT* are lacking, the test should not carry heavy weight in an assessment.

Peabody Picture Vocabulary Test — Revised ("The PPVT-R") (1959; rev. 1965, 1981): American Guidance Service.

This is a standardized, individual test of single word receptive vocabulary of standard (American) English. The age range is 2½-40 years; it takes 10-20 minutes to administer; and produces age level, standard, percentile, and stanine scores.

Strengths and Weaknesses:

Because *The PPVT-R* has a format of presenting pictures to elicit a response to a word, it is non-threatening. It is a good *first* test in a battery, and is well-designed and normed. But because it is simply a test of single word vocabulary, not too much should be made of the results. The fact that the subject must understand a word and a picture (or drawing) means more than vocabulary is being assessed.

Progressive Matrices ("The Ravens") (1956): H.K. Lewis & Co.

The test requires a subject to complete progressively complicated visual analogies. It is entirely non-verbal, and is available in Standard and Advanced levels. There is a coloured version for younger children.

Strengths and Weaknesses:

Reliability and validity data are acceptable, but norms are poor for school use. (It was standardized on patients in a veteran's hospital.) *The Ravens* can be used very effectively for a test-teach-test approach (See Chapter 13) and because it is non-verbal, may reveal some enlightening cognitive strengths in poor readers.

Slingerland Screening Tests for Identifying Children With Specific Learning Disability ("The Slingerland") (1962; rev. 1970, Form D, 1974): Educators' Publishing Service.

This is a non-standardized, informal group test of visual, auditory, and kinesthetic skills related to reading and spelling, designed to identify students with a specific language disability. The age range is 6-12; it takes 60-90 minutes to administer; and it produces no scores but has guidelines for evaluating test performance.

Strengths and Weaknesses:

The tests in this instrument are strictly informal measures and permit a great deal of subjectivity. Some students become very frustrated during administration because extensive writing is required. Administration procedures are complex and difficult. Because it lacks validity and reliability data, and because of severe criticism of its value, use of *The Slingerland* has declined significantly.

Spache Diagnostic Reading Scales ("The Spache") (1963; rev. 1972, 1981): McGraw-Hill.

This is an individual, standardized, criterion-referenced test, designed to measure oral and silent reading, and listening comprehension. The grade range is 1 to 7; it takes 30-45 minutes to administer; and the test produces grade level scores.

Strengths and Weaknesses:

Because the battery includes 3 graded word recognition lists, 2 reading selections at each of 11 levels (from grades 1.6 to 7.5) and 12 supplementary word analysis and phonics tests, it purports to give fairly good information about students' reading skills. What must be considered however, is to what extent a knowledge of phonics can be equated with reading ability, and to what degree of accuracy, one can establish grade levels of a passage to 1.6 or 7.5. Many of the questions are yes-no type which gives a 50 per cent probability in guessing. The test offers a silent reading rate score which, given individual differences, is not very meaningful. Generally, *The Spache* is not highly regarded because of its very serious flaws; however the author has written an excellent manual in which he shares his extensive knowledge of reading, and this one element is quite worth while.

Stanford-Binet Intelligence Scale, Fourth Edition ("The Binet") (1986): Riverside Publishing.

The fourth edition retains many features of previous editions. Its authors claim that this edition is designed to help differentiate between mental handicap and learning disability, to identify giftedness, to understand why a student is having learning problems, and to study the development of cognitive skills from 2-adult. There are 15 subtests, not dissimilar from those in the WISC-III, including Vocabulary, Quantitative, Memory for Sentences, Pattern Analysis, Copying, Verbal Relations, Memory for Objects, and others.

Strengths and Weaknesses:

There is surprisingly little research or review material on what has been a long established I.Q. test, perhaps because of the excellent reputation of its predecessors. The publishers claim to have responded to cultural-bias criticism directed at earlier versions. It is likely that time and experience will increase the use of this test as an alternative to the WISC-III.

Test of Reading Comprehension ("The TORC") (1978): Pro-Ed.

This is a standardized, norm-referenced test for individual or group, designed to give a normed measure of silent reading comprehension independent of specific curriculum, via eight sub-tests like Paragraph Reading, Synthetic Similarities, Social Studies Vocabulary, Reading the Directions of Schoolwork, etc. The age range is 6½-14½; it takes 1½-2 hours to administer and produces scaled (each sub-test) and standardized (total test) scores.

Strengths and Weaknesses:

Generally the test has come to be used at the upper age ranges because of the preclusive effect of very specific, subject-based vocabulary. Several of the sub-tests measure abilities not taught in classrooms and therefore the value of the results for school purposes may be questionable. Because the theoretical constructs underlying *The TORC* are new and complex, the worth of the scores, not to mention their interpretation, may well be suspect, especially in light of the intricate psycholinguistic base from which the tests are developed.

Wide Range Achievement Test — Revised ("The WRAT-R") (1983): Jastak Associates.

This is an individual, norm-referenced, standardized test designed to assess skills in reading (actually, word recognition), written spelling, and arithmetic computation. The age range is 5 to adult; it takes 20-30 minutes to administer; and produces grade level, standard, percentile, and stanine scores.

Strengths and Weaknesses:

This test is very easy and very fast in administration and scoring, and can be a fairly efficient first step in an assessment. However it should never be used as the sole element in any evaluation, assessment or admission procedure (but often is!). The arithmetic computation sub-test does not test ability as much as it tests what the subject's curriculum offered. The spelling sub-test grants a grade level score of 1.3 for merely copying 18 marks and writing two letters from the subject's name. Finally, the reading sub-test asks the subject merely to read a list of single words. There is no measure of sentence or paragraph reading, or of comprehension. Reviewers also point out that overestimations of reading ability, at the primary level especially, are a weakness.

Woodcock-Johnson Psycho-Educational Battery ("The Woodcock") (1990): Teaching Resources Corporation.

This is an individual, standardized, norm-referenced test designed to measure cognitive ability, academic achievement and interests over a wide range. The age range is 3-adult; it takes 1½-2 hours to administer; and produces grade level, age level, percentile, and standard scores, along with scores the authors call 'functional level' and 'relative performance index'.

Strengths and Weaknesses:

This is a busy and involved instrument, with 27 sub-tests. Twelve are in "Cognitive Ability" (e.g., analysis-synthesis; quantitative concepts; memory for sentences, etc.) Ten are in "Tests of Achievement" (e.g., calculation, dictation, proofing, etc.). There are five in "Interest Level" (e.g., Reading Interest, Social Interest, etc.).

Clusters of sub-tests (e.g., reading) provide the primary analysis, with scores plotted on four profiles: the 'sub-test profile' for quick presentation of performance, the 'percentile rank profile' for comparison with age or grade; the 'instructional implications profile' for relating instructional range to current grade placement, and the 'achievement-aptitude' profile to compare actual and anticipated achievement. This is a comprehensive and interesting means of reporting which offers some interesting comparisons of cognitive ability with actual achievement.

To make this instrument work its best however, requires a major commitment from the examiner. It is difficult, complex and time-consuming. This fact, along with the concern over whether the scholastic aptitude clusters are reliable and valid measures of reading, math, written language, and knowledge, has restricted the popular use of the instrument. There is considerable research being conducted on it at present, and a major effort is being made by the publisher to add information for examiners, and to develop awareness among psychometrists.

Woodcock Reading Mastery Tests (1973): Guidance Service.

This is an individual, standardized, criterion and norm-referenced test designed to measure a wide range of reading skills. The grade range is K-12; it takes 30-45 minutes to administer; and it produces a wide set of scores including grade level, percentile, relative mastery, achievement index, and reading range.

Strengths and Weaknesses:

This test offers five sub-tests covering letters, words, and passages. The Word Comprehension sub-test uses analogy, and the Passage Comprehension makes use of the cloze procedures, both highly regarded techniques. A useful concept is the 'relative mastery' which provides a useful indication of what can be expected of a student. Another useful point is the concept of instructional range in which the test gives indication of where a student can be expected to perform. Reliability and validity data are very good.

As with all tests of reading skills however, the results must always be viewed with some circumspection simply because of the elusiveness of the task of measuring reading ability.

Some General Terms Used In Testing
(See Also Chapter 13)

Age Norm (Age Score) A score indicating average performance for students classified according to chronological age.

Base Level The level at which all items of a test are passed, just preceding the level where the first failure occurs. All items below the base level are assumed correct. Contrast with ceiling level.

Battery A group of carefully selected tests administered to a student.

Ceiling Level The highest item of a sequence in which a certain number of items has been failed. All items above the ceiling item are assumed incorrect.

Chronological Age (CA) Age from birth expressed in years and months; for example, 7 years, 6 months.

Correlation Coefficient (r) A statistical index that measures the degree of relationship between any two variables.

Diagnostic Testing An intensive, in-depth evaluation process using formal, standardized tests and informal tests designed to determine the nature and severity of specific learning problems.

Intelligence Quotient (I.Q.) An index of mental capacity, expressing a student's ability to perform on an intelligence test.

Mean (M) The sum of a set of scores divided by the number of scores.

Median (MD) The middle point in a set of ranked scores.

Mental Age (MA) A measure of a student's level of mental development, based on performance on a test of mental ability and determined by the level of difficulty of the test items passed.

Mode (MO) The score that occurs most frequently in a distribution. In the distribution 18, 14, 12, 11, 10, 10, 7, the mode is 10. Its value is entirely independent of extreme scores.

Percentile Rank A type of converted score that expresses a student's score relative to his or her group in percentile points. Indicates the percentage of students tested who made scores equal to or lower than the specified score.

Projective Technique A test situation in which the student responds to ambiguous stimulus materials, such as pictures, inkblots, or incomplete sentences, thereby supposedly projecting personality characteristics.

Protocol The original record of the test results.

Rank Ordering The arrangement of scores from highest to lowest.

Raw Score The basic score initially obtained by scoring a test according to the directions in the manual.

Reliability The degree to which a student would obtain the same score if the test were readministered (assuming no further learning, practice effects, or other change).

Scaled Score Usually this is a score which is used to measure students' growth from year to year. It is a useful comparison also with the norming sample.

Standard Deviation (SD) The most commonly used measure of variation. A statistic used to express the extent of the distribution's deviations from the mean.

Standardization In test construction, this refers to the process of trying the test out on a group of students to determine uniform or standard scoring procedures and methods of interpretation.

Standardized Test Contains empirically selected materials, with specific directions for administration, scoring, and interpretation. Provides data on validity and reliability, and has adequately derived norms.

Standard Score Derived score that transforms a raw score in such a manner that it has the same mean and the same standard deviation.

Stanine A weighted scale divided into nine equal units that represent nine levels of performance on any particular test. The stanine is a standard score.

Validity The extent to which a test measures what it is designated to measure. A test valid for one use may have negligible validity for another.

Appendix C

Some Controversial Theories and Treatments

People with a special need are often the target of exotic theories and practices, some of which make very dramatic claims. Very few of these practices are the product of out-and-out charlatanism, but most of them when submitted to the cold light of rigorous analysis, fail to live up to the hyperbole that usually described them initially. But they proliferate because they grow in fertile ground. Parents, teachers, the students themselves, are quite understandably anxious to hear about potential "cures" or successful methods of remediation, so the audience is always ready and waiting. Special education itself attracts unique theory. It is a field still relatively new, still uncertain about itself, and desperate for scientific validity. With the exception of hearing and visual matters, which are pretty much carefully managed by "hard" medical research (although by no means always, and certainly not with absolute success) areas of special education that deal with brain injury, behaviour, and most especially learning disabilities, are more accessible to "soft" research and pseudo-science.

The consequence over the past twenty-five years has been a plethora of strategies, therapies, and sometimes bizarre techniques that attract a fiercely loyal initial following, then usually die a quick and ignominious death. This is unfortunate because in many cases there may well have been a kernel of truth or a mote of potential usefulness that with more care and research might have been developed into a truly beneficial outcome for people with exceptionalities. It is also unfortunate, because each exposed-as-useless therapy besmirches the field in general and retards the impetus for research into other ideas. However, if nothing else, the passing of a theory serves to underline yet again that there are no panaceas in special education: no magic cures and no quick fixes.

What follows is a brief outline of some of the ideas that continue to retain some currency, and rear up from time to time in conferences and in courses in special education.

(i) Patterning. This theory and technique was initially developed by Glen Doman and Carl Delacato at the Institute for Human Rehabilitation in Pennsylvania. The underlying concept follows the principle that failure to pass properly through a certain sequence of developmental stages in mobility, language, and competence in the manual, visual, auditory, and tactile areas reflects poor neurological organization and may indicate brain damage.

In 1983 the American Academy of Pediatrics, after reviewing all of the relevant literature, concluded "that the patterning treatment offers no special merit, that the claims of its advocates are unproven, and that the demands on families are so great that in some cases there may be harm in its use."

(ii) Optometric Visual Training. Most optometrists clearly delineate their role in educational achievement in terms of visual enhancement for the sake of clear, comfortable, and efficient visual performance. A sub group of optometrists have a "developmental vision" point of view, and tend to look rather broadly at the role of the optometrist. They feel that learning in general and reading in particular are primarily visuo-perceptual tasks related to sensory-motor coordination of the child, and employ a wide diversity of educational and sensory-motor-perceptual training techniques in an attempt to correct educational problems in children. Several reviews have concluded that there is no scientific evidence to support a claim for improving the academic abilities of children through treatment based solely on: (a) visual training (muscle exercises, ocular pursuit, glasses); (b) neurologic organizational training (laterality training, balance board, perceptual training).

(iii) Scotopic Sensitivity and the Irlen Lenses. According to information provided by the Irlen Institute for Perceptual and Learning Disabilities, a student with scotopic sensitivity experiences headaches, burning and itchy eyes and general discomfort while reading, along

with and perhaps because of words that appear to double or become fuzzy or move and disappear. The student thus finds reading a physically — and ultimately an intellectually — difficult chore. Treatment involves screening the text with coloured filters, or wearing coloured lenses (hence "Irlen Lenses").

The research provided by the Irlen Institute in 1983 was sharply criticized for flawed methodology. Subsequently, reports in the Journal of Learning Disabilities (1990) 23, 10, offer results both supporting and denying the efficacy of the treatment.

(iv) Vestibular Dysfunction. Several investigators have suggested that the vestibular system is important in academic learning. They claim that there is a causal relationship between vestibular disorders and poor academic performance involving written language in children with learning disabilities.

The role of the vestibular system in the higher cortical functions required for academic performance is not known and there is no evidence supportive of the vestibular theories or of the proposed treatment approaches.

(v) Applied Kinesiology. Recently, some chiropractors and chiropractic clinics, especially in the U.S., have advertised actively that they can cure dyslexia and learning disabilities. The literature that is distributed refers to the use of "applied kinesiology" and to the work of Dr. Carl A. Ferreri. The claim is that this treatment can result in an astounding reversal of all dyslexic and learning disability conditions. The basis for the theory and treatment is a book written by Carl A. Ferreri and Richard B. Wainwright (1984): *Breakthrough for Dyslexia and Learning Disabilities*, in which there is no research support.

(vi) Megavitamins. The use of massive doses of vitamins to treat emotional or cognitive disorders began with the treatment of schizophrenia. The American Academy of Pediatrics, in 1976, issued a report specifically focused on megavitamin therapy and learning disabilities; no validity to the concept or treatment was reported.

(vii) Trace Elements. Trace elements, including copper, zinc, magnesium, manganese, and chromium along with more common elements such calcium, sodium, and iron are necessary nutrients. Their presence is essential for the maintenance of normal physiological function. No one to date has published data supporting the theory that deficiencies in one or more of these elements is a cause of learning disabilities. Yet some children are tested for such deficiencies and treated with replacement therapy. There are no research data to support this view or that replacement therapy leads to improvement of learning disabilities.

(viii) Hypoglycemia. Another orthomolecular concept is that learning disabilities are due to hypoglycemia. The treatment proposed is to place the child or adolescent on a hypoglycemic diet. It may be that some children with learning disabilities are also hypoglycemic; however, clinical studies on the learning disabled using a formal glucose tolerance test are not conclusive.

(ix) Food Additives and Preservatives. In *Why Your Child is Hyperactive*, Dr. Benjamin Feingold (1975) proposed that synthetic flavours and colours in the diet are related to hyperactivity. He reported that the elimination of all foods containing artificial colours and flavours as well as salicylates and certain other additives stopped the hyperactivity. Neither in this book nor in any of his other publications did Dr. Feingold present research data to support this theory; all findings were based on his clinical experience. He and his book received wide publicity. It was left to others to document whether he was correct or incorrect.

There does appear to be a subset of children with behavioural disturbances who respond to some aspects of Feingold's diet. However, as noted above, the controlled clinical studies indicate that this group is small.

With notable exceptions, the specific elimination of synthetic food colours from the diet does not appear to be a major factor in the reported responses of a majority of these children.

(x) Refined Sugars. Clinical observation and parent reports suggest that refined sugar promotes adverse behavioural reactions in children. Hyperactive behaviour is most commonly reported. Two theories have been proposed for the possible reaction. There is the possibility that certain sugars (e.g., glucose) could influence brain neurotransmitter levels and thus activity level in children with hyperactivity.

This concept is based on the observation that platelet serotonin levels in the hyperactive have been found to be elevated above the norm. The other concept is that carbohydrate intake influences the level of essential fatty acids. These fatty acids are necessary for the synthesis of prostaglandin in the brain. Insulin is required in the critical step to activate the prostaglandin precursors. Thus, a role for essential fatty acid levels in producing hyperactivity could be influenced by carbohydrate intake, which could influence insulin production.

These concepts are not supported by clinical observation or parent reports.

(xi) Auditory Retraining. A Parisian specialist in ear, nose, and throat, Dr. A.A. Tomatis developed a theory that centres on the remediation of dyslexia through auditory training, or in essence: retraining. The first stage of the Tomatis method or "Electronic Ear program" concerns itself with the child's need to be reborn into the world of communication. Through a filtering of sounds technique which is claimed to approximate the sound heard by the fetus in the womb, the child is given a 'sonic birth'. As the child listens to his mother's highly filtered voice, gradually the entire spectrum of her voice is put back until he hears her normal voice. A successful sonic birth will release the child from prenatal attachment to his mother.

The next stage of treatment involves retraining the child's mode of listening. Words are filtered to remove low frequencies, forcing concentration on the sounds which pertain to language. During alternate sessions the child listens to highly filtered music, especially the music of Mozart, on the theory that it will help develop an alert, sensorially well-nourished brain. The final step is to ensure lateralization, so more sound is fed into the right ear than the left so that right ear dominance is strengthened. As the ear becomes lateralized, so do the rest of the motor and psychic functions.

Although there was a great degree of interest in the Tomatis method during the early 1980's, especially in Ontario and western Canada, the results of rigorously controlled studies have not been able to lend support, and the popularity of this theory has diminished significantly.

(xii) Teaching to a modality preference. A teaching strategy that triggered a very favorable response in the late 1970's but which was never substantiated by research was "teaching to the student's modality preference". The theory was that students usually have a preferred modality for learning, be it visual, or auditory, or tactile or kinesthetic/tactile.

Its popularity was no doubt owing to a self-fulfilling prophecy. Students who develop a visualization strategy for remembering things, or a subvocalization strategy were comfortably identified as visual or auditory learners respectively, and were often instructed thereafter in "the visual mode" or "the auditory mode" on the assumption that one or the other was their preferred (i.e., strong) point. It is not a surprising field practice when one considers that at the time it was still de rigeur for academics to be discussing things like "visual memory" and "visual closure" as though they were discrete, measureable and teachable entities.

Regrettably there is no conclusive evidence to justify grouping learners in this way. Indeed there is evidence which shows that "visual learners" for example, who "visualize" something by writing it down are in fact using the visual modality and the motor act of writing (kinesthetic/tactile) and may well subvocalize at the same time. The Ontario Ministry of Education which enthusiastically supported modality preference in its 1980 support document on learning disabilities, recanted cautiously in the 1986 edition, and went on to advocate a multisensory, multifocal approach to learning, supporting the idea that teachers can do their students a greater service by teaching them in a variety of ways.

(xiii) The Frostig Program of Visual Perception was developed in 1964 by Marianne Frostig to train children who have difficulties in perceptual and motor skills. It has a series of worksheets and workbooks which offer practice in exercises like "perceptual constancy" (recognizing that an object stays the same even if its shape and colour change), figure-ground perception, position in space, etc. Accompanying the program is the *Frostig Developmental Test of Visual Perception* which purports to measure five functions of visual perception.

Criticism of the program has largely been directed at the fact that visual-motor perception has never been demonstrated to be a vital element in learning, if it exists as an entity at all. Caution is often advanced against spending children's time on this material when it could be more profitably spent in other endeavours.

Bibliography and Further Readings

General Overview and Introductory

Baine, D., Sobsey, D., Wilgosh, L., & Kysella, G.M. (eds). (1988) *Alternative futures for the education of students with severe disabilities,* University of Alberta.

Berdine, W.H., & Blackhurst, A.E. (1985) *An Introduction To Special Education,* (Little Brown).

Blackhurst, A.E. (Ed.) (1982) "The special educator as professional person", *Exceptional Education Quarterly,* 2, 4, (entire issue).

Davis, W.E. (1980) *Educator's Resource Guide To Special Education,* (Allyn & Bacon).

Deno, E.N., (1970) "Special education as developmental capital", *Exceptional Children,* 37, 229-37.

Foerter, J., et al. (1991) *Special Education: Bridging The Centuries,* (Ontario Teachers' Federation).

Hallahan, D.P., & Kauffman, J.M. (1986) *Exceptional Children,* Third Edition, (Prentice-Hall).

Hammill, D.D., Bartel, N.R., & Bunch, G.O. (1984) *Teaching Children With Learning and Behaviour Problems,* Canadian Edition, (Allyn & Bacon).

Reynolds, M. C., "A framework for considering some issues in special education", *Exceptional Children,* 28, 367-70.

Weber, K. (1993) *Special Education In Ontario Schools, Third Edition,* Highland Press.

Wight-Felske, A. & Hughson, E. (1986) "Disabled persons in Canada: A review of the literature on independent living", in Brown, R.I. & Wight-Felske, A. (1987) "Rehabilitation education: an integrated approach within the province of Alberta", *Canadian Journal of Special Education,* 3, 139-151.

Winzer, M. et al., (1990) *Exceptionalities: a Canadian Perspective,* (Prentice-Hall).

Useful Insights Into Special Education Issues

Abramson, M. "Implications of mainstreaming: A challenge for special education", in Mann, L., & Sabatino, D. (Eds.) (1980) *The Fourth Review of Special Education,* (Grune & Stratton).

Algozzine, R., & Mercer, C. D. (1980) "Labels and expectancies for handicapped children and youth", in L. Mann D. Sabatino (Eds.) *Ibid.*

Biklen, D. (1985) *Achieving the complete school — strategies for effective mainstreaming,* (Teachers College Press).

Biklen, D., Ferguson, D. & Ford, A. (Eds.) (1989) *Schooling and Disability,* Chicago (National Society for Education).

Csapo, M. (1984) "Segregation, integration and beyond: A sociological perspective of special education", *B.C. Journal of Special Education,* 8, 211-29.

Csapo, M. & Goguen, L. (Eds.) (1989) *Special education across Canada; issues for the 90's.* (Centre for Human Development and Research, Vancouver).

Eckberg, D.L. (1979) *Intelligence and Race,* (Praeger).

Jensen, A.R. (1973) *Educability and Group Differences,* (Methuen Publications).

Kakalik, J., Furry, W., Thomas., M. & Carney, F. (1981) *The Cost of Special Education,* RAND N-1792 ED.

Little, D.M. (Ed.) (1987) *Special-ordinary education: issues in organization, administration, instruction and learning,* (Acadia University Printing Services).

MacKay, A. W. (1984) *Education Law in Canada,* (Montgomery).

Palmer, D. (1983 "An attributional perspective on labelling", *Exceptional Children* 49, (5) 423-29.

Sage, D. D. (1987) "Resource cost analysis: What we really need to know", *Special Services in Schools*, 4, 63-76.

Whimbey, A. (1975) *Intelligence Can Be Taught*, (Sutton).

Wilson, A. Keeton- (1983) *A Consumer's Guide To Bill 82*, (OISE Press).

The Practical Side: Useful Advice And Techniques

Canfield, J., & Wells, H. (1976) *100 Ways To Improve Self Concept*, (Prentice-Hall).

Cartwright, C.A., et al., (1981) *Teachers of Special Learners*, (Wadsworth).

Gaylord-Ross, R.J. (1985) *Strategies for Educating Students With Severe Handicaps*, (Little Brown).

Little, D.M. (1988) A crime against childhood — Uniform curriculum at uniform rate: mainstreaming redefined, re-examined. *Canadian Journal of Special Education*. 2, 2, 191-208.

Lovitt, T.C. (1982) *Because of My Persistence I've Learned From Children*, (Merrill).

Maier, N. (1982) *Teaching The Gifted, Challenging the Average*, (Guidance Centre).

Morsink, C.V. (1984) *Teaching Special Needs Students In Regular Classrooms*, (Little Brown & Co.)

Purkey, W.W. (1978) *Inviting School Success*, (Wadsworth).

Radabaugh, M.T., & Yukish, J.F. (1982) *Curriculum and Methods For The Mildly Handicapped*, (Allyn & Bacon).

Tonjes, M.J., & Zintz, M.V. (1981) *Teaching Reading/Thinking/Study Skills In Content Classrooms*, (W.C. Brown).

Weber, K.J. (1974) *Yes They Can!* (Gage Publications).

Weber, K.J. (1982) *The Teacher Is The Key*, (Gage Publications).

Weiderholt, J.L. (1983) *The Resource Teacher*, Second Edition, (Allyn & Bacon).

Winzer, M. (1989) *Closing the gap: special learners in regular classrooms*. (Copp-Clark).

Assessment

Aiken, L.R. (1988) *Psychological Testing and Assessment*, 6th edition, (Allyn & Bacon).

Clarizio, H. (1982) "Intellectual assessment of Hispanic children", *Psychology in the Schools*, 19, (61-71).

DeRuiter, J., & Wansart, W. (1982) *Psychology of Learning Disabilities*, (Aspen Learning Systems).

Faust, D., & Ziskin, J. (1988) "The Expert Witness in Psychology and Psychiatry", *Science*, 241, 4861, (31-35).

Feuerstein, R. (1979) *The Dynamic Assessment of Retarded Performers*, (University Park Press).

Howell, K.W., Kaplan, J.S., & O'Connell, C.Y. (1979) *Evaluating Exceptional Children*, (Columbus: Chas Merrill).

Kavale, K., & Mattson, D. (1983) "One jumped off the balance beam: Meta-analysis of perceptual-motor training", *Journal of Learning Disabilities*, 16, (165-173)

Lerner, J., Mardell-Czudnowski, C., & Goldenberg, D. (1981) *Special Education For The Early Years*, (Prentice-Hall).

Lyman, H.B. (1978) *Test Scores and What They Mean*, Third Edition, (Prentice-Hall).

Mann, P.H., Suiter, P.A., & McClung, R.M. (1979) *A Handbook of Diagnostic Prescriptive Teaching*, Second Edition, (Allyn & Bacon).

Partenio, I., & Taylor, R. (1985) "The relationship of teacher ratings and IQ: A question of bias?", *School Psychology Review*, 14, (79-83).

Salvia, J., & Hughes, C. (1990) *Curriculum-Based Assessment: Testing What Is Taught*, (Macmillan).

Salvia, J., & Ysseldyke, J.E. (1985) *Assessment In Special And Remedial Education*, (Houghton Mifflin).

Taylor, R., (1989) *Assessment of Exceptional Students*, (Prentice-Hall).

Behaviour Disorders

Algozzine, B. (1980) "The disturbing child: a matter of opinion", *Behavioural Disorders*, 5, 2, 112-15.

Ayllon, T., Garber, S. & Pisor, D. (1975) "The elimination of discipline problems through a combined school-home motivational system", *Behavior Therapy*, 6, 616-626.

Bennett, J. & Winzer, M. (1980) *Education in correctional institutions: A preliminary survey*. (Toronto: Federation of Provincial Schools Authority Teachers).

Bower, E.M. (1981) *Early Identification of Emotionally Handicapped Children In School*, Third Ed., (Charles C. Thomas).

Bratlinger, E. (1991) "Social Class Distinctions in Adolescents' Reports of Problems and Punishments in School", *Behavioral Disorders*, 17, 1, (36-46).

Cohen, N., Davine, M., Horodezky, N., Lipsett, L. & Isaacson, L. (1993) "Unsuspected Language Impairment In Psychiatrically Disturbed Children: Prevalence and Language and Behavioural Characteristics", *Journal of the American Academy of Child and Adolescent Psychiatry*, (in press).

Craighead, W.E., et al., (Eds.) (1981) *Behavior Modification: Principles, Issues, and Applications*, (Houghton Mifflin).

Csapo, M. (1981) "The emotionally disturbed child in Canada's schools", *Behavioural Disorders*, 6, 139-149.

Cullinan, D., Epstein, M. H., & Kauffman, J. M. (1984) "Teachers' ratings of student behaviors: what constitutes behavior disorder in schools?", *Behavioral Disorders*, 10, (9-19).

Drabman, R.S., & Patterson, J.N. (1981) "Disruptive behaviour and the social standing of exceptional children", *Exceptional Education Quarterly*, 1, 45-55.

Dubois, J. (1982) "Ontario Association of Children's Mental Health Centres: Tenth Anniversary", *Canada's Mental Health*, 30, 20-21.

Dworet, D. H. & Rathgeber, A. J. (1990) "Provincial and Territorial Government Responses to Behaviorally Disordered Students in Canada - 1988", *Behavioral Disorders*, 15, 4, (201-209).

Fremont, T., Klingsporn, M., & Wilson, J. (1976) "Identifying emotionally disturbed children: The professionals differ", *Journal of School Psychology*, 14, 275-381.

Gadow, K.D. (1986) *Children On Medication Vols. I & II*. (College Hill Press).

Gardner, W.I. (1974) *Children with learning and behaviour problems: A behavior management approach*. (Allyn & Bacon).

Garreau, B., Parthelmy, D., Sauvage, D., Leddet, I. & Lelord, G. (1984) "A comparison of autistic syndromes with and without associated neurological problems", *Journal of Autism and Developmental Disabilities*, 14, 105-113.

Kauffman, J. M. (1989) *Characteristics of Behavior Disorders in Children and Youth*, (Merrill).

Knitzer, J., Steinberg, Z., Fleisch, B. (1990) *At the Schoolhouse Door: An Examination of Programs and Policies For Children With Behavioral and Emotional Problems*, (Bank Street College of Education).

Koppitz, E. M. (1980) "Strategies for diagnosis and identification of children with behavior and learning problems", in *Conflict In The Classroom: The Education of Emotionally Disturbed Children*, (Wadsworth).

Martin, B., (1975) "Parent-child relationships", in Horowitz, F.D. (Ed.) *Review of Child Development and Research*, (U. of Chicago Press).

McDermott, P.A. (1981) "The manifestation of problem behaviour in ten age groups of Canadian school children", *Canadian Journal of Behavioural Science*, 13, 310, 319.

McGinnis, E. & Goldstein, A.P. (1984) *Skillstreaming the adolescent: teaching prosocial behaviors*. (Research Press).

McGinnis, E. & Goldstein, A.P. (1983) *Skillstreaming the elementary school child: teaching prosocial skills*. (Research Press).

Patterson, G. R. (1982) *Coercive Family Process*, (Castalia Press).

Rapp, D. (1991) *Is This Your Child? Discovering and Treating Unrecognized Allergies*, (Morrow).

Rich, L. H. (1982) *Disturbed Students: Characteristics and Educational Strategies*, (University Park Press).

Rose, T.L., Epstein, M.H., Cullinan, D., & Lloyd, J. (1981) "Academic programming for behaviorally disordered adolescents: An approach to remediation", In G. Brown, R.L.-McDowell, & J. Smith (Eds.), *Educating adolescents with behavior disorders*, (Merrill).

Ross, D.M., & Ross, S.A. (1976) *Hyperactivity: Research, Theory and Action*, (Wiley).

Swanson, J. et al. (1993) "Effect of Stimulant Medication on Children with ADD: A 'Review of Reviews'", Exceptional Children, 60, 2. (See whole issue for ADD and ADHD.)

Thomas, D. R., Becker, W. C. & Armstrong, M. (1968) "Production and elimination of disruptive classroom behaviour by systematically varying teachers' behavior", *Journal of Applied Behaviour Analysis*, 1, (35-45).

Thomas, A. & Chess, S. (1984) "Genesis and evolution of behaviour disorders: From infancy to early adult", *American Journal of Psychiatry*, 141, (1-9).

Wagner, M. (1989) *The National Longitudinal Transition Study*, (Stanford Research Institute).

Walker, H. M. (1979) *The Acting-out Child: Coping With Classroom Disruption*, (Allyn & Bacon).

Ysseldyke, J. E. & Algozzine, B. (1981) "Diagnostic classification decisions as a function of referral information", *Journal of Special Education*, 15, 4, (429-435).

Deafness and Hard of Hearing

Allen, T. (1986) "Patterns of academic achievement among hearing impaired students", in Schildroth, A., & Karchmer (Eds.), *Deaf Children in America*, (San Diego: Little Brown).

Bond, D.E. (1981) "Aspects of behaviour and management of adolescents who are hearing-impaired", *The Teacher of the Deaf*, 5, 41-48.

Clarke, B.R., & Winzer, M. (1983) "A concise history of the education of the deaf in Canada", *ACEHI Journal*, 9, 36-51.

Conrad, R. (1979) *The deaf school child: Language and cognitive function*, (Harper & Row).

Farth, H.G. (1973) *Deafness and Learning*. (Wadsworth Publishing).

Geers, A. & Moog, J. (1989) "Factors predictive of the development of literacy in profoundly hearing-impaired adolescents", *The Volta Review*, 91, (69-86).

Karchmer, M.A., Petersen, L.M., Allen, T.E., & Osborn, T.I. (1981) *Highlights of the Canadian survey of hearing impaired children and youth*, (Washington, D.C.: Gallaudet College, Office of demographic studies).

Meadow, K.P. (1980) *Deafness and Child Development*, (University of California Press).

Moores, D.F. (1982) *Educating the Deaf: Psychology, Principles and Practices* (2nd ed.), (Houghton Mifflin).

Padden, C., & Humphries, T. (1988) *Deaf in America: Voices from a Culture.* (Harvard University Press).

Paul, P.V., & Quigley, S.P. (1987) "Some effects of hearing impairment on early English language development", in Martin F. (Ed.), *Hearing disorders in children: pediatric audiology*, (Pro-Ed).

Stassen, R.A. (1978) "I have one in my class who's wearing hearing aids!" In W. Northcott (ed.), *The hearing impaired child in a regular classroom: Preschool, elementary and secondary years.* Washington, D.C.: (Alexander Graham Bell Association for the Deaf).

Trybus, R.J., & Karchmer, M.A. (1977) "School Achievement Scores of Hearing Impaired Children", *American Annals of the Deaf*, 122, 62-69.

Gifted And Talented Children

Bain, D.A. (1980) "Gifted and enriched education in Canada", In M. Csapo and L. Goguen (Eds.), *Special education across Canada: Issues and concerns for the '80s*, (Vancouver: Centre for Human Development and Research).

Banks, R. (1979) "How would you like it if you were gifted?" *Special Education in Canada*, 53, 12-14.

Betts, G. (1986) "The Autonomous Learning Model", in Renzulli, J. (Ed.) *Systems and Models For Developing Programs For the Gifted And Talented*, (Creative Learning Press).

Borthwick, B., Dow, I., Levesque, D., & Banks, R. (1980) *The gifted and talented students in Canada: Results of a CEA study.* (Toronto: The Canadian Education Association).

Ciha, T., Harris, R., Hoffman, D. & Potter, M. (1974) "Parents as identifiers of giftedness: ignored but accurate", *Gifted Child Quarterly*, 18, 191-195.

Clarke, B. (1988) *Growing Up Gifted: Developing the Potential of Children at Home and at School*, (Merrill).

Cox, C. (1984) Developing gifted behaviours: a conversation with Joseph S. Renzulli. *Curriculum Review.* Nov.-Dec. '84, 14-18.

Dishart, M. (1981) "Special education and personal needs of gifted and talented children", *Association of Educators of Gifted, Talented and Creative Children in B.C.*, 3, 6-12.

Dow, I.I. (1981) "The education of gifted students in Canada", *Association of Educators of Gifted, Talented and Creative Children in B.C.*, 3, 13-19.

Feldhusen, J. & Koffoff, P. (1986) "The Purdue Three Stage Enrichment Model", in Renzulli, J. (Ed.) *Systems and Models For Developing Programs For The Gifted and Talented*, (Creative Learning Press).

Gardner, H. (1983) *Frames of Mind*, (Basic Books).

Hatch, T.C., & Gardner, H. (1986) "From Testing Intelligence to Assessing Competences: A Pluralistic View of Intellect", *Roeper Review*, VIII, 3, 147-150.

Karnes, M. B. (1985) "Maximizing the potential of the young gifted child", *Roeper Review*, April.

King, E., et al. (1985) *Programming for the Gifted*, (Toronto: Ontario Ministry of Education).

Khoury, J.T. & Appel, M.A. (1979) "Gifted children: current trends and issues", In A. Lane (Ed.), *Readings in human growth and development of the exceptional individual*, (Special Learning Corporation).

Ontario, Ministry of Education. (1978) *Curriculum ideas for teachers:* Gifted, Talented children. Ontario, Ministry of Education.

Perks, B. (1984) *Identification of Gifted Children*, Ed.D. Dissertation, University of British Columbia.

Reis, S.M. & O'Shea, A.A. (1984) "An innovative enrichment program: the Enrichment Triad Revolving Door Model", *Special Education in Canada*, 58, 135-138.

Renzulli, J.S. (1977) *The enrichment triad model: a guide for developing defensible programs for the gifted and talented*, (Creative Learning Press).

Renzulli, J.S. (1978) "What makes giftedness? re-examining a definition", *Phi Delta Kappan*, 60, 180-184, 261

Renzulli, J., Reis, S. Smith, L. (1981) *The Revolving Door Identification Model*, (Creative Learning Press).

Smyth, E. (1984) "Educating Ontario's ablest: an overview of historic and emerging trends", *Special Education in Canada*, 58, 145-147.

Sternberg, R.J. (1986) "Identifying the Gifted through I.Q.: why a little bit of knowledge is a dangerous thing", *Roeper Review*, VIII, 3, 143-146.

Terman, L. & Oden, M. (1951) "The Stanford studies of the gifted", In P. Witty (Ed.), *The Gifted Child*, (D.C. Heath).

Torrance, E.P. (1960) "Explorations in creative thinking", *Education*, 81, 216-220.

Torrance, E.P. & Reynolds, C.R. (1978) "Images of the future of gifted adolescents: effects of alienation and specialized cerebral functioning", *Gifted Child Quarterly*, 22, 40-54.

The Matter of Integration

During the preparation of this edition of *Special Education in Canadian Schools*, I examined over a thousand items on the subject of integration. What follows is a very rigorously summarized, but balanced, distillation of the material. —K.W.

Affleck, J., Madge, S., Adams, A. & Lowenbraun, S. (1988) "Integrated classroom versus resource model: Academic viability and effectiveness", *Exceptional Children*, 54, 4, (339-48).

Alper, S., & Ryndak, D. (1992) "Educating students with severe handicaps in regular classes", Elementary School Journal, 92, 3, (373-87).

Baker, J., & Zigmond, N. (1990) "Are regular education classes equipped to accommodate students with learning disabilities?", *Exceptional Children*, 56, (515-26).

Bender, W., "The case against mainstreaming: empirical support for the political backlash", *Education* 105, 3, (279-87).

Berres, M. & Knoblock, P. (Eds.) (1986) *Program Models For Mainstreaming: Integrating Students With Moderate To Severe Disabilities*, (Aspen Publishers).

Bishop, V.E. (1986) "Identifying the components of success in mainstreaming", *Journal of Visual Impairment and Blindness*, 80,9, (939-46).

Black-Branch, J.L. (1993) *Traditions, rights and realities: Legal, de facto, and symbolic influences of the Canadian Charter of Rights and Freedoms on educational administration in Canada.* Unpublished doctoral dissertation, University of Toronto.

Brown, B. (1990) "La dolce vita: integrated schools in Italy make it possible for everyone", *entourage*, 5, 2&3, (15-17, 20).

Christoplos, F. & Renz, P. (1969) "A critical examination of special education programs" *The Journal of Special Education*, 3, 371-79.

Conway, R., & Gow, L. (1988) "Mainstreaming special class students with mild handicaps through group instruction", Special Instruction, 9, 5, (34-41)

Darvill, C. (1989) "Teacher attitudes to mainstreaming", *Canadian Journal of Special Education*, 5, 1, (1-14).

Dickinson, G.M. & MacKay, A.W. (1989) *Rights, freedoms and the education system in Canada: cases and materials,* (Emond-Montgomery).

Ferro, N. (1990) *Trends in philosophy and practice* Paper presented at the International Conference on Integration in School, Leisure and Transition to Work, Stockholm.

Foster, S. (1989) "Reflections of a group of deaf adults on their experiences in mainstream and residential programs in the United States", *Disability, Handicap, and Society*, 4, 1. (110-19)

Fullan, M. (1982) *The Meaning of Educational Change*, Teachers College Press. Gaylord-Ross, R. (Ed.) (1986) *Integration Strategies For Students With Handicaps*, (Brookes Publishing Co.).

Gartner, A., Kerzner-Lipsky, D. & Turnbull, A. (1991)*Supporting Families With A Child With A Disability,* (Brookes Publishing).

Gersten, R., & Woodward, J. (1990) "Rethinking the regular education initiative: focus on the classroom teacher", *Remedial and Special Education*, 11, 3, (7-15).

Graden, J., Zins, J. & Curtis, M. (Eds.) (1989) *Alternative Educational Delivery Systems: Enhancing Instructional Options For All Students*, National Association of School Psychologists.

Grunewald, K. (1986) *The Intellectually Handicapped In Sweden: New Legislation In A Bid For Normalization,* Svenska Institutet.

Hamre-Nietupski, S., McDonald, J., & Nietupski, J. (1992) "Integrating elementary students with multiple disabilities into supported regular classes", *Teaching Exceptional Children*, Spring, (6-9).

Haring, K.A., & Lovett, D.L. (1990) "A follow-up study of special education graduates", *Journal of Special Education*, 23, 4, (463-76).

Hayes, M. (1989) "Integration: a review of current literature", *Saskatchewan School Trustees Research Centre*.

Hayek, R. (1987) "In class support teaching: tackling fish", *British Journal of Special Education*, 13, 2, (21-30).

Hegarty, S. (1987) *Meeting Special Needs in Ordinary Schools,* (Hodder and Stoughton).

Horner, R., Meyer, L. & Fredericks, H. (Eds.) (1986) *Education Of Learners With Severe Handicaps: Exemplary Service Strategies*, (Brookes Publishing Co.).

Jenkins, A., Odom, V. & Speltz, R. (1990) "Effects of social integration on preschool children with handicaps", *Exceptional Children*, 40, (420-27).

Johnson, D., & Johnson, R. (1986) "Mainstreaming and cooperative learning strategies", *Exceptional Children*, 52, (553-61).

Larivee, B. (1986) "Effective teaching for mainstreamed students is effective teaching for all students", *Teacher Education and Special Education*, 9, 4, (173-79).

Little, D.M. (1988) The redefinition of special education: special-ordinary education — individualized and personalized in the regular classroom. *Education Canada*, 28, 1, 36-42.

McEvoy, Shores, Wehby, Johnson & Fox (1990) "Special education teachers implementation of procedures to promote social integration among children in integrated settings", *Education and Training In Mental Retardation*, (267-76).

Meese, R. (1992) "Adapting textbooks for children with learning disabilities in mainstreamed classrooms", *Teaching Exceptional Children*, Spring, (49-51).

McLean, M., & Hanline, M. (1990) "Providing early intervention services in integrated environments: challenges and opportunities for the future", *TECSE*, 10, (78-89).

O'Reilly, R., & Duquette, C. (1988) "Experienced teachers look at mainstreaming", *Education Canada*, 28, (9-13).

Porter, G. & Richler, D. (1991) *Changing Canadian Schools: Perspectives On Disability And Inclusion*, The Roeher Institute.

Reideger, E, Hillyard, A. & Sobsey, R (1986) "Integration of handicapped children: Administrative strategies", *Canadian Journal For Exceptional Children*, 2, 3, (90-96).

Reynolds, M. (1989) "An historical perspective: the delivery of special education to mildly disabled and at-risk students", *Remedial and Special Education*, 10, 6, (7-11).

Reynolds, M. & Birch, J. (1988) *Adaptive Mainstreaming: A Primer For Teachers And Principals*, (Longman).

Rottenberg, C. (1992) "Integration of the handicapped: a comparative review", *B.C. Journal of Special Education*, 16, 1, (59-69).

Sailor, W., Anderson, J., Halvorsen, K., Doering, J., Filler, J. & Goetz, L. (1989) *The Comprehensive Local School: Regular Education For All Students With Disabilities*, (Brookes Publishing Co).

Salend, S. (1990) *Effective Mainstreaming*, (Macmillan).

Sanche, R., & Dahl, H. (1991) "Progress in Saskatchewan toward integration of students with disabilities", *Canadian Journal of Special Education*, 7, 1, (16-31).

Schloss, P. (1992) "Mainstreaming revisited", *Elementary School Journal*, 92, 3, (233-44).

Schumaker, J., & Deshler, D. (1988) "Implementing the regular education initiative in secondary schools: a different ball game", *Journal of Learning Disabilities*, 21, (36-42).

Scruggs, T., & Mastropieri, M. (1992) "Effective mainstreaming strategies for mildly handicapped students", *Elementary School Journal*, 92, 3, (389-409).

Simon, L. (1992) "Mainstreaming: is it in the best interests of all children?", *B.C. Journal of Special Education*, 16, 2, (131-37).

Simpson, R., & Myles, B. (1989) "Parents' mainsteaming modification preferences for children with educable mental handicaps, behaviour disorders, and learning disabilities", *Psychology In The Schools*, 26, (202-11).

Stainback, W., & Stainback, S. (1990) *Support Networks For Inclusive Schooling*, (Paul H. Brookes).

Stainback, W., Stainback, S., & Forest, M. (1989) *Educating All Students In The Mainstream*, (Paul H. Brookes).

Stephens, V., (1991) "Peer status of learning disabled children: the integration question", Thesis for M.A. degree, University of Toronto.

Stewin, L. & McCann, S. (1993) *Contemporary Educational Issues: The Canadian Mosaic*, (2nd Ed.) (Copp Clark Pitman).

Thomas, G. (1986) "Integrating personnel in order to integrate children", *Support For Learning*, 1, 1.

Wang, M, & Baker, E. (1986) "Mainstreaming programs: design features and effects", *Journal of Special Education*, 19,4, (503-21).

Winzer, M. (1987) "Mainstreaming exceptional children: teacher attitudes and the educational climate", *Alberta Journal of Educational Research*, 33,1, (33-42).

Wittrock, M. (Ed.) (1986) *Handbook On Research On Teaching* (Macmillan).

Wood, J. (1989) *Mainstreaming: A Practical Approach For Teachers*, (Merrill).Yau, M. (1988) "Alternative service delivery models for learning disabled students", *Research Report #188*, Toronto Board of Education.

York, J. Vandercook, T., Macdonald, C. & Wolff, C. (Eds.) (1989) Strategies For Full Inclusion, U. of Minn. Institute on Community Integration.

York, J., & Vandercook, T. (1991) "Designing an integrated program for learners with severe disabilities", *Teaching Exceptional Children* 23, 1, (22-28).

Zigmond, N., Levin, E. & Laurie, T. (1985) "Managing the mainstream: an analysis of teacher attitudes and student performance in mainstream high school programs", *Journal of Learning Disabilities*, 18, 9, (535-41).

Learning Disabilities

Baker, L. (1982) "An evaluation of the role of metacognitive deficits in learning disabilities", *Topics in Learning and Learning Disabilities*, 2, 27-35.

Barnes, D.B. (1983, Spring) Technology, education and the learning disabled. *National Canadian Association for Children and Adults with Learning Disabilities*, p. 10.

Bryan, T.H. & Pfluam, S. (1978) "Social interactions of learning disabled children: a linguistic, social, and cognitive analysis, *Learning Disability Quarterly*, 1, 70-79.

Cantwell, D. P. & Baker L. (1991) "Association between attention deficit-hyperactivity and learning disorders", *Journal of Learning Disabilities*, 24, 2, (88-95).

Cohen, R.L. & Netley, C. (1981) "Short term memory deficits in reading disabled children, in the absence of opportunity for rehearsal strategies", *Intelligence*, 5, 69-76.

Cole, J.L. (1985) "Developing cognitive strategies in learning disabled adolescents", M.Ed. major paper, University of British Columbia.

Cotugno, A.J. (1987)"Cognitive Control Functioning", *Journal of Learning Disabilities*, 20, 9, 563-7.

Crealock, C., (1986) *The learning disabled / juvenile delinquency link: Causation or correction*, Solicitor General.

Critchley, M. & Critchley, E.A. (1978) *Dyslexia Defined*, (William Heinemann).

Cruickshank, W.M. (1979) "Myths and realities in learning disabilities," In A. Lane (Ed.), *Readings in human growth and development of the exceptional individual*, (Special Learning Corporation).

Decker, S.N. & DeFries, J.C. (1980) "Cognitive abilities in families with reading disabled children", *Journal of Learning Disabilities*, 13, 517-522.

Dow, I.I., et al., (1981) *Manual for teachers of students with learning disabilities*, (Ontario Ministry of Education).

Gaddes, W.H. (1981) "Neuropsychology, fact or mythology, educational help or hindrance?", *School Psychology Review*, 10, 322-330.

Hammill, D.D., Leigh, L.E., McNutt, G., & Larsen, S.C. (1981) "A new definition of learning disabilities", *Learning Disability Quarterly*, 4, 336-342.

Harber, J.R. (1980) "Auditory perception and reading: Another look", *Learning Disability Quarterly*, 3, 19-25.

Harris, A.J. & Sipay, E.R. (1980) *How to increase reading ability: A guide to developmental and remedial methods*, (7th ed.), (Longman).

Hinchelwood, J. (1917) *Congenital word-blindness*, (H.K. Lewis).

Kamhi, A. G., (1992) "Response to Historical Perspective: A Developmental Language Perspective", *Journal of Learning Disabilities*, 25, 1, (48-52).

Lerner, J. (1981) *Learning disabilities: theories, diagnosis and teaching strategies* (3rd ed.), (Houghton Mifflin).

Little, D.M. (1980) Severe learning disabilities: status quo in B.C. *British Columbia Journal of Special Education*.

MacIntyre, R.B., Keeton, A., Agard, R. (1980) *Identification of Learning Disabilities In Ontario: A Validity Study*, (Ontario Ministry of Education).

Mann, L. (1970) "Perceptual training: misdirections and redirections", *Am. Journal of Orthopsychiatry*, 40, 30-38.

McKinney, J.D., & Feagans, L. (1984) "Academic and behavioural characteristics of learning disabled children and average achievers: longitudinal studies", *Learning Disabilities Quarterly*, 7, 251-264.

McMurray, J.G. (1980) "Learning disabled adolescents: Perspectives from Canadian principals", *Special Education in Canada*, 55, 10-14.

Murphy, D. (1986) "The prevalence of handicapping conditions among juvenile delinquents", *Remedial and Special Education*, 7, 7-17.

Reeve, R. E., (1989) "ADHD: facts and fallacies", *Intervention In School And Clinic*, 26, 2, (70-78).

Richardson, S. (1992) "Historical Perspectives on Dyslexia", *Journal of Learning Disabilities*, 25, 1, (40-47)

Ross & Ross (1976) See *Behaviour Disorders*.

Santostefano, S. (1978) *A Biodevelopmental Approach To Clinical Child Psychology*, (Wiley).

Short, E.J., et al. (1986) "Longitudinal stability of LD sub-types based on age and IQ achievement discrepancies", *Learning Disability Quarterly*, 6(2), 115-127.

Siegel, L. S., (1992) "An evaluation of the discrepancy definition of dyslexia", *Journal of Learning Disabilities*, 25, 10.

Stephens, T.M. (1977) *Teaching skills to children with learning and behavior disorders*, (Charles Merrill).

Torgenson, J.K. (1986) "Learning disabilities theory: its current state and future prospects", *Journal of Learning Disabilities*, 19, 399-407.

Torgenson, J.K., & Wong, B. (Eds.) (1986) *Psychological and Educational Perspectives on Learning Disabilities*, (Academic Press).

Vaughn, S., & Bos, C. (1987) *Research In Learning Disabilities*, (College Hill Press).

Wang, M., Walberg, H., & Reynolds, M. (Eds.) (1987) *The Handbook of Special Education*, (Pergamon Press).

Wiig, E.H. & Semel, E.H. (1976) *Language disabilities in Children and adolescents*, (Merrill).

Ysseldyke, J.E., et al. (1982) "Similarities and differences between low achievers and students classified learning disabled", *The Journal of Special Education*, 16(1), 73-85.

Ysseldyke, J.E., Thurlow, J., Graden, J., Wesson, C., Aglozzine, B., and Deno, S. (1983) "Generalizations from five years of research on assessment & decision making: The University of Minnesota Institute", *Exceptional Education Quarterly*, 4, 75-93.

Mental Handicaps

Bouchard, T., & McGue, M. (1981) "Familial studies of intelligence: a review", *Science* 212, 1055-1059.

Canadian Association for the Mentally Retarded, (1980) *Questions and answers about mental retardation.* Pamphlet, n.p.: CAMR.

Corman, L. & Gottlieb, J. (1978) "Mainstreaming mentally retarded children: A review of research", In N.R. Ellis (Ed.), *International review of research in mental retardation (Vol. 9)*, (Academic Press).

Downie, D.D. & Snart, F. (1983) "Bioethical considerations for teachers of the severe and profoundly retarded: a position paper", *Special Education in Canada*, 58, 3-4.

Fernald, G. (1943) *Remedial Techniques In Basic School Subjects*, (McGraw-Hill).

Forest, M. & Lusthaus, E. (1990) "Everybody belongs with the MAPS Action Planning System", *Exceptional Children*, 22, 4, (36-39).

Grossman, H. (Ed.) (1985) *Classification in Mental Retardation*, (American Association on Mental Deficiency).

Haywood, H.C., Meryers, C.E., & Switzky, S.N. (1982) "Mental retardation", *American Review of Psychology*, 33, 309-342.

Kneedler, R.D. with D.P. Hallahan, & J.M. Kauffman, (1984) *Special education for today*, (Prentice-Hall).

Laurendeau, M.C., Blanchet, A., & Coshan, M. (1984) "Studying the effects of deinstitutionalization programs on mentally retarded persons", *Canadian Journal on Mental Retardation*, 34, 33-41.

Matson, J.L., & Mulich, J.A. (Eds.) (1983) *Handbook of Mental Retardation*, (Pergamon Press).

National Prevention Committee, Canadian Association for the Mentally Retarded. (1982) *Final report to the Minister of National Health and Welfare on the five regional symposia on the prevention of mental retardation in Canada*, (Ottawa: Health and Welfare).

Neisworth, J.T. & Smith, R.M. (Eds.) (1978) *Retardation: Issues, assessment, intervention.* (McGraw-Hill).

Peterson, N. & Harolick, J. (1987) "Integration of Handicapped and Nonhandicapped Preschoolers: an analysis of play behaviour and social interaction", *Education and Training of the Mentally Retarded.*

Reiss, S., Levitan, G.W., & McNally, R.J. (1982) "Emotionally disturbed mentally retarded people", *American Psychologists*, 37, 361-367.

Robbins, M. (1966) "The Delacato interpretation of neurological organization", *Reading Research Quarterly*, 1, 57-78.

Snyder, L. et al., (1985) "Integrated settings at the early childhood level: the role of nonretarded peers", *Exceptional Children.*

Sontag, E., Certo, N. & Burton J.E. (1979) "On a distinction between the education of the severely and profoundly handicapped and a doctrine of limitations", *Exceptional Children*, 45, 640-666.

Zdriluk, D.M. (1983) "Workshops: A Canadian perspective". *Canadian Journal on Mental Retardation*, 33, 35-37.

Zigmond, N. & Baker, J. "Mainstream (1990) Experiences for learning disabled students (project MEMH) Preliminary Report" *Exceptional Children*, 176-193.

Physical, Neurological and Health Problems (including Speech)

Bloom, L. & Lahey, M. (1978) *Language development and disorders*, (John Wiley).

Comings, D.E. (1990) *Tourette Syndrome and Human Behaviour*, (Duarte).

Epilepsy Foundation of America, (1973) *Answers to the most frequent questions people ask about epilepsy.* (American Epilepsy Association).

Freeman, J.M. (1974) *Practical management of meningomyelocele*, (University Park Press).

Guerin, G.R. (1979) "School achievement and behaviour of children with mild or moderate health conditions", *Journal of Special Education*, 13, 179-186.

Hughes, S. (1990) *Ryan: A Mother's Story Of Her Hyperactive, Tourette Syndrome Child*, (Duarte).

Kanner, L. (1943) "Autistic Disturbances of Affective Contact", *New Child*, 2, 21.

Kirk, S.A., & Gallagher, J.J. (1979) *Educating Exceptional Children*, (Houghton Mifflin).

Konstantareas, M.M. (1986) "Early Developmental Backgrounds of Autistic and Mentally Retarded Children", *Psychiatric Clinic of North America*, 9, 1, 671-687.

LaPointe, L. (1982) "Neurogenic disorders of speech", In G. Shames & E.H. Wiig (Eds.) *Human Communication Disorders*, (Charles E. Merrill).

Levi, S.L. (1991) "Tourette Syndrome Association" *Journal of Learning Disabilities,* 24, 16.

Moore, P. (1982) "Voice disorders", In G. Shames & E.H. Wiig (Eds.), *Human Communication Disorders*, (Charles E. Merrill).

Parker, K. (1985) "Helping children cope with Tourette Syndrome", *Journal of School Health*, 55, 30-32.

Rutter, M., & Schopler, E. (Eds.) (1978) *Autism: A Reappraisal of Concepts and Treatment*, (Plenum Press).

Schopler, E., et al. (1980) "Toward Objective Classification of Childhood Autism: Childhood autism Rating Scale", *Journal of Autism and Developmental Disorders*, 10, 91.

Suran, B.G. & Rizzo, J.V. (1983) *Special children: An Integrative approach* (2nd ed.), (Scott Foresman).

Thompson, G.H., et al., (1983) *Comprehensive Management of Cerebral Palsy*, (Grune & Stratton).

Van Riper, C. (1978) *Speech Correction Principles and Methods* (6th ed.), (Prentice-Hall).

White, B.B., & M.S. (1987) "Autism From The Inside" *Medical Hypotheses*, 24, 223-29.

Wiig, E.H. (1982) "Language disabilities in the school-aged child", In G. Shames & E.H. Wiig, (Eds.), *Human Communication Disorders*, (Charles E. Merrill).

Wiig, E.H. & Semel, E.M. (1976) *Language Disabilities in Children and Adolescents*, (Charles E. Merrill).

Wiig, E.H. & Semel, E.M. (1980) *Language Assessment and Intervention for the Learning Disabled*, (Charles E. Merrill).

Wing, Lorna (1976) *Early Childhood Autism*, (Pergamon).

Visual Impairments

Barraga, N.C. (1976) *Visual handicaps and learning: A developmental approach*, (Wadsworth).

Carroll, B. (1983) Eye trumpets: *A consumer guide to low vision and low vision aids*, (Toronto: Low Vision Association of Ontario).

Cratty, B.J. & Sams, T.A. (1968) *The body-image of blind children*, (American Foundation for the Blind).

Hanninen, K.A. (1975) *Teaching the Visually Handicapped*, (Charles E. Merrill).

Harrison, F. & Crow, M. (1993) *Living and Learning With Blind Children*, (University of Toronto Press).

Mangold, S.S. & Roessing, L.J. (1982) "Instructional needs of students with low vision", In S. Mangold (Ed.), *A teacher's guide to the special educational needs of blind and visually handicapped children*. (American Foundation for the Blind).

Index

See also Appendices and Bibliography

Index (see also Appendices and Bibliography)

Index (see also Appendices and Bibliography)